COWBOY JUSTICE

COWBOY JUSTICE
Tale of a Texas Lawman
Jim Gober

Edited by

James R. Gober and B. Byron Price

Illustrations by

Harold Dow Bugbee

Texas Tech University Press

This book was set in New Century Schoolbook and Americana and printed on acid-free paper that meets the guidelines for permanence and durability of the Committee on Production Guidelines for Book Longevity of the Council on Library Resources. (∞)

Cover photo Jim Gober ca. 1888.
All Harold Dow Bugbee drawings, unless stated otherwise, are reprinted with permission courtesy of Panhandle-Plains Historical Museum, Canyon, Texas.
Photographs not credited otherwise are from the Gober family collection.
Printed in the United States of America
Book and jacket design by Lisa Camp

Library of Congress Cataloging-in-Publication Data
Gober, Jim, 1864–1933.
    Cowboy justice : tale of a Texas lawman / Jim Gober ; edited by James R. Gober and B. Byron Price.
        p.   cm.
    Includes index.
    ISBN 0-89672-373-9 (cloth : alk. paper). — ISBN 0-89672-450-6 (paper : alk. paper)
    1. Gober, Jim, 1864–1933—Anecdotes. 2. Cowboys—Texas—Texas Panhandle—Biography—Anecdotes. 3. Sheriffs—Texas—Texas Panhandle—Biography—Anecdotes. 4. Ranch life—Texas—Texas Panhandle—Anecdotes. 5. Frontier and pioneer life—Texas—Texas Panhandle—Anecdotes. 6. Law enforcement—Texas—Texas Panhandle—Anecdotes. 7. Potter County (Tex.)—Biography—Anecdotes. 8. Texas Panhandle (Tex.)—Biography—Anecdotes. I. Gober, James R., 1927– II. Price, B. Byron. III. Title.
F392.P168G63 1997
976.4'82506'092—dc20
[B]   96-38813
                                                                              CIP

01 02 03 04 05 06 / 9 8 7 6 5 4

Texas Tech University Press
Box 41037
Lubbock, Texas 79409-1037 USA

1-800-832-4042
ttup@ttu.edu
http://www.ttup.ttu.edu

To Amanda Mathis Camp Gober,
    a noble lady who nourished and molded good
    traits of character into her son, Jimmie. The
    result is this story.

To the memory of Jim Gober,
    "A kid from the Skillet," without his remarkable
    story there would be no book.

Jim Gober's badge as sheriff of Potter County, 1887.

Contents

Contents

Contents

Contents

Foreword

In the West, state lines sometimes meant little, and as the advancing "civilization" rolled over the frontier in a tide of railroads, telegraph wires, and law and order, certain regions remained practically untouched. One such region, bound by climate, topography, economic endeavors, and a philosophy of fair dealing enforced by a .45 Colt when necessary, was the Texas Panhandle and the northwestern corner of Oklahoma including the narrow strip once known as No Man's Land, now called the Oklahoma Panhandle. Primarily cattle country, it was a land of fierce weather, hundreds of square miles of prairie, few roads, very little water, and scattered, isolated settlements, a land where defending your life and property was often a matter of individual effort rather than collective law enforcement. While most sheriffs and city marshals were poorly paid but honest, many others were minions of corrupt city or county governments who supplemented their salaries with bribes or payoffs. In some instances judges ran their courts as private fiefdoms for the benefit of family or friends. Such corruption of the legal system was by no means restricted to the Texas and Oklahoma Panhandles, but the necessity for the individual to resort to "the law of the gun" for justice continued into the twentieth century.

That such circumstances existed past the time that the Wild West was theoretically dead owes much to the fact that this region was one of the last to be settled, other than by cattle and cowboys, and to its geographic isolation. Much of the West was already linked by railroads before the first tracks were laid into Amarillo in 1887 by the Fort Worth and Denver Railroad. Drought, fire, a depression, and grasshopper infestations decimated the economy and the population during the 1890s, driving many farmers and small ranchers to abandon their land for more congenial surroundings. The Texas and Oklahoma Panhandles were not for the weak of heart, weak of spirit, or weak of mind. Only those strong in character and body survived to bequeath a legacy of honor, determination, and sheer grit to their descendants. Stories of these pioneers linger in the oral histories of families, in the files and microfilm of museum and library archives, in the faded ink of old records in dusty basements of county courthouses. But few of the original settlers left manuscripts written in their own hand telling of their experiences, hardships, and heartaches. Few contemporary eyewitness accounts record the events, the men and women both good and bad, and the pioneer culture of the region. None save that of James Ransler Gober presents a history of this region from 1881 to the late 1920s.

Writing with surprising candor, Gober conceals neither his own weaknesses and misjudgments nor those of others as he records his experiences as a cowboy, as the first sheriff of Potter County, as a small rancher, and as a saloon owner. Concerning the "big fight" at Tascosa on March 20, 1886, he offers a new perspective and new testimony that supports my own theories as to the underlying causes of the gunfight set forth in my historical novel, *The Reckoning*. Had I been aware of Gober's manuscript before I wrote the novel, I would have saved myself much mental anguish and doubt over my interpretation of the personal and economic forces at work in Tascosa at the time.

Gober's manuscript is a historical gold mine, an invaluable record of one man's impressions and memories of a time and a land close to being lost in myth and legend, not to mention misinterpretation of data. It may surprise many, but not those of us who dwell here, that the myth and legend are truer than the sanitized versions of those historians who record facts but disregard or fail to understand the cultural and psychological forces behind events. The history of the West, particularly this region, is less a history of movements or trends—such as westward expansion or economic exploitation or racial injustice or Manifest Destiny—than one of individuals respond- ing to these forces according to their own perceptions and beliefs. Gober's story is less about settling this region than about his experi- ences, observations, and responses during the process of settlement. It is individual history, personalized history, and his sketches of such well-known regional figures as Temple Houston, W. M. D. Lee, Pat Garrett, and Jim East bring these men to life in a way no study of their letters or papers can do. This is one man writing of other men he knew personally.

The publication of *Cowboy Justice* ensures the reassessment of previous Texas and Oklahoma Panhandle histories. James Ransler Gober is a voice from the past, describing events, naming names, revealing motives that I am certain at least some of his contemporaries believed well concealed from the future's judgment. Certainly his accounts of early local government in Amarillo and Potter County, Texas, and in Woodward, Oklahoma, reveal fraud, chicanery, dishonesty, and violence on the part of elected officials, largely excluded from most local histories.

James Ransler Gober was not a famous man, nor even well-known beyond a few local historians, but he was a literate, poetic observer whose words ring with veracity, with emotion, with candor. His story is not a pretty one nor a romantic one, but it is, I believe, a true one. *Cowboy Justice* is a window on the past, our past, through which we look upon an age more harsh, more violent, more exciting, more tragic, more wonderful than any western film Hollywood could possibly produce. It is a chronicle of a time, a land, and a people. It is truth as one man saw and recorded it.

D. R. Meredith
Amarillo

James Gober
First Sheriff
Potter County

— H.D. Bugbee —

Editor's Preface

The Saturday afternoons of my 1930s childhood were consumed in the local theater, where my imagination was held willing captive by western films of the day. I hung on each weekly cliff-hanger and feature thriller starring such western movie idols as Buck Jones, Tex Ritter, Charles Starrett, and William Boyd (before Hopalong Cassidy), to mention a few. No heroes were larger than the western idols of my youth.

Not unlike many small children who hear about the feats of ancestors, I heard stories about my grandfather, Jim Gober. Imagine my delight when these stories hinted at the kind of cowboy legendry immortalized on the big screen. The Wild West tales featuring Jim Gober spanned the gamut from the Indian raids of his childhood in Denton County, Texas, and the shootouts of his teenage years in the Panhandle town of Tascosa, to the shot, in self-defense, from his Colt .45 when the then young lawman served as the first sheriff of Potter County, Texas.

My father, Richard Fly Gober, was Jim Gober's youngest child. Regrettably, I never knew either my father or grandfather. The former died in Denver when I was five months old; the latter, in Amarillo in 1933, when I was five years old and living in California. My mother, Fanny Berger Gober, remarried when I was five. I was adopted and reared by a loving disciplinarian, my father's older sister, Jimmye Gober Bowersock.

In 1980, shortly before her death, my aunt gave me a huge bundle of papers that had belonged to Jim Gober. I do not believe she expected anyone, least of all me, to construct anything from that bundle. Nor, at that stage of my life, did I anticipate doing anything more than browsing my way through it as I had time.

Yet as I made my way through the pages that grew more discolored each year, I began to see the crude shape of what truly might be termed an opus. The more I became drawn to it, the more I agonized over the state of Jim Gober's manuscript. Spelling problems alone made the quest for legibility and author's intent a major challenge. In many places the print was so dim from age as to be almost illegible. There were serious problems in chronology. Certain events were inexplicably commingled. No chaptering or subchaptering existed, nor any attempt at transition. Dramatic episodes buried in the story were diluted by misplacement and misspellings. Poetry on many subjects was interspersed with prose.

Although I proceeded to agonize over Jim Gober's papers for the next ten years, full-time employment continued to excuse my not making any serious attempt to sort or edit them. It was not until the summer of 1993, on my second retirement, that I began to think of Jim Gober's memoirs as a project. I had a spiritual motivation to unpack them and read the manuscript thoroughly—to solve the problems described above—and to yield to the strong urge to do something with this material. I was not a writer, but somehow this rough autobiography of the grandfather I never knew, but whose name I bore, managed to exact from me a commitment.

I wasn't really sure it was possible to make a coherent story out of Jim Gober's pages without bridging the gaps with fiction. Yet despite an agent's strong suggestions that I substitute a less heavy-handed voice for Jim Gober's own and that I infuse invented sequences to support its natural drama, I resisted the temptation to fictionalize the account. Somehow I couldn't relinquish the thought that despite its crude presentation and cumbersome wording, there was within those pages a gripping, true story that needed to be told as its author intended. I was resolved that even if it never were published, the work would not be contaminated with artifice.

Above all I knew I must preserve not only the truth of the story but also the voice of the man who told it—after all, what could reveal more about the real Jim Gober and the complexity of his personality than his voice? The task was to wade through the manuscript, line by line, evaluating each word within the context of its sentence and determining the difference between careless errors (mistakes Gober himself would have corrected) and vernacular speech. If I were to make a change in wording or spelling or add a phrase of transition, I could not disturb Gober's resonance or derail the thrust of what he was saying.

Jim Gober was remarkably accurate in the detail with which he recalls places, people, events, and their associated time frames. This leads me to believe that either he had a uncommon memory or he kept meticulous diary entries from which he eventually wrote the pieces of his manuscript. From his notations of elapsed time, his age, and circumstances at the time of recollection, I have concluded that he wrote his manuscript, which he entitled "Life's Battles Fought to a Draw," sometime between 1924 and 1930.

Editing these papers, compiling and organizing information, acquiring artwork and photographs, and drawing maps to facilitate the reader's understanding of complex journeys over unfamiliar country was not unlike piecing together a jigsaw puzzle. But it was truly a labor of love. I emphasize again, however, that this story is authentic and true. None of the facts have been changed.

The history in Jim Gober's story deserves to be made available for the enlightenment and entertainment of others: it is a true drama of the old West, played out against the dangerous and often cruel life of the late nineteenth century. Its suspense, personal sorrow, and dry cowboy humor are not inventions, but rather reflections of significant historical changes that shaped events and characters in Texas, Oklahoma, New Mexico, Kansas, and Colorado.

I have wondered why Jim Gober never completed or refined his memoirs. Perhaps it was because he was never able to find a publisher for his historic short story "Cowboys of Old Tascosa" (now the basis of Chapter Three), despite its action-packed content and illustrations by Panhandle artist Harold Dow Bugbee (whose work now illuminates this autobiography). As you read this story you will find, as I have, that Jim Gober was a man driven by idealism and a sense of honor. His writing reveals that he was not self-centered or prone to toot his own horn. Nor was he motivated to do things merely for the glory that might result. Perhaps this is why he never sought to sell his story to the dime novelists that made famous so many of his contemporaries, and why so little can be found about him in popular historical accounts.

James R. Gober
Albuquerque

Acknowledgments

I am convinced that when a writing project becomes successful it is usually the result of an effective team effort. Without that team, the story of Jim Gober's life and adventures that were more exciting than fiction might never have been told.

My first debt of gratitude is to my wife, Tuyet, who gave me the months, really years, necessary to take this manuscript apart, line by line, and put it back together in a publishable form; the time to draw the maps and collect the pictures from Denton County, Texas, to Woodward, Oklahoma, and from Kent County, Texas to many other locations. Heartfelt thanks go out to my relatives, direct and by marriage; to Paul Tolbert, Upland, California; and to Peggy and Tom Taylor, Maryville, Tennessee, for genealogical information and the generous use of priceless Gober family photographs.

I pay tribute to the museums, large and small, their directors, curators, archivists, and others without fancy titles who pitched in to find that special picture I needed; and to the libraries, genealogical societies, and publishing companies that tracked and found scores of photographs that have brought back to life countless images from the past. Specifically, I am grateful to Greg Thomas, assistant director of library services, Amarillo Public Library, for his personal attention to selecting, arranging for duplication, and mailing needed photographs; to Louise B. James, author, currently director and curator of the Plains Indians and Pioneers Museum, Woodward, Oklahoma, for her obvious interest in this project and magnificent job of providing photographs and other vital information documenting Jim Gober's life in the Oklahoma Territory; to Dessie Hanbury of the XIT Museum, Dalhart, Texas; to Elizabeth Connell (now deceased) of the Heart of West Texas Museum, Colorado City, Texas; to Dan Angler, Texas Ranger Hall of Fame Museum, Waco; to Vergel Neskorik, Bicentennial City-County Library, Paducah, Texas; to Dana Brinkman, Kent County Library, Jayton, Texas, who coordinated the location and copying of two priceless photographs of early twentieth-century lawmen; to Steve Bogener, Southwest Collection, Texas Tech University, Lubbock; to Christi Ray Callicoatte of the Nita Stewart Haley Library, Midland, Texas, who served as a capable locator of photographs of two Oldham County lawmen no one else seemed to have; to John Germann, Houston, whose expert knowledge of Texas post office history was very helpful; to Olive Bugbee, volunteer; to Claire Kuehn, archivist, and her successor, Lisa Lambert, Panhandle-Plains Historical Museum, Canyon, Texas; and to Mack Woodward, Sam Houston Memorial Museum.

Enhancing this gripping story is the artwork of Harold Dow Bugbee. Each of these wonderful graphic depictions of the old West was done in one of the following mediums: ink, oil, or watercolor. I am most grateful to Michael Grauer, curator of art, Panhandle-Plains Historical Museum, Canyon, Texas, who first extended to me the hope of using this most unique artwork to grace Jim Gober's story and arranged the availability of additional line drawings from a private collection. Over the course of several years he did yeoman service in meeting my needs, even in times of personal difficulty.

Special thanks go to Judith Keeling, Anne Towery, and Lisa Camp at Texas Tech University Press, who caught and shared my vision for Jim Gober's story; and to the hardworking staff of the press who translated the vision into reality.

I am grateful to Judy Sacks for her unrivaled editing, priceless suggestions on handling thought-provoking issues, and her work in creating the index.

Last mentioned, but among the top performers in the team that put this book together, is B. Byron Price. Byron's prowess as a historian and the peerless research he conducted into the life and little known activities of Jim Gober have resulted in the annotations that have made a fine historical document priceless. His friendly and helpful advice was invaluable in countless ways during the refining process of the manuscript and in providing me with answers to several puzzling questions arising from the creation of maps amplifying Jim Gober's journeys and adventures.

James R. Gober
Albuquerque

Honour has come back, as a king to earth,
And paid his subjects with a royal wage;
And nobleness walks in our ways again;
And we have come into our heritage.

Rupert Brooke

Introduction

In the 1920s, James R. Gober, a bank guard and private detective living in Amarillo, Texas, began writing his autobiography. He finished the manuscript, which he called "Life's Battle Fought to a Draw," three months before his death on April 22, 1933. Besides being a bittersweet personal recollection of a fascinating and often tragic life, Gober's account was also the story of a region in transition—the settling up of the Texas Panhandle and western Oklahoma—told from the viewpoint of a sensitive, observant, and well-placed participant.

The author had come to the Panhandle as a cowboy in the spring of 1882, only a few years after the first ranchers had introduced permanent stocks of cattle and sheep into the region. A few months before Gober delivered a herd to the Frying Pan Ranch, the neighboring T Anchor spread enclosed a horse pasture with wire fence, the first barbed barrier erected in the area. The following year, Gober's employers, Joseph Glidden and H. B. Sanborn, surrounded a quarter of a million acres of Frying Pan grass and some twenty-five thousand head of cattle with cedar fenceposts and four strands of galvanized steel.

Jim Gober reached the Panhandle as a wave of huge, corporate-owned ranches engulfed the small-scale, individual operators so long the staple of cattle raising on the Texas frontier. Fueled by the promise of extravagant profits and buoyed by eastern and foreign capital, these titans bought out or bullied more modest enterprises, prohibited employees from owning personal cattle and horses, and forbade gambling and the wearing of sidearms in cow camps. During the early 1880s their dominance of land and livestock in the western Panhandle led to economic and social tensions that culminated in the celebrated cowboy strike of 1883. Although not among the strikers, Gober observed the labor action and its violent aftermath first-hand, sympathized with the participants, and subsequently invested in a cattle pool established in New Mexico by the organizer of the strike.

Three years later, while working for the LX Ranch, Gober witnessed another watershed event in Panhandle history. The brutal forty-eight-hour blizzard that began on January 7, 1886, killed thousands of cattle and, coupled with rampant overgrazing, plummeting beef prices, and the introduction of barbed wire, helped bring about a fundamental transformation in the cattle industry on the Great Plains.

The pace of change quickened in the mid-1880s as the Fort Worth and Denver and the Kansas and Southern Railroads penetrated the Panhandle, carrying eager settlers and new markets on their tracks. Fortune-seeking town boosters, bent on taking economic and political advantage of still-fluid conditions, were not far behind.

The offer of a job as deputy sheriff of Oldham County in the spring of 1887 placed Jim Gober, then barely twenty-two years old, in a unique position to observe the swift metamorphosis of a transient track-laying community known as "Rag Town" into the bustling county seat known as Amarillo. Gober became an official part of that history in the fall, when voters elected him Potter County's first sheriff. At the time, he was heralded as the youngest sheriff in the United States.

A wide majority returned Gober to office in the regular elections held the following year. Youth and political inexperience, however, left the neophyte lawman vulnerable to the bitter factional infighting that characterized county politics during his tumultuous second term. Gober was soon embroiled in rancorous squabbles surrounding the construction of a permanent courthouse and the moving of the original town site and seat of county government to a new section owned by H. B. Sanborn, his old employer. These rivalries eventually led to murder charges filed against Gober following his mortal wounding of the town constable during a tense saloon confrontation in March 1889. Although Gober feared for his life when he fired the fatal shot, and he subsequently was acquitted by a jury, many townspeople branded him a killer.

While still under indictment, Gober married Belle Helen Plemons in the first wedding held in Potter County. This union allied the beleaguered young sheriff with a politically prominent Amarillo family whose patriarch, William Buford Plemons, was then serving as county judge and who later became forty-seventh district judge and a state legislator. As a member of the Texas House of Representatives,

Plemons authored the famous Four Section Settler Act, land legislation that facilitated the settling of the semi-arid plains of Texas.

Gober's kinship with Plemons brought him into contact with many of the region's leading jurists, including Temple Houston. Gober would encounter the brilliant and colorful son of Sam Houston again in Oklahoma in the early 1890s, both men having been prodded there by legal travails in Texas and the chance for a fresh start afforded by the opening of the Cheyenne and Arapaho reservation to white settlement.

Tragedy, however, dogged Gober's nearly three-decade-long tenure in western Oklahoma. He lost two daughters to illness, his wife and eldest son to murder, and several crops to voracious grasshoppers. He survived a life-threatening operation, endured bouts with alcohol and depression, considered suicide, and was often separated from home and family. During this unsettled period Gober drifted from job to job, at one time or another earning a living as a homesteader, freighter, hotelier, restauranteur, saloon keeper, deputy sheriff, cattle commission agent, and livestock detective.

In 1923, after serving two years as city marshal at Shattuck, Oklahoma, an irrepressible Jim Gober took up residence in San Francisco to be near his daughter's family and to gain experience as a private investigator. After a few months of on-the-job-training, part of it with the Pinkertons, Gober pulled up stakes and returned to Amarillo, intent on establishing his own detective agency. The opportunity eluded him for several years, however, and he bided his time helping enforce a community-wide smallpox quarantine and working as a bank guard until 1928, when he finally established the James R. Gober Detective Agency.

By this time, Gober had been working on his memoirs and writing poetry in his spare time for several years. He may have begun to reminisce, at least in part, as an antidote to loneliness. "The older I get," he once wrote, "the more lonesome I get for friends of my own nature and disposition, and I really pass many lonely hours because it is not convenient to be with company of my choice."[1]

Gober's celebrity as the first sheriff of Potter County occasionally attracted the attention of local reporters who sought him out for stories. He reminisced briefly for a 1924 newspaper article on the early-day Panhandle and gave a much longer interview, published under the title "Bad Men of West Easily Outwitted," in the Amarillo Sunday *News-Globe* in 1929. In the latter commentary the ex-lawman recounted his 1888 pursuit and capture of outlaw Lee Fuller and attempted to set the record straight on renowned mankillers like John Wesley Hardin, John Selman, and "Deacon" Jim Miller, who were being sensationalized by popular literature and motion pictures. "'The so-called bad man is more properly a weak man,'" Gober told the *News-Globe* reporter, adding, "'I never had to shoot a man in the discharge of my official duty, and I knew and handled some of the worst that West Texas ever saw . . . . Brains could outwit the quick draw every time. All the bad men I have known have been too dumb or too big cowards to have to be shot.'"[2]

Jim Gober's outburst of historical and biographical revelation was not only a reaction to the growing national popularity of western stories and films but also part of a general historical awakening among the residents of the Texas Panhandle during the 1920s. The origins of this movement were manifest even before World War I, with the founding in 1914 of the Panhandle Old Settlers Association. The motivating spirit of the fledgling organization was, ironically, Amarillo attorney Thomas F. Turner, who had helped defend Jim Gober at his 1889 murder trial.

Of even more lasting import was the establishment of the Panhandle-Plains Historical Society in 1921. While there is no evidence that Gober was ever a member of this organization, its widely reported activities, particularly the aggressive collecting program underway by 1925, could not have escaped his notice.

Gober's narrative, while one of the earliest accounts of pioneer life in the Panhandle, was certainly not the first. In fact, the novice writer may have drawn literary and even occupational inspiration from Charles Siringo, a former LX Ranch wagon boss with whom Gober had worked on an 1883 roundup. In 1885 Siringo had written his own widely circulated autobiography, *A Texas Cowboy*, covering his Panhandle years. In later books Siringo elaborated upon his subsequent career as a detective.

Jim Gober's recollections, in turn, may have influenced some of his old friends to record some of their own experiences. John Arnot, one of Gober's pallbearers, for example, produced several important first-hand sketches of cowboy life in the Panhandle in the 1880s, two of them published in the *Panhandle-Plains Historical Review* in the 1930s and others in local newspapers.

As his own memoir neared completion, Gober approached artist Harold Bugbee of Clarendon, Texas, about illustrating the work with line drawings in pen and ink. Bugbee agreed. In the spring of 1933, the artist sent Gober's illustrated article "Cowboys of Old Tascosa" to the *Dallas Morning News* seeking publication. The feature editor at the newspaper, however, declined to run the piece because a previous writer had covered similar material.

The rebuff came a few weeks after Gober, then age sixty-seven, had succumbed to a brief illness at the Amarillo home of his sister. The news of Jim Gober's passing rated front-page coverage in the Amarillo Sunday *News-Globe,* which used the occasion to reprint the 1929 article "Bad Men of West Easily Outwitted."

Methodist funeral services for the old sheriff were conducted on April 24, 1933, and Gober was buried beside other area pioneers in Amarillo's historic Llano Cemetery. Besides John Arnot, his pallbearers included John Snider, former Amarillo town marshal and friend from his cowboy days; and bankers Charles T. Ware and B. T. Baker, for whom Gober had worked as a bank guard.

Although the drafts and notes from which this book was created remained in family hands, Gober's original manuscript seems to have disappeared after his death. Earl Vandale, an industrious Amarillo collector of western Americana, did acquire a twenty-four-page typewritten account of the 1883 cowboy strike and its aftermath, written by Gober and accompanied by a three-page introduction giving details of the author's family background and personal philosophy. This undated, crudely written document may be the Gober account to which author John McCarty cryptically refers in his 1946 saga *Maverick Town, Story of Old Tascosa.*

Although not the work of a professional writer, Gober's reminiscences clearly embody the author's sense of history and belief that he had lived in extraordinary times. Jim Gober was also anxious to share the background, moral code, friendships, and kinships that shaped his attitudes and colored his vision of right and wrong and enabled him to overcome hardship.

A keen observer, Gober possessed a remarkable, though not infallible, memory for incident, anecdote, and detail. His memoir does not, for example, recall his holding the stakes at the first Panhandle prizefight, a bare-knuckles brawl held in Tascosa between two former LX cowboys. Nor does it recount his role in helping Amarillo postal contractor W. H. Fuqua establish the first mail route between Amarillo and Colorado City about 1890. And though Gober's autobiography documents several determined pursuits of outlaws in Texas and

Oklahoma, it ignores the sheriff's futile 1887 chase of a ranch cook who had sold him a stolen horse.

On at least two other occasions in what is otherwise a remarkably candid manuscript, Gober consciously declines to reveal key details bearing on controversial incidents. Sworn to secrecy in one such instance, he refers to the source of his account of the so-called "Big Fight" at Tascosa in 1886 only as "Silent Bill." A pencil annotation on the Gober typescript in the Vandale collection, however, identifies the informant (and one of the alleged slayers of the four men killed by gunfire in the incident) as a loner known as Bill Gale. In the second such instance, Gober intimates that he, too, played a role in the demise of an adversary who had attempted to murder him in Amarillo's bowery district.

Some revisionist historians of the American West will no doubt embrace Jim Gober's narrative as yet another confirmation of their own recent studies in failure. Gober himself would certainly have agreed that his life was no triumphant romp in a land of milk and honey. Yet he never considered himself a failure. His humble autobiography attests instead to a resilient spirit that persevered in the face of repeated adversity and disappointment.

B. Byron Price
Oklahoma City

Jim Gober (1864-1933), ca. 1888.

The Formative Years

A Pioneer Beginning

I t was the end of February 1881, and it seemed that spring had begun an early entry into Denton County. The beautiful wildflowers that would complete the picture of an early spring hadn't yet made their appearance in the rolling meadows along Clear Creek. Green, however, was showing in the grasses, and the trees were beginning to bud.

It was a time when everyone should have been looking forward with a spirit of joyful anticipation and hope for the spring, the summer, and beyond. A bright present and future was not what I saw as I sat in great misery that afternoon in the old oaken tub of cold water, looking at my horribly mistreated body. I knew I was the worst, most pitiful sight that anyone could imagine. That unexpected mule-dragging I got, when Father hit the stubborn mule I was tied to with a fence rail, had torn off all my clothes. What skin was left was in huge whelps from the bull nettle. Besides, I was already plumb tuckered out before the ornery mule did this to me. Nobody knew how Bob Wright had mistreated me, driving me like an animal relentlessly in front of his riding plow every day for two weeks until I was forced to bed from exhaustion.

Father and I had agreed for me to help Wright plow his field as a gesture of appreciation for the favors he had shown our family when our house burned to the ground. However, it had been difficult keeping this cruel treatment as a secret, for if Father had found out, it would have caused serious trouble between him and Wright, and that would have meant estrangement between his wife and our entire family.[1] Mainly, I was very sick at heart over being abused by a man who I had thought was my friend, a man whose wife was a cousin but in truth was as near a sister as possible not to actually be a sister.

There was the embarrassment with Father over my failure as a rail-splitter. How could I live that down? Four days I worked very hard, thinking I had done a commendable job of laying down timber to become the finest rails in the county, only to find to my disappointment that they were piss elms and couldn't be split with dynamite. But what the mean-spirited mule did to me was the last straw, the final disillusionment in my young life. I had lost my sweetheart, Augustine Alexander. That new teacher from Tennessee, Mr. Boren, had maneuvered himself into a position where he stole her affections. As if that wasn't enough, I had to be further embarrassed by his prejudice as a teacher that was now denying me an education. How could I accept this? I had learned real fast in school and always craved, since I was ten years old, to be a man of importance. With all of this, I knew in my heart that there was only one way out. I must leave home.

While I sobbed and Mother bathed the skinned places and got the sand out of the raw places, I pondered something I had been told by Uncle John Gober. He had said, "Jim, sometime you will reach a point in your life when you believe that everything is over, finished. That will be the beginning."

A glimmer of hope began to replace the darkness that had come over me. Some small stream of light from the beautiful day outside entered the room, and my mind, as I thought about the past and the wonderful heritage that I had. After all, didn't I come from parents who were of pioneer New England stock? Didn't my ancestors believe in fighting for what is right—my great-grandfather in the Revolutionary War and my father in the War between the States? I remembered the difficulties we had as a family and what Father and Mother had told me about our life when I was too young to know: the struggle to survive on Pot Creek in Hunt County, Texas, before and after my birth in 1864; the chaotic conditions in Texas following the war, with attacks by Comanche and marauding, lawless men. And there were the difficulties of running the mill on Long Branch.[2]

When we moved to Denton County, it was like "jumping out of the frying pan into the fire," with the Comanche raids that lasted until 1875 and the loss of our beautiful new home on Clear Creek. The loss left us destitute and with a feeling of hopelessness. North central

The Gober family, ca. 1890. Seated center, parents George Wisdom, Jr. and Amanda, with daughters Annie (left) and Sallie (right); standing, left to right, sons Arthur, Tom, Jim, and John. Courtesy Paul Tolbert, Upland, California.

Texas was a difficult frontier, and just existing was a dangerous challenge. But we made it, and I made up my mind that for the future, I would make it, too.

Apprehensive of her reaction, I told Mother I was going away to hunt work, something I could do without having so much trouble in my life. With great confidence she said, "Perhaps someone near home will need you and you could work for them and be where I would know you are all right, but," she paused, "you are to stay with me here until you get well, so I can doctor these skinned places and nettle stings." Secretly, I was hoping to be hired as a cowhand, for, like many a Denton County boy, I was fascinated by tales of the Old Chisum Trail as well as the Old Chisholm Trail.[3]

Leaving Home

I could just sense my chance to break away from my troubling past, to make a new beginning, was near when a few days later Mr. Lock Forester[4] came into town looking for hands to work on his cattle ranch. When I found him and asked for a job I was grinning all over with expectation. He looked me straight in the eyes and said, "Jimmie, I would like to give you a job, but I have some bronc horses to break before I start gathering cattle, and each man I am hiring will have to break at least one horse."

My smile of eager anticipation was suddenly replaced by a look of reluctance and concern. "Well," I said, "I don't mind trying to ride one," not sounding very convincing, I'm sure.

Forester replied, "Son, you ask your mother, and tell her you have to ride a bronc, and if she is willing, you can go out with me this evening."

Part of me said, "Jimmie, this is your big chance. Hurry home and get Mother's approval." The other part said, "Slow down—do you really feel you are capable of breaking in a bronc?" The underlying anxiety over the thought of having to ride that bronc left me with a real dilemma: Did I really want to be a cowboy?

I alternated running and walking home, but all the way struggling inside with the question of what should I do. When I found Mother and told her I had gotten a job with Mr. Forester, I wasn't sure whether to stand and receive my chastisement or to walk away and forget the idea. "Mr. Forester," she said, as her eyes sparkled with approval. "He is a good man, and I think you will be treated well. So I will let you go if you promise to come home every chance you get, and be careful and not get hurt." I felt somewhat relieved, but I worked hard to hide a guilty conscience for not telling her that I had to ride a bronc—but I knew it would be all off if she knew.

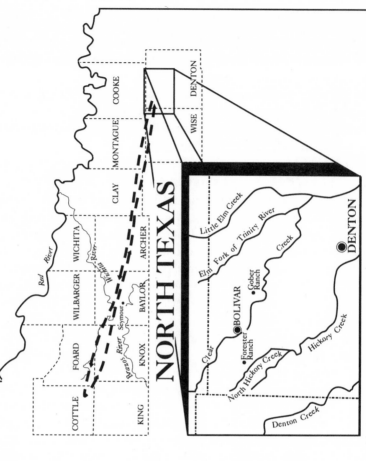

PANHANDLE

NORTH TEXAS

Early Adventures of Jim Gober
Part 1 : circa 1881

LEGEND

Reconstruction of Jim Gober's Cowboying Route
from near Bolivar, Denton County, to the original
Frying Pan Ranch, in Cottle County, and back

Statute Miles

10 0 10 20 30 40 50 60 70 80 90 100

© 1996 James R. Gober

I had mixed emotions about the step I contemplated taking. The chance to leave a disappointing life was an exciting and refreshing idea, but the thought of leaving home, my loving, caring family, had a finality about it that was unsettling to a sixteen-year-old. Nevertheless, I began getting my saddle and bridle in shape and fed my trusted pony that I had raised from a colt.

She was the first property I ever owned, and I came by her when what was considered to be the last Indian raid was made in these parts. The settlers had organized and overtaken the Indians and recaptured horses they had stolen, and there had occurred a running fight. The settlers shot one paint mare in the front leg, just above the knee, and the Indian that was riding her had climbed on another horse with its rider. This Indian mare was left crippled, but she finally got well and had a colt. The colt was a beauty, snow-white with fawn-colored spots on her hips. Since it was open range, the horses and cattle ran at large, and the calves and colts were rounded up and branded once a year. The Indian mare was a stray, so my father advertised her according to the stray law.[5] He bought her at the sale and gave me the colt, a beautiful pony that could gallop all day. Now, I had just prepared to saddle her to leave home, to be on my own for the very first time.

By noon my pony was saddled, and Mother had packed what clothing she thought I would need in a flour sack. I tied it behind my saddle and hitched my pony to the yard fence in front of the house to eagerly await Father's arrival from the field. His consent would be the last barrier I must hurdle to depart into a new life.

I took care to keep out of his sight long enough for Mother to plead my case. Finally, I slipped into the kitchen and found that Father had consented. After embracing me, patting me on the back and giving me his blessings, Father went back into the house. He soon emerged carrying, in one hand, a gunbelt full of .44-40 cartridges. In the other hand was a beautiful Colt with bone handles, which he slipped carefully into the holster attached to the belt. "Jimmie," he said, "I've had this Colt and belt for you a long time, and I knew this day would come. It is a mean world out there, Son. You're sixteen now and old enough to keep this and use it with responsibility."

"Thank you, Father," I said with tears of thanks and of mixed emotions over leaving, and with a great sigh of relief for getting my father's permission, I bade them both goodbye and rode away with my heart considerably lighter than it had been for several days. This

Courtesy Private Collection

When I turned my Indian paint pony down the road toward the evening sun,
My burden of grief and sadness had just begun,
. . . .

No heavier task has come my way,
Than leaving home and loved ones that sad day.

was a mighty step for a sixteen-year-old boy, and it took willpower, courage, and strength of character to leave a home environment such as I had always enjoyed: a loving mother, the strongest tie of all; a dependable father; a younger sister and brother; and last, but not least, my first sweetheart. As I rode away, weighing all that I had left behind, I began to have second thoughts, knowing that the only hope that I had was that of making a better and happier future.

When I turned my Indian paint pony down the road toward the evening sun, my burden of grief and sadness had just begun, and it was many days and nights before my grieving was done. Can you picture a tender-hearted, home-loving boy that had always been his mother's pride and joy, astride an Indian pony's back, with all his belongings in a flour sack, seeking some place to make his way by hardships and toil each day? No soldier ever stood in battle line that his burden was heaver than mine, and when my memory carries me back to that sad day I am sincere and can say truthfully, no heavier task has come my way than leaving home and loved ones that sad day.

As the crimson hues of sunset were being swallowed by purple shadows of the early evening, Mr. Forester and I finally arrived at his ranch. The ranch was located on the high, rolling prairie about four miles west of Bolivar, near the north Hickory Creek.[6] The splendid ranch house was an old-fashioned frame building, one of the first frame buildings to be constructed in the county. You could see several miles in every direction from its vantage point. From the house you could also see two large corrals and one small corral, all connected so that stock could be separated from one corral to the other. The small corral was used to run in and confine such stock as was to be lassoed for branding or for other purposes.

The next morning Mr. Forester gave detailed instructions to several men, then sent them out into the grazing pastures to bring in the range horses. By the middle of the afternoon they had one of the largest corrals full—at least one hundred head of mares and colts and two-, three-, and four-year-old unbroken geldings. The excitement of beginning a life as a cowboy was beginning to make its presence felt.

We all went to the corrals and began to run such broncs into the corrals as Mr. Forester directed. After getting one bronc each for the six of us, two Negroes, Phil Chisholm and Slick Allen, started lassoing the broncs. One would catch the bronc by the head, and the other would lasso the front feet. Another man would then get on the rope with each of the Negroes and throw the bronc. Still another man would bring a hackamore, a halter made of small rope and fastened to a larger rope, long enough and strong enough to hold the bronc when tied to a heavy log out on the prairie. After getting them all caught and tied to logs, the day's routine was over.

For quite a while, I stayed out where I could watch those broncs run on the rope and rare, and paw, and snort. It served as an indoctrination for me, and it gave me a chance to think about and reflect upon this new life. As I lay in my bunk that evening, I was in an undecided frame of mind as to whether I would try to ride one of those broncs or go home.

Cowboy: To Be, or Not?

When I got up the next morning I felt shaken and blue, having spent the night sleepless and in mental conflict. After breakfast, Mr. Forester called the Negroes up and told them to help each man get on his bronc and then for them to get on two good horses; in case anyone got thrown, they could catch the bronc. He spoke directly to Phil Chisholm and told him to saddle the three-year-old for me and to lead him with the rope fastened to his saddle horn. Then I felt better, and my courage was bolstered considerably as I realized that Mr. Forester had a greater interest than I expected in protecting my life.

After Phil and Slick got all of the men mounted, except me, some were running and some pitching, and all were a considerable distance away. It was then that we saddled my bronc as Phil fastened a blindfold made by folding a gunny sack. After putting it over the bronc's eyes, he got on his gentle horse and pulled the bronc's head up close to the horn of his saddle. I was then able to ease into my saddle on the back of this powerful animal, my first bronc.

The spirited horse reared and jumped and tried to run but was helpless, as Phil and his trusty horse knew just how to handle him. When we got out of sight of the house, away from the balance of the men, and my bronc was still trying to rear and jump, Phil said, "You get off of him, and I will take him to a cleaning." We both dismounted, and I climbed on his horse. Phil soon vaulted onto the bronc after he succeeded in getting a red bandanna over the animal's eyes. When he had adjusted himself in the saddle, he reached and pulled the bandanna off of the bronc's eyes, and he hit him down the hind legs with a heavy, rawhide quirt. Then the fun began for me.

The bronc pitched and bawled on every jump, just like a calf, and Phil hit him every jump he made. After pitching about fifty yards, he straightened out at a run, and Phil kept using his quirt. After running about two miles, the bronc was definitely through running away and had given out, and Phil told me to get on him. When I got up into the saddle Phil got on his horse, and he drove me and the bronc in front of him by using the quirt constantly. It took us until the dark shadows of dusk had fallen to get him back to the ranch. By then my bronc was

Courtesy Private Collection

*The bronc pitched and bawled on every jump, just like a calf, and Phil
hit him every jump he made.*

broken, so far as pitching was concerned, and it was easy for me to
handle him the next day.

My most-dreaded task was over, and I had finished the first degree
of a cowpuncher without any trouble. I began to feel considerably
more important.

Howdy, Rustler

We rode the broncs every day for the next four or five days, and
after we had them real docile, they were turned into a pasture with

About the tenth of March, we saddled old, trained cow ponies and used an old, gentle horse for a pack animal for our bed blankets, coffeepot, and frying pan. This trip was a milestone in my new chosen career.

the other saddle horses. It was early in March 1881, but the grass was already a healthy green, and the cattle and horses were doing better than most had seen them for that time of the year. About the tenth of March, we saddled old, trained cow ponies and used an old, gentle horse for a pack animal for our bed blankets, coffeepot, and frying pan. This trip was a milestone in my new chosen career, as we were preparing for my first short-duration roundup of stray cattle. I was detailed to lead the pack horse, and Jesse Murphy drove our extra mounts of one horse apiece and followed me.

We went south to Denton Creek, a distance of twenty miles, where we camped for the night. With us we carried a flour sack full of biscuits that were cooked at the ranch, some bacon and coffee, and that was our menu three times a day, if we found it convenient to stop that often.

There were two Forester brothers, Lock and John. Lock would take a man or two, and John likewise, and the separate outfits would go in different directions hunting the cattle that had strayed away during the winter. As they rounded up groups of stray cattle, they

There in the fire, were several pieces of wagon tires about four feet long, with one end turned up in a foot shape. When the tires were red hot, Phil and Slick began roping the cattle with the small brands, then tying them, hog fashion.

Branding on the Open Range

would turn them over to Jesse Murphy and me to herd and keep moving toward the designated camping place for the night. After being out ten days, we returned to the Forester Ranch with about one hundred head of cattle.

The Forester brand we were looking for was distinctive and could best be described as looking like railroad tracks running clear across the animal's side, and the brand was called Two Rails. I had noticed that we had several head of cattle in the herd that didn't have the Forester brand but had small brands of one or two letters of the alphabet, like A or B, C, or E.

The next morning, when I was awakened for breakfast, I walked out in the yard in the gray shadows of the early dawn. The light wasn't good yet, but I noticed a large fire out at the corral. After eating breakfast we went to the corral right to where old Phil Chisholm was keeping the fire going. There in the fire were several pieces of wagon tires about four feet long, with one end turned up in a foot shape. When the tires were red hot, Phil and Slick began roping the cattle with the small brands, then tying them, hog fashion. John Forester then grabbed a hot wagon tire and began burning the Two Rail brand on the animal. When he had finished, the Two Rail brand had entirely absorbed or covered up the small letter that made up the original brand. Then and there I got my second lesson in cowpunching, and I was amused and surprised, for the Foresters were considered leading citizens of the county, and they were well-to-do. I had never heard of them being accused of rustling cattle.

This incident of rustling by the Foresters in an outfit of which I was a member, albeit, a new, young member, created in me an internal moral struggle. The issue was whether I should live with this secret or make it known.

Cattle and the Open Range

A Cowboy, in Deed and in Truth

I worked for the Foresters until late in the autumn of 1881 and kept the secret of the rustling that I had observed on that ranch. It is with truthfulness and honesty that I say that only in this writing have I ever divulged my knowledge of that incident of rustling in Denton County.

When I departed the Foresters to go home, it was in anticipation of seeing my oldest brother, Tom. I was excited because he had written me that he had jobs for both of us to help drive a herd of six hundred head of cattle from the vicinity of our home area to the Pease River in Cottle County, a distance of two hundred miles.[1]

My brother had been working on a cattle ranch in Goliad County, on the coast of the Gulf of Mexico, and had been home for some time awaiting my return. The work he had told me about would be done for Bob and Crow Wright, the same Bob Wright that had worked me to a frazzle.[2] I told my brother I didn't want to go but didn't give him any reason, because I was still sensitive to the family implications that were involved. He insisted that I should go, and finally I consented.

Brother had negotiated with the Wrights, and when my pay was agreed upon at fifteen dollars per month we went to Bob Wright's ranch and began helping brand cattle and got ready to move. They allowed me to bring my trusted pony with me, the one I had raised from a colt. I guess I was still a kid in some ways, for having my horse to ride provided a sense of security that I needed.

William Crow Wright, ca. 1862. Collection of Mike Cochran, Denton, Texas.

After two or three days we were on the trail with a mess wagon and a cook named Garrison that was about sixty years old and cuckoo to the point that it was a pitiful act to put any responsibility on him. Besides Crow Wright there was Tom McDonald, Mack Rinehart, my brother, an old Negro named Dan Brumley, and myself, and we got along nicely and made fairly good time. The only thing that rubbed me a little was that Crow Wright seemed to be interested in keeping me impressed with the fact that boys should be humble and respectful to older men, by always leaving me on herd when we stopped at noon. I was told not to be too serious about the way he was because he had some wounds that acted up at times. Also, when I reflected on who Crow Wright really was, the respect he had in the community and the fact that he was a living hero of the War between the States and local Indian wars, I was less bothered and felt proud to be in his company.

Old Dan, the Negro, usually would be left with me on herd, and Dan thought very highly of me. He kept me entertained with the exciting experiences he had had in Indian fights. It seemed to me that Dan's experiences were centered mostly on fighting his horse to outrun the Indians he had encountered.

The country was beautiful, rolling and green, and the prairie just seemed to go on and on. This was the farthest from home that I'd ever been, and there was a thrill about it that I just can't describe. After being out on the prairie fifteen days we hit the Brazos River about noon, near where the thriving city of Seymour now stands.[3] At that time Seymour was composed of possibly a half dozen families living in dugouts and a small stock of groceries in another dugout.

A Fine Meal, Indeed

We turned the herd off course, probably one mile, and watered them in the Brazos River. What a sight it was to see all those cattle, some of them waded out a ways into the river and others just gathered along the banks. Never had I seen so many cattle in one place, and there was a feeling of importance that came over me knowing that I was part of this outfit.

I was left alone to graze them until the balance ate dinner. Then they would move the herd on while I had the rare privilege of eating what the crazy cook had left for me: rank bacon so old it was yellow, cold sourdough biscuits so hard they could be considered lethal weapons, black homemade molasses that I had to fight the bees for, and black coffee so strong that it could dispose of itself without any help.

While on herd at noon that day I saw a chaparral cock in a mesquite tree, the first chaparral I ever saw, and I thought it was the most beautiful bird I had ever seen. I looked around until I found a rock that suited me to throw, and when I threw it I was lucky and killed the chaparral. What a luxury dinner I pictured I would have that night!

So when I was relieved, I hurried to the wagon and told the cook to get a frying pan ready to cook my bird. I didn't take time to pick the feathers off, but I skinned him, took out the entrails, unjointed and washed him, then handed the tin he was on to the cook with the instructions to fry him.

The cook proceeded to grant my request, but with a little more of a grouch than usual. When he finished frying it, he handed the chaparral to me on a tin platter. I proceeded to attempt to eat it, but

While on herd that noon day, I saw a chaparral cock in a mesquite tree, the first chaparral I ever saw, and I thought it was the most beautiful bird I had ever seen.

couldn't. Chewing that bird was like what I imagined it would be like to chew on a rawhide string. I was so disappointed I could have cried.

After I caught up with the herd I told Dan about my troubles and blamed the old cook, for I really thought it was the way he had cooked the bird that made it so tough. Old Dan just laughed until tears ran down his cheeks. Finally, when he could quit laughing long enough to talk, he said, "Jimmie, those things are not fit to eat. They live on centipedes, tarantulas, and snakes—even kill rattlesnakes and eat

Courtesy Private Collection

We camped that night just at the edge of what was called the narrows, a high, narrow ridge with wasted, barren canyons, gulches, and washes on either side as far as you could see.

'em. You're lucky you couldn't eat the confounded thing, for it would surely have made you sick."

We camped that night just at the edge of what was called the narrows, a high, narrow ridge with wasted, barren canyons, gulches, and washes on either side as far as you could see. This ridge was fifteen miles long, and there was no water or grass, so we had to make the fifteen-mile drive before we could get grass or water for the cattle.

By daybreak next morning we were moving, and the cattle seemed to travel better than usual. We stopped at noon and had lunch and rested our herd, then proceeded on our way. In the evening the cattle began to get thirsty and travel faster, and just about one hour before sundown, we went out of the narrows down into a big valley. We could see trees in the distance, indicating that there was a creek and water. It was truly a spectacular sight as we came down into the valley, bathed in the sunset shades of red-orange.

This valley had an appearance different than anything that I'd seen before. It was covered with shinery, a kind of oak bush that bears small acorns that are fine feed for hogs or turkeys, and in any direction I looked, I could see big bunches of wild turkeys. They were strung out, moving towards little groves of cottonwood trees to roost for the night. Soon, a bunch of turkeys, probably about seventy-five, came within fifty yards of the herd, and I took after them on my pony. The turkeys, of course, flew, but they were so fat that one flight was all that they could make.

I spied a big gobbler that was the first to light on the ground, and he was squatting in a bunch of shinery. As I jumped off of my pony, I headed directly for the gobbler. He took off running, but I soon caught up with him and, believe me, for a wild turkey, that gobbler was a monster! I grabbed him, cut his throat with my pocket knife, awaited his demise, then tied him behind my saddle. By this time the herd had made it to a creek, and while it was filling up on water, the boss picked out a camping place for the mess wagon.

After getting camp established, Crow Wright provided a welcomed message when he said, "We will not have to night herd the cattle, as they are tired and hungry, and after they fill up on water, they will graze a while and then lay down."

Old Dan and I then proceeded, with great anticipation, to clean the gobbler, and when we got him cleaned well enough to eat, we just cut the meat off the bone and fried it like steak. Oh, boy! What a welcome feast it made for a hungry sixteen-year-old kid that was most starved for something fit to eat! I guarantee, there never has been a boy eat as much in the same length of time as I did. Every day after that, some one of us would catch a turkey or two, and we would just slice off the breast and throw the rest away.

A Cook from Bad to Worse

In four or five days we got to the Wichita River and turned our cattle loose and established a dugout to provide a winter camp for McDonald and Rinehart, who were going to stay with the cattle and make a permanent ranch.[4] Then Wright, my brother and I, the old cook, and Dan hit the back track for home.

It was then the middle of November 1881 and the fall rains had set in, making the weather disagreeable. Crow Wright was getting progressively worse. His suffering from arthritis and the wounds he'd gotten in his legs during the Civil War seemed to increase when the cold, damp weather set in. His face was one continuous grimace of pain.

The first day on the road home we traveled twenty-five miles, since we didn't have any stock to slow us down, only the horses we were riding and the team with the mess wagon. The cook was driving, and Crow Wright was riding on the wagon with him. That night it began to rain a slow, cold winter mist. We had a sheet and bows on the wagon, and my brother and I had a good tarpaulin on our bed consisting of several heavy comforters and blankets. Old Dan moved his pallet under the wagon, and Wright and the cook slept in the wagon.

Next morning we were up by daylight and barely managed to get a fire started with mesquite roots. Pretty soon I saw old Dan looking over the mess wagon with a concern on his face. "What's wrong, Dan?" I hollered as he started cussing and kicking the wagon.

"It's that old cook Mr. Garrison. He's sullen and won't make any effort to cook, just sits on the wagon, tongue swelled like a toad." No one knew what ailed the old cook, so Dan had to do the cooking. He made coffee and sourdough biscuits, half done, and fried bacon.

Wright was suffering from his Civil War wounds and didn't get out of the wagon; he just lay in his bed, not knowing of the cook's actions. After we finished that rough eating, my brother said to the cook, "Mr. Garrison, we're gonna hitch the team to the wagon while you put the pots and pans away. Now, we'll do our job and we expect you to do your job; then we'll be on our way."

We saddled our horses and hitched the team to the wagon and presumed the cook would follow us. Everything was ready to travel, and the cook had strolled off behind some mesquite bushes, so my brother, Dan, and I started on our way. There was no road, but we had just taken a dead-reckoning course, expecting to hit a trail during the day. We kept looking back for the wagon, and after we had ridden two or three miles, we stopped and waited half an hour; but still there was no wagon in sight.

My brother said, "Jimmie, you and Dan wait here while I go back to see what has happened to the wagon." We had slickers that kept the rain from getting our clothes wet, but it was cold and disagreeable nevertheless. After we had stomped around for at least two hours, we concluded we should go back and see what had become of my brother.

"Dan, this is the place where we camped last night," I told my companion as we came upon the smoldering campfire. "Look!" I shouted, pointing to wagon tracks in the muddy ground. "The wagon has been turned around and headed in the opposite direction." I also noticed the tracks of my brother's horse where he'd followed the wagon. Dan and I began gathering mesquite roots, and we struggled to renew the feeble fire we had left three or four hours before.

About noon we were relieved when saw the wagon coming across the prairie. My brother's horse was tied beside the team, and Brother was driving the wagon. He drove up while we were proceeding to cook dinner at the same spot where we had breakfast. Regardless what anybody else did, we were not going to starve.

Brother had overtaken the cook, driving in a fast trot in the opposite direction from our planned route. Wright had several hundred dollars in his pockets for expense money, and I am convinced that crazy old cook intended to get away with him and take his money, the wagon, and the team. He may have planned to put Wright's saddle on one of the work horses, leave the balance of the outfit, and make a getaway.

Wright was both mad and scared when he realized what had happened. "Gober," he said, looking in the direction of my brother, "What are we going to do with this jackass of a cook?"

After some discussion between Brother and Wright, Brother voiced a suggestion: "I think we ought to put Jimmie on the wagon as driver, then put Garrison on Jimmie's horse where we can watch him." Finally, Wright decided to follow Brother's suggestion and let me drive the wagon and put the old crazy cook on my horse. It was a foregone conclusion that when we got back to the settlements, we would ditch him.

We made another start toward home that evening but were only able to get about fifteen miles down the road. That night we made the cook sleep on the ground, and I slept in the wagon with Wright. My brother and Dan took turns staying awake, watching old Garrison. Next morning, Garrison was up by daybreak, had a fire going, and got breakfast in good order. He seemed more rational than he appeared to have been for days and continued to act all right, so we let him drive the wagon, but never again did we let him get out of our sight. It took us fifteen days before we finally reached home. It was now the first of December 1881, and my cowpunching for the year and my second episode as a cowboy was over.

I had saved my wages and was in good spirits except I was still haunted by the sadness of being beat out of the girl I loved. On the other hand, I had two other girlfriends that were perfectly sweet,

Finally, Wright decided to follow Brother's suggestion and let me drive the wagon and put the old crazy cook on my horse. It was a foregone conclusion that when we got back to the settlements, we would ditch him.

Moving the Wagon

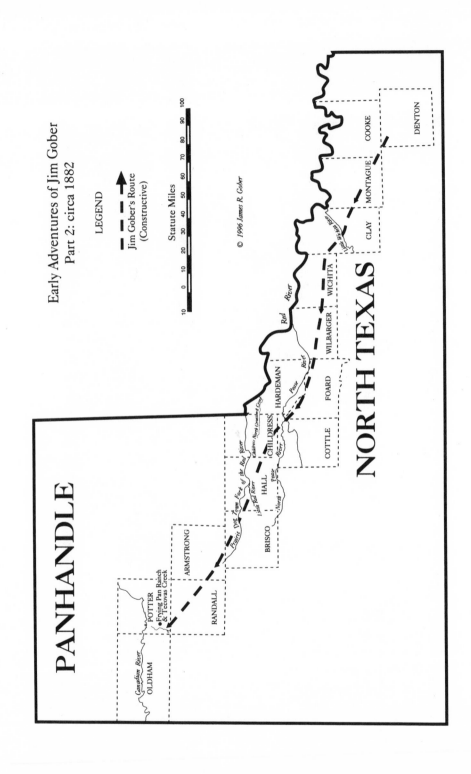

Early Adventures of Jim Gober
Part 2: circa 1882

LEGEND

Jim Gober's Route
(Constructive)

Statute Miles

10 0 10 20 30 40 50 60 70 80 90 100

© 1996 James R. Gober

PANHANDLE

NORTH TEXAS

OLDHAM
Canadian River
POTTER
Frying Pan Ranch
& Tecovas Creek
RANDALL
ARMSTRONG
Prairie Dog Town Fork of the Red River
BRISCO
Little Red River
North
Pease
HALL
Prairie
North
Pease River
Childress
Childress North (Groesbeck) Creek
CHILDRESS
COTTLE
HARDEMAN
Pease River
FOARD
WILBARGER
Red River
WICHITA
Little Wichita River
CLAY
MONTAGUE
COOKE
DENTON

good-looking girls, and both of them liked me. In fact, I had first place with them at all our parties, and, while I liked them and enjoyed their company, I wasn't in love with either of them.

Westward, Young Cowboy!

After hanging around Bolivar for three months, I was getting anxious to get on with my life as a cowboy. In March 1882, Mr. Arch Childs came to Crow's horse ranch, just two miles from Bolivar. Childs was in charge of the Frying Pan Ranch on the Pease River, some 250 miles west. He had come to Crow's ranch to buy fifty-five head of saddle horses to take to the Pease River ranch. Their plans were to use those horses in gathering three thousand head of cattle and moving them to the Panhandle of Texas, some two hundred miles farther west.

Mr. Childs was hiring a few hands to drive the horses to the Pease River ranch and then drive the cattle on to the Panhandle as soon as they could be gathered. I asked him for a job, and he hired me and several other young men who were good friends of mine. Among them were John Howard, Charley Woods, Albert Webster, John Grissom, John Alexander, Bing Grissom, and Sam Harmon, a schoolmate.

Our wages were to be thirty dollars per month. That was more than any of us had ever earned, so we were all in high spirits, and pleased that we were going to see the staked plains of the Panhandle of west Texas.

Mr. Childs had given instructions to his brother-in-law, a Mr. Cox, to bring a couple of mule teams, wagons, and camping outfits from his home near Sherman, in Grayson County, Texas. Mrs. Childs, two small sons, and Mrs. Cox, a sister to Mrs. Childs, joined us at Bolivar, and we started for the Pease River ranch with high spirits. This was the first experience any of us had had with women and children in the camp, so all the cowboys agreed we'd have to watch how we acted and what we said.

The third night we camped at Ramrod Johnson's ranch near Cambridge, Clay County, Texas.[5] After supper several of us walked to town, a distance of three-fourths of a mile. There we found a strange, somewhat alarming sight. As many as fifty cowpunchers and ranch owners were in town, standing on corners and moving from place to place in a restless way. It appeared to me that it would take only a small spark to ignite the fumes of discontent into a blazing,

As many as fifty cowpunchers and ranch owners were in town, standing on corners and moving from place to place in a restless way . . . . All of these restless men were heavily armed with .45-caliber, six-shooter pistols and a belt full of cartridges.

Courtesy Private Collection

deadly firefight. All of these restless men were heavily armed with .45-caliber, six-shooter pistols, and a belt full of cartridges.

We obtained information that Jim Curtis and Van Rice, cattlemen, had had a gunfight a few days before, and Rice had killed Curtis. Rice, who was badly wounded from the encounter with Curtis, was shot and killed from a window by some unknown party while he lay in bed the night before our arrival.

Bing Grissom and I sized up the situation there in town, and Bing turned to me and in a low voice expressed his concern: "Jimmie, I don't like what I see going on here. We'd best get what we need and make tracks for Johnson's ranch." I shared Bing's concern. We didn't ask any questions but got what incidentals we happened to need, then hastened back to camp.

Encounter with a Lasting Love

It began to rain that night at Johnson's ranch and continued the next day. However, we moved on, riding through Henrietta,[6] which was only five miles from Cambridge. As we crossed the Little Wichita and camped one mile from town, it was still raining, and the ground had gotten too soft to make any headway with the wagon, so we stayed there two days and nights.[7] The second night we were invited to a dance in town, and several of us went and found a hearty welcome.

Henrietta was then a small, western cattle town, and the people were full of frontier hospitality and congeniality. Since I was always backward and timid among strangers, I didn't have any intentions of taking part in the dancing. However, a very courteous young man from the local town took notice of me. I must have looked sad and left out, for when he approached me, he had a look of sympathy on his face as he said, "You look left out of having a good time. I'm Fite Garrity. What's your name?"

"Jim Gober's mine," I said, as my hand met his in a solid shake.

"How about if I get a dancing partner for you?"

"Oh that's all right, Garrity, I'm just enjoying being off the trail and listening to the music."

"Aw come on," he retorted. "You must participate in the dancing, or you'll miss the most enjoyable part." Since he had insisted on my dancing, I finally consented, just to show my appreciation for his friendliness and kindness.

He went to several grown young ladies but found them engaged for the dance or set, which it was called in those days. Four couples would form a square, and one man would call "Balance all, swing your partner" and "Promenade" and so forth.

My new-found friend finally went to a little girl by the side of the dance floor who seemed to be surrounded by friends. She was very young, yet there was a striking beauty about her that caused me to stare. He came to me in an apologetic way and said, "They are going to run two sets this time, and most of the ladies seem to be engaged, but I have gotten you a little twelve-year-old girl that is as good a dancer as any of them, if you don't mind dancing with a girl."

I told him, "That suits me just fine, for I am only a boy myself."

As my friend brought her around to the end of the dance hall where I was standing, I marveled at the sweet face and the radiance of this beautiful little brown-eyed girl. Fite, my self-appointed benefactor, who seemed to be doing very well for the moment, and the young girl approached me. "This is Miss Belle Helen Plemons," he said as she smiled very sweetly at me. As I introduced myself and we talked and danced until the evening festivities were over, I couldn't have been more congenially and agreeably entertained than I was that evening. While I was certain that we were too young to develop a serious relationship, something just told me that I would see Miss Plemons again. The next morning we moved on and had no mishaps until we arrived at the Pease River ranch, a week later.

Friendly Jesting

As soon as we finished unloading and had everything arranged about the ranch headquarters, Mr. Childs began to scatter the men out in different camps on the outer reaches of the range, and he gave me a line to ride, about ten miles from and back to the ranch, so I could be with Mrs. Childs and Mrs. Cox at night. The two men would both be busy receiving and branding cattle at distant ranches from which the cattle were bought.

Mr. Childs would come in once a week, and he took special delight in teasing me about being familiar with his wife and Mrs. Cox, and it seemed the more men that were present, the rougher he would get. On several occasions it caused me to leave the dinner table before I finished my meal. But as time went on, I got used to him and liked him, and his method of joking didn't bother me. Both Mrs. Childs and Mrs. Cox were good and kind to me, and I soon felt that I was one of the family.

After about thirty days, it was necessary to extend my riding line clear through between the Frying Pan and the R2 range, so Mr. Childs came to me and said, "I will have to put you off in the cedar breaks away from these women, or they are going to be fighting over you. They have got you spoiled now until you aren't any account for anything except a ladies' man." All of this he said in the presence of the women and five or six men. I just turned red and didn't know what to say, I was so embarrassed by his remarks.

Mr. Childs gathered a tent, my bedding and Bing Grissom's as well, a frying pan, coffeepot, and bread skillet, and packed them on a horse. We saddled our horses, each riding one and leading the extra horse

Courtesy Private Collection

After getting us lined up and giving us instructions how to ride next day, Mr. Childs bade us goodbye and started climbing up the trail.

as we struck out to the Pease River country. We went into the roughs on the north side of the river, crossed canyons and table lands, and climbed small mountains, finally hitting a cattle path that led down off of a ridge into a deep basin, five hundred feet below. This little basin probably contained five acres of land and on one side was a deep gulch with a seeping spring that ran a small stream of water for fifty yards, then sank into the crevices of the rocky bottom of the gulch.

Interlude with a Tiger

All around this basin were scrub cedar trees and brush. We found a suitable spot, stretched our tent, and hobbled all the horses. We left one tied with a stake rope so that we could ride it after the others, should they become restless and stray off. After getting us lined up and giving us instructions how to ride next day, Mr. Childs bade us goodbye and started climbing up the trail.

Grissom and I were the same age and had been raised in the same county. His parents and mine were pioneer settlers in Denton County and always congenial friends. I don't believe Grissom and I spoke a word to each other until we had our supper and made down our beds in the tent. We both had Colt .45 revolvers, Winchesters, and two shepherd dogs that had been brought with us so that we would each have one to chase cattle we might find drifting across the boundary of our range.

When it was dark, we went to bed with our six-shooters and our Winchesters by our sides, and we finally began to talk. I don't remember who broke the silence that had prevailed for two hours; however, once broken, we were both full of talk and no sleep.

About nine o'clock, when it was so dark it was impossible to see five feet in any direction, a panther that had evidently come to the spring for water spied the dogs, which began to bark and growl. When the panther gave out the most hideous and blood-curdling scream I had ever heard, both dogs burst in at the tent opening and sneaked down at our feet with their tails between their legs. Grissom and I both sat up straight in our beds, with six-shooters in hand, and we were silent again for ten minutes. During that time the panther growled two or three more times, seeming to get farther away each time. Finally, I conceived the idea of shooting several shots in the direction of the spring with the hope of scaring off the panther. I fired the three shots in the direction of the spring by poking my six-shooter under the bottom of the tent. Then we put the dogs out and tied the tent flaps good, and then we sat up in bed until daylight. I really believe the first gray hair came in my head that night.

The next morning we went to the spring. "Look at those tracks," Grissom shouted as I noticed the surprised look on his face and gazed in the direction that he was pointing. "Wow!" I ejaculated in astonishment, bending down to examine more closely the paw marks left in the soft dirt. "Look at these marks, Bing; they're many times larger than these dogs' paws could have made and larger than my hand can cover."

We decided then and there to get back off of our line in time to cut poles and build a scaffold as high as the tent would permit, and then to put our beds up off the ground. That would at least help protect us from rattlesnakes and skunks.

Unexpected Impression

Mr. Childs had informed me that during the day's ride I would meet an R2 man that didn't have much sense, and that he was just as liable to turn a bunch of our cattle to the R2 range as he was to turn them our way. Childs said further that if I saw him running cattle I must overtake him and stop the cattle, and if they were ours, to give him a good cursing, and if he got saucy, to use my quirt on him.

My route was to climb out of this hellhole and through the roughs and onto the flats covered with mesquite grass and mesquite brush that extended from the breaks of the Pease River to North Groesbeck.[8] I started early and rode nine or ten miles and didn't see any cattle to turn back. Suddenly, I saw a horseman coming through the mesquites to meet me. I instinctively knew that he was the R2 crazy man Mr. Childs had warned me about. He had long hair and a full beard, carried a Winchester, six-shooter, Bowie knife, and two belts of cartridges, but spoke very polite, and his way of expressing himself showed him to be a man of intelligence. We had a conversation of about fifteen minutes, and I felt like I had known him always and liked his appearance. His name was Jake Smith, and I learned before we parted that he and Childs were old-time friends. Knowing Childs's devilish nature, I knew he had ribbed me, thinking I would run into a bunch of cattle Smith might be chasing, and if I had treated him like Childs had suggested, it would have been a joke, in his mind, on Smith.

When I saw Childs a few days afterwards, I said, "Say, about turning cattle back and quirting that R2 man, I refused to obey orders." Childs laughed until I thought he would burst.

Grissom and I arrived back at our new home of purgatory about four PM. We proceeded to cut poles and set forked posts and made scaffolds for our beds. For several nights we could hear all kinds of growls and barks of different varmints that came there for water, as that was the only water for ten miles in any direction. But the dogs began to get braver and would bark and venture out from the tent. The panther never yelled anymore, and we both got to where we could sleep. However, the least noise would have us up with our guns at the ready, as long as we remained in that hellhole, which was about thirty days.

The New Frying Pan Ranch

One day we were instructed to pick up our traps and belongings and go to the ranch, where they had a herd of two thousand cattle, branded and ready to start. We were about to head for the Panhandle ranch location, in the west end of the Panhandle of Texas, in what became Potter County. A handful of us were to go with the first herd. In a few days we were on our way with three thousand head of cattle

Courtesy Private Collection

A handful of us were to go with the first herd. In a few days we were on our way with three thousand head of cattle and eight men, besides the cook.

and eight men, besides the cook. We had five horses to the man and four mules on the chuck wagon. Mr. Tom Smith was our trail boss, a fine man indeed, and all of us got along well with him.

We stood guard around the cattle at night, two men at a time keeping a vigil for a period of three hours. All the horses were hobbled at night, and one man would round them up early in the morning to be unhobbled and to catch the ones we were to ride until noon. At that time we would get fresh ones and turn loose the ones we had ridden.

After about twenty-five days en route we arrived at the range set aside for the new Frying Pan Ranch.[9] We turned the cattle loose and established temporary camps on the outskirts of the land our company owned or controlled, an area which measured twelve by sixteen miles. Men were already at work fencing, and they continued until the entire range was under a four-strand barbed-wire fence.

It was during this period in the spring of 1882, right after I had helped establish the new Frying Pan Ranch, sixteen miles west of where Amarillo stands today, that I first met Temple Houston.[10] Our first meeting was soon after he had begun to practice law at Mobeetie, Texas.[11] One of the owners of the cattle, Mr. H. B. Sanborn, had come to Mobeetie, had hired a buggy team, and had hired Temple Houston

Temple Houston, ca. 1885.
Courtesy Sam Houston
Memorial Museum,
Huntsville, Texas.

to come with him to transact some business pertaining to land titles.[12]
The distance from the Frying Pan Ranch to Mobeetie was one hundred miles.

At the time of our meeting, I was riding a line on the range to keep the cattle from drifting north. I rode from the east line of the range to the west line, a distance of twelve miles, and my route was along the Old Fort Bascom Trail, which skirted the breaks of the Sweet Lacruse.[13] I had made my line and left the trail and started for the ranch. Just as I approached the dry fork of the Tecovas Creek, it began to rain and hail and lightning and thunder furiously.[14] I was riding at a fast gallop, and presently I saw a buggy and team, and as I rode to it, I found Mr. Sanborn sitting in the buggy with a buffalo robe around him. Temple Houston, then not over twenty one years of age, was standing in front of the team holding the horses by the bridle bits while they, of course, were pawing and lurching from the hail. Houston was swearing savagely at the hail, the team, the rain, and when a keen clap of thunder would explode, Houston would smile and curse louder. He was a striking figure of a man, with long auburn hair

Headquarters, Frying Pan Ranch, Tecovas Springs, Texas, ca. 1882-83. Left to right: John Grissom; unknown; Mrs. W. W. Wetsel, first white female resident of Potter County and wife of the first foreman of the Frying Pan Ranch; Harry Wetsel, son of Mr. and Mrs Wetsel; Thomas Fitzgerald, brother of Mrs. Wetsel; unknown (possibly Jim Gober); Charles Dar, ranch cook; unknown; George Johnson, cowboy and later ranch boss. Courtesy Amarillo Public Library.

and steel gray eyes that danced back and forth as his anger at the storm increased to frightening proportions. That surprising incident was my first encounter with Temple Houston, who later became a close personal friend. I didn't see Houston again, however, until 1888, in Austin, Texas.

Mr. Childs went to Tascosa, an old Mexican town of probably three hundred people, with two supply stores that hauled in their goods by ox team from Dodge City, Kansas, or Springer, New Mexico, each a distance of about 250 miles.[15] He had hired several Mexicans and brought them out to build a ranch house of adobe. In thirty days we had a large, convenient house for the ranch headquarters. Then the Mexicans turned their attention to building a huge adobe corral and stable. Thus the once famous Frying Pan Ranch was established in June 1882, just west of where the beautiful city of Amarillo now stands with its population of twenty-five thousand people. Amarillo was established when the Fort Worth and Denver Railroad was built through the Texas Panhandle in 1887, five years after the Frying Pan Ranch. I was fortunate to be involved in both events.

By the time the headquarters ranch was finished, Mrs. Childs and Mrs. Cox had arrived, and Mrs. Wetsel, the wife of the foreman, came.

Cowboys in Dodge City

Then several of us decided to go back into Dodge to take in the sights.... After we had all prowled the town quite awhile, most of the outfit went back to camp except Gus and me. We had decided to stay all night.

She was a most welcome addition, a handsome young woman with a jolly, sociable nature who kept all of us in good cheer and spirit.

By the middle of June, the second herd of fifteen hundred head of cattle had arrived from the Pease River ranch. John Grissom had bossed it through, and things ran along nicely for several months. In the fall, however, some dissatisfaction arose between Mr. Childs and Mr. Sanborn, one of the owners of the ranch. Mr. Childs quit, and he and Mr. Cox and their families went back to their homes in Grayson County. John Grissom was put in charge of the ranch.

On the Trail to Dodge City

In October 1882 we gathered the fat steers and started them to Dodge City, Kansas. Gus Gober was given six men, a cook, and a horse rustler, and put in charge of the herd. I was one of the six cowpunchers chosen to make the trip under Gus Gober, a double cousin of mine, five years older and a handsome, good fellow.

It was 250 miles to Dodge City and took us eighteen days on the trail. After arriving and shipping our cattle, or rather after we loaded them in the railroad cars, we took the mess wagon four or five miles back down the trail toward home and camped. Then several of us decided to go back into Dodge to take in the sights. That decision might have proved to be a fatal for one Gus and me.

After we had all prowled the town for quite a while, most of the outfit went back to camp except Gus and me. We had decided to stay all night. When the balance of the group had departed to return to camp, Gus and I, without hesitation, went off to treat ourselves to some decent grub. Our memory of the taste of good food seemed almost lost, but when we walked by a place by the name of Kelley's, the smell of food drew us in like a magnet.

After we had eaten till our bellies were full, we walked on down Front Street to the Long Branch Saloon, a place where we could get some of the wild mare's milk.[16] I was attracted to the name Long Branch, the same name as a place in Hunt County, Texas, where we had lived when I was a small child. We checked our gunbelts, as was required by the city ordinance, and had taken a bottle and a couple of glasses over to a small table and had just settled down to a welcomed drink when a disturbance erupted at a gambling table across the end of the room. One of the gamblers who was arguing in a loud voice with another moved suddenly and fell over backwards in his chair.

For some reason known only to Gus, he got tickled at the poor, clumsy gambler and let out a whoop and a holler. The next thing we knew, the irate gambler, a big, burly fellow with bushy eyebrows arched over his mean, rattlesnake eyes, was aiming a short forty-five right in Gus's face. "You little skunk," he growled. "I'm gonna give you something to holler about. Nobody laughs at me and gets away with it."

Just then I looked up, and another man had a gun at the gambler's back, saying, "He's gonna get away with it, Jake, unless you're ready to die to try to make your threat stick." It was the city marshal, who had come into the saloon, thank goodness, in the nick of time. I learned that the marshal was Jack Bridges, and he hauled old Jake away to jail for assault and for having a concealed weapon, not checked as required.[17]

We finished our drinks with haste and departed, somewhat shaken by the incident. Gus and I then decided that the evening was still young and not to let the experience dampen our spirits, so we strode on down to the Lady Gay Dance Hall. When we got there, everyone seemed to be having a gay time, in keeping with the name, but later, every time the music stopped you could hear loud, angry voices. It seemed as though a jealousy skirmish had broken out, not too uncommon in dance halls. However, this skirmish soon broke out into a full-fledged battle as sides seemed to form and guns started blazing. Three men were down and the crowd was dispersing, many fleeing out the doors of the hall.

Next morning we learned that three men had been killed at the dance hall, but there was no talk or excitement over the affair. Killing men in Dodge City was such a common occurrence that it created no excitement or concern, and usually someone had to be hired to bury them. But the whispered news we got through a woman made us content to saddle our horses and strike for camp and get the outfit on the way to the ranch.

Home, Sweet Home

When we arrived back at the ranch and had done some preparing for the winter by establishing men in side camps, Gus, Charlie Woods, and I had decided to go home and spend Christmas with our folks, so we left the ranch on the tenth of December. Charlie's father, mother, and two sisters lived at Graham, Young County. We went some out of our way to go by Graham with Charlie, and we spent two nights and one day with his family. They were fine, hospitable people, and one of his sisters gave us a dance the second night and we had a great time.

Next morning, Gus and I hit the road early, and the second day we rode into Bolivar at four PM. It was only two days until Christmas. I began to get invitations to various entertainments as soon as the news spread that I was home. Every day was most enjoyable for the next two months.

It seems Augustine, my old sweetheart, and the teacher had married some four months after I had left home. But I had gotten over my lovesickness for Augustine and had really concluded I had been living in a dreamland. My attitude was due for a change to where I should not look on any of my girlfriends too seriously. I felt that I would have that same spirit all my life, but time changes all things and the spirit as well, as I certainly learned when I grew older.

I was having a good time during my extended stay at home. My oldest brother, Tom, was home from the Cripple Creek gold camp in Colorado, and he had bought ten head of cow ponies for me, having found them at a bargain. He had decided to go to the Panhandle with me, and we planned to leave the first of March. I hated to leave worse than ever but was obliged to be back at the Frying Pan at a certain time in March. We packed one pony, drove the balance, and we were on our way March 1, 1883. We had a good trip, reaching our destination March 12, safe and sound, with all our ponies.

During the winter, the adjoining ranch on the south, the T Anchor Ranch, had been sold to an English syndicate.[18] They had agreed to take all saddle horses with the ☈ brand at fifty dollars per head. Cattle and horses were to be turned over the first of June. Their boss was a good fellow and liked me, so we took six head of my ponies that had cost fifteen dollars per head and put the ☈ brand on them in the T Anchor range. The first of June, the English syndicate had six Mexican ponies at fifty dollars apiece.

The Cowboys of Old Tascosa

The Stage and the Setting

I n the summer and fall of 1882, there began a period of significant change in and around the large cattle ranches that called the Panhandle of Texas home. Cattle had advanced in value considerably as demand soared throughout the country. The fame and reputation of these cattle-producing businesses spread, not only to the eastern United States but also to Europe. What resulted was that many of the large ranches and herds were acquired by the English syndicate.

One of the large ranches in the Panhandle that fate and circumstance thrust right into the middle of these major alterations of life and process and the ensuing controversy and turmoil that would result was the Lee-Scott Cattle Company, well known as the LS Ranch.[1] The headquarters was located some thirty-five miles west of Tascosa.

The historic trading point known as Tascosa, a wild cattle town, also became a focal point of considerable change. Since Tascosa was the only trading point in a radius of two hundred miles, the major ranches in the Panhandle relied upon the bustling settlement to supply its principal needs for ranch supplies.

Cowboys from the ranches were drawn to Tascosa because of its seemingly limitless supply of red liquor,[2] gambling games, and sporting women. It seems the population of those who conducted such businesses became excess baggage in Mobeetie in 1882, when they were run out of that rowdy town by the Texas Rangers. These peddlers of pleasure increased the population of Tascosa, finding more than a welcome home there. Since some major cattle trails[3] came through

Equity Bar, Tascosa, Texas, with Sheriff James Henry East on horseback, ca. 1880s. Courtesy Panhandle-Plains Museum, Research Center, Canyon, Texas.

Interior of Jack Ryan's saloon, Tascosa, Texas, ca. 1880. Courtesy Panhandle-Plains Museum, Research Center, Canyon, Texas.

the Texas Panhandle heading for the Kansas markets, itinerant cowboys from trail driving teams often crowded the pleasure houses of Tascosa, providing additional instigators of conflict.

A principal catalyst for change, although there is some question of the value of the change he prompted, was Captain W. M. D. Lee, manager and part owner of the Lee-Scott Cattle Company.[4] Lee resided at Fort Leavenworth, Kansas, but made frequent trips to the LS Ranch each year to look over general conditions and give instructions for future ranch activities. It is possible that Lee, because he didn't live in the Texas Panhandle on a day-to-day basis, may not have sensed the undercurrent of discontent that was growing among the cowboys. On the other hand, he just may have been unsympathetic to the plight of the cowboy and insensitive to the situation in view of the potential economic impact to the ranch owners that a change, beneficial to the cowboys, might bring.

The change in ownership of some of the cattle interests and the advance in value of cattle brought no corresponding raise in wages for cowhands. They remained at thirty dollars a month for common hands and fifty for bosses. This disparity began to cause general dissatisfaction among the boys on all ranches, with the feelings of injustice and indignation finally bringing about an attempt at defensive action.

In February 1883, the cowboys organized a strike for higher wages, and Tom Harris was appointed leader and manager of the strike.[5] Most of the cowboys on ranches within 150 miles of Tascosa quit work, banded together, and established a camp convenient to Tascosa. Tom Harris, who worked for Lee as foreman or wagon boss, was a capable, trustworthy man, well-liked by those who worked under him and by all other cowboys that knew him. His esteem by all of the cowboys and his natural leadership capabilities made him a perfect choice to lead them in strike.

The cowboy strike came as a surprise to Brother and me, as we did not learn about it until we arrived at the Frying Pan Ranch on March 12. We also learned that the strikers, about 150 in number, had made camp near Tascosa. With the possibility of work being very remote, my brother concluded that he would go on to Cripple Creek, Colorado, where he had prospected during the gold boom.

I went to work as soon as I could get my old mount together, regardless of the strike orders. All the cowboys that I had gotten acquainted with the year before seemed to like me, and I told them whenever the question would arise, "I am neither for nor against the strike, but I am a Democrat and claim the freedom and liberty to choose whether I will work or not." I don't think any of them held any malice against me; if so, I never knew about it.

Being idle, the cowboys were naturally restless, and they indulged in all the pleasures Tascosa afforded, gambling, drinking and entertaining sporting women. As was to be expected, all were broke in

Colorado Gold

With the possibility of work being very remote, my brother concluded that he would go on to Cripple Creek, Colorado, where he had prospected during the gold boom.

thirty days, disbanded, hunting jobs, and ready to acknowledge defeat. No doubt, if these cowboys returned to the jobs they left thirty days before, they would have been more efficient than ever before and more loyal to the interests they had forsaken. However, Captain Lee was president of the Cattlemen's Association, and his wishes were accorded the respect usually given to men in his position.[6] He gave written notice to all ranch foremen to refuse employment to all cowboys who had joined the strike, furnishing a complete list of the strikers' names. His vindictive actions rekindled the flame that had subsided, was smoldering to ashes, and would soon have blown away. I am confident that Captain Lee soon realized the seriousness of his mistake, but his "rule or ruin" disposition dominated his personality, spirit, and actions.

Then, in the early spring of 1884, Lee poured more fuel on the already flaming fire by sending for Pat Garrett.[7] Garrett, the notorious slayer of Billy the Kid, brought two bad-man killers with him from Roswell. With the addition of six LS cowboys who had remained loyal, refusing to strike, Garrett organized a special ranger company for the Panhandle and then returned to New Mexico.[8] These eight rangers were then instructed to take their orders and directions from Captain Lee. Being rangers under Pat Garrett soon inoculated the six former LS cowboys with the bad-man spirit, and they began to snub and otherwise mistreat the boys with whom they had worked, side by side, before the strike. Fortunately, the LS Rangers lasted only a year, and then they were disbanded. Nevertheless, camps of discontent and future reprisal had already been formed.

Some of the boys that had joined the strike owned a few cattle, having had their brands recorded in the name of some friend not connected with the cattle business. The acquiring of cattle was done in this manner because it was known that a cowboy owning cattle could not get work on any of the large ranches. These various small brands were termed maverick brands by the cattle companies, because it was logical reasoning that the ambitious cowboy would put his brand on any unbranded yearling not following its mother. As a matter of fact, these yearlings were usually calves by some stray cow whose owner was not known. The cowboys contended that they had as much right to the mavericks as anyone, but every large company claimed all unbranded yearlings that were found on its individual range. This claim by the large ranches brought forth a feeling of distrust on one side and injustice on the other.[9]

There is no doubt in my mind that Tom Harris realized fully the difficult position in which the strike and all the many circumstances leading up to it had placed every cowboy in the Panhandle of Texas. Furthermore, he certainly must have sensed his own untenable position as the leader of the strike. Inevitably, his own life and every action, personal or otherwise, connected with his selected position of responsibility, would come under intense scrutiny; anything he did would draw the attention of big ranch owners and all of the eyes and ears that were available to them. My personal concern was for Tom Harris, my friend, and how he would weather the storm that undoubtedly lay ahead.

Harris was a determined man on any question in which he believed himself to be right, but after the strike had failed, he organized a cowboys' cattle company.[10] I haven't the slightest doubt that his intention was to get out of the poisonous atmosphere caused by the strike, to establish a productive ranch, and to accumulate something for himself and the friends who had invested in his cattle company.

After a Maverick

The cowboys contended that they had as much right to the mavericks as anyone, but every large company claimed all unbranded yearlings that were found on its individual range. This claim by the large ranches brought forth a feeling of distrust on one side and injustice on the other.

The headquarters of the ranch and cattle company was near Endee, a few miles over the line in New Mexico.[11] I believed in his good intentions sufficiently to invest one thousand dollars in the venture, and I wish to state that my confidence in Harris's honor and loyalty to obligations was wholly justified at the final settlement, sometime later, of my interest in the company.

Tom Harris was a fine specimen of manhood, about six feet tall, with blue eyes and light brown hair, broad of shoulder and well proportioned from his head to his booted feet. He knew no fear and always stood for justice and equality among men. I was but seventeen when I first met him in 1882, and he must have been about thirty-three years old.[12] In spite of our age difference, we soon became staunch friends.

The Lee-Scott range bordered the state line of Texas; the Harris range extended to the same line of New Mexico, which circumstance strengthened the antagonism between W. M. D. Lee and Tom Harris. Cattle from both ranges crossed the line, making it necessary for

Harris and LS men to be thrown together during the roundups. No doubt Lee thought Harris had located his range with the sole purpose of depredating LS cattle, which was another injustice to Tom.

In the spring and summer of 1884, Captain Lee sent his Pat Garrett rangers with a wagon to follow the roundup on the various ranges. They had instructions to gather all maverick brands, including cattle belonging to cowboys who had registered small bunches in the name of a friend. As president of the Panhandle Cattlemen's Association, Lee ordered these actions under the pretense that money obtained from the sale of cattle confiscated under the stray law would be put in the school fund. Most of the owners of these small bunches had gone to Montana, Wyoming, Dakota,[13] and Arizona seeking work.

The Garrett rangers gathered about one hundred head of these cattle under Lee's orders, drove them to Las Vegas, New Mexico, sold them, and spent two weeks and the proceeds gambling, drinking, and playing the dance halls. So far as I was ever able to learn, none of this money was ever accounted for.

During the fall and winter following this cattle confiscation, Captain Lee reached the height of unpopularity. The LS Rangers made a bad matter worse by staying in Tascosa most of the time, becoming more and more antagonistic towards those cowboys remaining in the vicinity and just plain asking for trouble.

A Precursor of Trouble

Early in the spring of 1885, I went to Tascosa and met with Tom Harris, who had come from the New Mexico ranch for a few days' vacation. He had been in town several days and was drinking excessively. This situation worried me, for in his case it indicated that something had gone very wrong.

Harris and I were inseparable, but it was dangerous for other than a friend to approach him when he was drinking, particularly his enemies, the LS Rangers. We both were carrying Colt .45s and a full belt of cartridges, and I was constantly uneasy, fearing trouble. However, taking any chance was preferable to deserting him.

As usual with most of our friends, we made our headquarters at Jesse Jenkins's saloon.[14] Jesse was a warm, dependable friend to Harris and me, was square as a die and fearless as a lion. In addition, Jesse and I were raised in adjoining counties. In short, the three of us were as one.

James Henry East, Oldham County sheriff 1883-86, ca. 1884. Courtesy J. Evetts Haley Collection, Nita Stewart Haley Memorial Library, Midland, Texas.

About sunset of my first evening in town, Harris and I were in the gambling room of Jenkins's saloon. The building faced north on the main and only business street and was directly opposite the Russell Hotel.[15] A twenty-foot section of the rear of the saloon was partitioned off for the gambling games, with an arched opening of seven or eight feet in the center of the partition giving an unobstructed view of the entire length of both rooms. Harris, with his back to the entrance, began to play at a monte game[16] while I stood facing the saloon and, through its swinging doors, the main street. It was just dusk when the old stagecoach drew up in front of the Russell Hotel and I saw three strange men get off with revolvers in their belts and Winchesters in their hands. I noticed that Jim East, the sheriff of Oldham County,[17] and a couple of Garrett's LS Rangers had met them. At once I decided that they must be new recruits to the rangers, but feeling the need to be sure, I called Lem Woodruff, a bartender I knew, to one side, asking him, "Go across to the hotel, and if possible get from the hotel register the names and addresses of the three strangers that just got off the stage." He returned in a few minutes with their names and said that they were rangers from Seymour. This news made me very apprehensive about the situation, yet I said nothing about this to Harris. I was convinced that it was critical that I stay in my position facing the front entrance to the saloon.

It was now nearly dark outside, and coal-oil lamps, swinging from the ceiling, were casting eerie shadows in both rooms of the adobe building. As I gazed through the front entrance of the saloon and squinted to get the most out of the rapidly disappearing twilight, I could just make out the three strangers coming across the street from the hotel. The hair stood up on the back of my neck as they entered the saloon, took drinks, and then started to come back to the gambling room. Instinctively, my right hand felt the grip of the Colt .45 cradled in the holster against my right leg, my finger sensing the trigger inside the guard. At the same time I spoke in haste to Harris, "Put the money in your pocket, quickly, and look behind you."

In instant response to my warning, Harris turned, and we both faced the archway. The three rangers came to within about eight feet of the opening, saw us, and stopped. We faced them in a tense silence which seemed to last for hours but probably was not over ten seconds, the tension releasing when the rangers turned and, without having said a word, walked out of the saloon. I pulled a red bandanna out of my pocket and wiped the cold sweat from my forehead.

As I caught my breath I was trying to think of a way to get Harris out of sight until he was sober, so I said to him, "I have to meet a party at Hogtown[18] and don't like to go by myself." He readily agreed to go with me, so I peered out the back door, whispering to Harris, "Stay back; let me make sure it's safe for us to go." As soon as I could make sure that no one was staking us out as a target, we left quickly by the back door. I knew that we must stick to the shadows and dark areas, so I led the way, cutting straight across the sand hill that divided Hogtown from Tascosa proper, and avoiding the main traveled road.

We arrived at Hogtown and went to a dance hall where about eight cowboys and their women were dancing to the music of four Mexican minstrels. The music was good, and Harris seemed fascinated by it. As soon as the dancers were called to the bar I spoke to Emma Horner,[19] a woman with whom I was slightly acquainted, saying, "I need to talk to you as soon as possible, Emma. Come over here where I will be standing as soon as you can excuse yourself." She took her check or drink at the bar and came over to where Harris and I were standing. I asked Harris to excuse us for a few minutes and led Emma to a vacant corner of the dance hall.

Emma was about twenty-eight years old, with dark hair and brown eyes. She was rather tall and was a perfectly proportioned woman. There was no doubt that Emma obviously had been a beautiful girl. She was well-educated and showed every mark of good breeding. I felt reasonably certain I could depend on her to play any part I suggested.

Emma was apprised about my suspicions of the rangers, and then I told her, "I want to get Harris out of sight until I can get him to bed and sobered. In his present condition, I dread another meeting with the rangers." So she agreed to get Milly Graham, a pretty brunette some years younger than herself, and go to her room, where Harris and I would join them with beer, whiskey, and cigarettes.

We met in Emma's two-room adobe hut, one of a row of similar buildings across the street from the dance hall and on the extreme edge of town. Beyond this an open valley extended to the Canadian River.[20] Emma, Milly, and Tom each could play the French harp, and although my musical ability was limited to patting and singing cowboy songs, we were soon taking turns dancing, and the party was in full swing. Every thirty or forty minutes we would take drinks, but I was drinking lightly and hoping to down Harris so I could put him to bed. I was becoming very discouraged, disappointed, and uneasy, as on and on the party continued. Day was breaking, and I seemed no nearer my goal than when I had started.

Just as this discouraging mood seized me, I was startled by a knock at the front door. Emma's place had no windows at the front, so we could not see what visitors we had and would just have to deal with the intruder or intruders without the advantage of knowing who was there until we came face to face with them. Immediately stepping to one side of the door, Harris and I instantaneously and instinctively leveled our drawn .45s on it, and I told Emma to throw the door wide open. It seemed like an eternity before Emma obeyed my directions. While we waited what seemed like forever for her actions, a dozen questions ran through my mind. Were the intruders Sheriff East and the two Garrett rangers that momentarily would bolt through the open door with full intentions of nailing Harris's hide to the wall? Instead, would it be just those bloodthirsty rangers alone, seeking their personal revenge against Harris? Could it be someone completely outside of my present thoughts, and with totally different intentions?

As we braced for a showdown and my finger took up the slack on the trigger, the door slammed against the wall, and again it seemed that time stood still before the person at the door, a small, effeminate-appearing man, William Gough, stepped into the room. Little was known about him except that he was a particularly successful monte dealer nicknamed the Catfish Kid.[21]

"Catfish," I growled, "I resent your intrusion into my party. You will never know how close you came to meeting your maker." Then I asked him with even greater anger, "What do you mean interrupting me with your untimely appearance?"

He replied, "Well, I heard your singing and thought I would be welcome."

Still angry, I barked, "No one is welcome at my entertainments uninvited. Do you understand that?" Without waiting for an answer, Harris and the girls, realizing that I was seriously angry and might kill the Catfish Kid right on the spot, interceded, expressing the belief that he was straight and meant no harm. Although still suspicious, I said no more to the Kid, but turning to Harris I suggested, "Tom, since it is now daylight, we might as well break up the party, get a room at the Russell Hotel, and try to sleep a while." He agreed, and as we bade the girls goodbye, I slipped each of them a five-dollar bill, feeling very cheap that it was not the twenty I felt they had earned.

We started for town, the Catfish Kid still with us, and, although my suspicion of him had to some degree subsided, I was still uneasy and would have preferred his absence. We were perhaps halfway to the sand hill between Hogtown and Tascosa and I had taken Harris's left arm, as the effects of his dissipation were beginning to show.

The Kid, slightly to the rear, remarked, "Since you are engaged in steadying Harris, you had better let me carry your gun." Without waiting for my consent he lifted my .45 from its holster. At that very moment two of the LS Rangers came over the sand hill, and instead of passing us, as it appeared they intended to do, they waited until they were just even with us, then wheeled with drawn guns. Fortunately, I had no time to think about what was happening, just time to react.

Instantly releasing Harris, I shouted a Confederate war cry my father taught me and sprang between them, taking a firm hold on the shoulder of each ranger, neither of whom seemed to realize what was happening. By shoving or pulling at the proper moment, I spoiled their aim at Harris, who was running in a circle and returning their fire. Fifteen shots were fired without a single hit; finally, one ranger named Fred Chilton said to the other, "I am out of cartridges." The other ranger, named George Jones, said, "I am too; we'd better be going." The three guns were empty, so I released my hold on their shoulders and they started running toward town. Harris, sitting flat on the sand, had managed to get another cartridge in his .45, and as the second ranger topped the hill, Tom put a bullet through his flying coattail. Though the rangers were out of sight, I knew they would be back with reinforcements to finish their dirty work.

Meanwhile, the Kid had fallen at the first exchange of shots, and I naturally supposed that he had been hit. Turning to him, I saw that he was watching me, so I asked if he was hurt. He replied that he was just stunned, but when he turned and started to rise, I saw my gun partly buried in the sand beneath him. It was the hardest thing I have endured in all my career, refraining from riddling that snake with lead; but I was still faced with the problem of saving Harris.

My next instinct was to hand Harris my gun and belt of cartridges, strongly suggesting that he make for an old adobe stable about fifty yards from the road. I stood and watched Harris as he entered the stable; then I started for town to get friends and to see what was developing.

The figure of the Kid was just disappearing over the crest of the hill when Sheriff Jim East came in view with Charlie Pierce, his chief deputy, and the rangers from Seymour. All were armed with Winchesters and .45s, with the exception of East, who strode two or three paces in advance with a double-barrel shotgun in his hand. Addressing the sheriff I said, "East, you are the high sheriff of this town and county. You are well aware of the fact that it is a long established custom that if a man in your official territory is wanted in some other county or state, the foreign officer calls on you to make the arrest. Now, I don't know what these three rangers want with Harris, but I do know that two of the LS Rangers tried to assassinate him a few minutes ago, and Harris has no way of knowing but what these three strangers are on the same mission. Harris has always respected you, your deputies, and the law, as I guarantee he will this morning; but I suggest that you ask these strangers to go back to the courthouse while you and Pierce go to Harris, who will, I promise, peaceably submit to arrest." Just as I finished the plea, Jesse Jenkins dashed past us, leaning on the opposite side of Harris's horse, Winchester in hand, riding at full speed in the direction of the adobe stable where Harris had taken refuge.

East followed my suggestion, starting the rangers back to town and then with Pierce headed for the stable where Jenkins had joined Harris. As though they had heard our agreement, Harris and Jenkins came out of the stable, met the officers with smiles instead of guns, and listened quietly while East read a warrant charging Harris with being in possession of stolen horses. Undoubtedly, the whole incident arose because some LS cowboy, seeking to make a reputation with Lee by giving Harris trouble, had recognized the brand on five or six horses bought by Harris the previous fall and suspected they had been stolen. Harris, not being familiar with this brand, which was located near Seymour, was not aware that the horses had been stolen, but had the owner merely claimed and identified them, Tom would gladly have returned the animals.

The three rangers took Harris, accompanied by Jenkins, back to Seymour, where Jesse had wired his brother, an able lawyer of Brownwood, to meet them. They made bond for Harris, and having thirty days to wait for grand jury action, they went to Fredericksburg,[22] where Tom had been raised, and visited his relatives until time to return to Seymour for court. When the district court convened, the grand jury failed to indict Harris for lack of sufficient evidence, so Harris and Jenkins saddled their horses and started back to Tascosa, considered in those days a comparatively short ride of two hundred miles.

The Provocation

During his absence, Jenkins had left Lem Woodruff in charge of the saloon. At one time, Lem had worked on the LS Ranch but had been discharged when it was found that he owned cattle. However, he held no malice against anyone on that account and had taken up his abode with a small rancher named Briggs,[23] an honest man, a good citizen whose Spanish wife and beautiful daughter were loved and respected by all. They considered Lem just as one of their own family, for he was a likable young fellow about twenty-eight years of age, of medium size, with dark brown hair, blue eyes, and the same pleasant smile for everyone.

At about ten o'clock the night before Harris and Jenkins returned, four LS Rangers loped up to the saloon, dismounted, and went into the bar, where they ordered drinks. Woodruff, smiling in his usual friendly way, set the glasses and bottle of whiskey in front of them. They poured drinks, drank them, and as they set their glasses down, one of the rangers reached across the bar and slapped at Lem while the other three stood with their hands on their .45s. This was the second time he had been subjected to similar treatment, with the odds against him precluding retaliation, but undoubtedly he had hoped for an even break at some future meeting. His Colt .45 and full belt of cartridges were not worn for decorative purposes.

The Showdown

The rangers stomped out, mounted their horses, and loped off towards Hogtown. They had enjoyed imposing upon Woodruff so much, it was natural for them to return soon for some more amusement, and about an hour later, they did come back. Lem saw them dismount; then he started for the rear of the saloon. The rangers noticed Woodruff's movement, then rushed around the building to head him off, for they supposed he was running to his sleeping quarters, a small adobe hut about twenty paces back from the saloon. A pile of cottonwood four feet high, cut in cord wood pieces, extended from the space between the door of the saloon and a window of the adjoining restaurant, for about twenty-four feet. As the rangers came around the corner of the saloon they were met by the blaze of Lem's .45, and in addition two more guns roared from behind the cord wood. Jesse Sheets,[24] the restaurant man, harmless and innocent as a lamb, stuck his head out of the back window; curiosity, never safe in the Old West, was in this case fatal. One of the rangers, thinking Sheets was doing the shooting, sent a bullet through his head, and poor Jesse slid out of sight. When the smoke had drifted away, three rangers and one innocent man were dead, and Woodruff was seriously wounded. The fourth ranger, with slightly cold feet, had lagged behind the other three; but now, as he ventured to peep around the corner of the building, a .45 bullet spattered part of an adobe brick in his face, and I have never, to this day, met anyone who has seen him since. The anticipated amusement had not been wholly at Woodruff's expense.[25]

At this time I was still working for the LX Ranch or American Pastoral Company,[26] and the day after the fight I was on the southern part of their range with a cow outfit of seven men, a wagon, and a cook. We camped at noon at a lake of water on the plains, twenty-five miles south of the headquarters and about fifty miles southeast of Tascosa. Suddenly breaking into the depression where we were

Courtesy Private Collection

When the smoke had drifted away, three rangers and one innocent man were dead, and Woodruff was seriously wounded.

camped, a lone horseman who we all knew rode in unsaddled. He was riding an extremely tired-looking horse, and when the rider dismounted, he turned the horse loose to drink and graze. Silent Bill, as I will call him, was a rather tall, slim man of about thirty. He was of dark complexion, with small black eyes, brown mustache, and an apparent preference for his own company. No matter how many men were present he would always be sitting off by himself, seldom speaking except when directly addressed; however, Bill was a loyal, dependable friend to Lem Woodruff. They had been associated for about five years on cattle work and in Tascosa. He now joined us at our noon lunch of black coffee, beefsteak, navy beans, canned corn, and tomatoes. After lunch he took a few thoughtful puffs on a brown paper cigarette he had rolled, rose to his feet and, nodding to me, walked away from camp. I interpreted his mannerisms as indicating a desire for a talk in privacy, so I followed him.

We sat down on the grass, about fifty paces from the wagon; then Bill spoke, "I came to tell you of some trouble that happened at about eleven o'clock last night in Tascosa. I'm going to tell you just how it happened with all the details, but I'm going to ask you as a trusted friend never to divulge the fact that I talked to you or was in this part of the country today, at least not until I'm a long time gone." Then Bill told me the story as I have written it, asked me to tell the other boys to forget they had seen him, and, catching his horse, he saddled it and headed southeast. Silent Bill was in a position to know the facts, for he saw the fight from behind his smoking .45 and a pile of cottonwood cut into cord wood.[27]

Aftermath

About three days after the shooting in Tascosa, I made up what money I could on the LX ranch, saddled my most trusty river horse, and swam the south Canadian River when it was a mile wide. My six-shooter belt was around my neck, the six-shooter in the holster fastened to the belt and a Winchester in my left hand. I headed for a place where I saw a sandbar made by a high wave of sand and muddy water. There I stopped my horse until the sand gave way, then struck out for the next wave. I finally got across and went to the T Anchor Ranch, stayed all night, took up a collection there, then went by the Frying Pan to pick up what donations I could get. In all, I had collected six hundred dollars. I then went back to Tascosa, swimming the river again, and gave the money to Jesse Jenkins. He had just gotten back from Tom Harris's hearing the day after the killings in Tascosa.

Through all these years and the many confidential ideas that have been expressed about that unfortunate affair in Tascosa, no one has mentioned Silent Bill except Lem Woodruff when he repeated the story at the Briggs ranch, almost word for word, as I sat by his bedside three days later. Lem had been shot in the left side of the abdomen, the bullet severing an intestine, in which condition he had been helped into the saddle and had ridden the four miles to the ranch. He was immediately arrested, charged with killing the three rangers, but Jesse Jenkins and Briggs made bond for him, and he was allowed to remain at the ranch until district court convened. At that time, he was tried and acquitted.

Another Ranching Experience

A Return to March 1883

Soon after my return to the Frying Pan Ranch from home, and in the early days of the cowboy strike, I was fortunate enough to be sent temporarily to an outfit of the LX Ranch. The outfit was composed of ten or twelve men, several of them from different ranches. The organization was what we called a pool outfit: the LX company furnished a wagon, boss, cook, and several men. Once in operation, we went southeast about 150 miles and attended all the roundups of the different ranges, getting all cattle that had drifted south from our locality during the winter. The boss was a fine little man named Charles A. Siringo.[1] We were gone from our home ranches from the first of May to the middle of July.

When I got back to the Frying Pan Ranch we put in time branding up the calves, and after our range had been worked, they sent me to work at the LX range, where they were branding calves and gathering fat steers. I made friends with all the LX boys, since I had a good start by being with several of them two and one-half months during the southern roundup.

After the LX activity, I would go to other ranges and work the cattle, and I was also kept busy picking up our Panhandle cattle that had strayed out of our range. These activities gave me the opportunity to get acquainted with all the cowboys within one hundred square miles.

After the fall roundups were over, Charlie Hall and I, who as boys had been raised as neighbors, were put out in camp in a dugout on the east side of the range to ride and keep in repair sixteen miles of

Branding Calves

After our range had been worked, they sent me to the LX range, where they were branding calves and gathering fat steers.

wire fence. During the winter we would go in opposite directions from camp, which gave us a track to ride of eight miles out and back. We spent the evenings playing cards and talking of home folks, our escapades with the girls, and we built air castles about the things we would do when we went back home.

Beautiful spring is almost here
Bringing the beauties I love so dear.
The trees are leafing green,
The flowers will soon bloom in a beautiful scene.
From them the bees will take their toll
Like collectors of taxes from each human soul.
But soon will come the beautiful birds
Singing musical songs almost in words.
Oh, how I long to be in some forest alone
And just have its denizens and birds to claim as friends of my own,
For it's only God's wild creation of which I have no fear,
It's only their nature and freedom that can give me joy and cheer,
Since all humanity I have learned to doubt and fear.

Jim Gober

71

Courtesy Private Collection

We had been hankering to rope us a mustang out of a range bunch that usually roamed in that locality.

Spring came, and it was again time to start out in different directions to attend roundups. Once again I was detailed to an LX outfit to go south to the Pease River, a distance of two hundred miles, and work back towards home. Our boss was Charlie Spraig, and most of the nine or ten men were young fellows and full of fun.

We got about one hundred miles south and found a sheep ranch on the Yellow House Draw, at the extreme head of Yellow House Canyon.[2] The old fellow residing there also had a few groceries in an adobe building.[3] We stopped to buy tobacco and such provisions as we needed and found the old man had a barrel of whiskey, so we all had several drinks, and all bought a quart apiece and struck a lope to where the wagon had stopped to camp, some two miles down the draw. All of a sudden everyone began yelling and shooting their pistols, and it was truly a wild bunch. We were sick and drunk for two days and never moved out of camp.

On Foot with a Mad Buffalo

On the third morning we moved into action, and all the cowpunchers scattered out to scout across the plains for cattle. We sent the wagon on ahead to camp at a designated lake, about sixteen miles from the last camp. Bob Perkins and I rode together, and each of us

Courtesy Private Collection

We rode on until about three o'clock in the afternoon and hadn't seen an animal of any description. Finally, I saw three antelope coming toward us, aiming to circle around in front of us, as they always do.

was on a splendid horse. We had been hankering to rope us a mustang out of a range bunch that usually roamed in that locality.

We rode on until about three o'clock in the afternoon and hadn't seen an animal of any description. Finally, I saw three antelope coming toward us, aiming to circle around in front of us, as they always do. I said, "Bob, watch me rope one," and I turned my horse loose full speed and roped one around the head and in the mouth. I jerked it down and jumped off my horse, leaving the rope tied to the saddle horn, and I ran and jumped on the antelope. It began to bawl, and I slipped the rope off its head. My horse, frightened by its bawling, took off with my new forty-five-dollar saddle, fifteen-dollar bridle, and ten-dollar Mexican saddle blanket.

Perkins lit out after him, and soon both Perkins and my horse were out of sight. Disgusted as I could be, I turned the antelope loose to go his way, and there I was by myself afoot. So I just sat down on the buffalo grass waiting for something favorable to happen, but really not knowing what to expect. I waited until almost sundown and was satisfied Perkins had run his horse down and mine had gotten clear away, and that Perkins would never find the way back after dark. So I decided to chart my course back to the sheep camp on the draw, at least twelve miles ahead of me. If I could be lucky enough to hit the sheep camp, perhaps I could get a horse and saddle to allow me to overtake the outfit, where I had six more saddle horses. I just struck out afoot, despising antelope more and more, and I still despise the looks of one to this very day.

Surprisingly, I walked pretty fast just taking my course, by guess, across the plains, with no trail or object to go by. Shortly, I struck the east edge of a large, dry basin, usually a lake when full of water. They are numerous on the plains. As I went down into this basin it was just getting shadowy, between sundown and dark. Suddenly, I heard an awful roaring that seemed to jar the earth! I stopped still and tried to locate this terrifying sound. Finally I saw a buffalo bull that looked to me at that moment to be as big as a brick barn. He was four or five hundred yards from me, on the opposite side of the lake, or dry basin. The buffalo was pawing dirt into the air and roaring continuously such that it gave the impression of the onset of a dry weather cyclone.

I realized at once that he had been whipped out of his bunch by another bull, and lucky for me, the wind was the wrong way for him to smell me, and he was too busy to raise his head to see me. So I took square off from the lake, traveling in a low draw that was a water course to the lake during rains. I had to go a quarter of a mile before I was out of sight of that bull. Finally I was out of his line of sight and felt lucky, and was lucky, for I only had a short .45 six-shooter, and that would have just made that buffalo madder.[4]

I walked until twelve o'clock and finally hit the Yellow House Draw and knew I was above the sheep camp. However, I didn't know how far away it was, but I turned down the draw and just kept walking. About one o'clock I got to the sheep camp and finally convinced the old man that I was civilized and harmless. He asked me in, and I told him my hard-luck story, and he laughed heartily at me. I bought some

Courtesy Private Collection

Suddenly I heard an awful roaring that seemed to jar the earth! I stopped still and tried to locate this terrifying sound. Finally I saw a buffalo bull that looked to me at that moment to be as big as a brick barn.

canned salmon and crackers from him and took one drink of his tobacco juice whiskey. After eating generously, he made me a pallet on the floor, and I felt as though I still had a chance to survive.

A Makeshift Cowpoke

The next morning the sheep man had fried mutton and gravy made of grease flour and water, black coffee, and sourdough biscuits. I was still so starved that I stuffed myself again, and when I had finished, he wrapped up a couple of biscuits and two pieces of fried mutton. He apparently felt pity on me and loaned me a little brown pony so old he was gray around the ears and in the flank. The sheepherder also provided me with a saddle with no horn and a sheepskin tacked in the seat where the leather had worn away. He had no extra bridle, so I made a halter of rope.

I departed from the sheep man's abode and went to the campground where the wagon had started from the morning before and began to follow its tracks. That was the only way I knew how to find it, as there was no road and I didn't know any particular place or direction to go to look for it. The little Mexican pony proved better than he looked, and about four o'clock in the afternoon I rode into camp. If a poor unfortunate boy ever got hurrahed, it was me.

The next day we worked the Estes Brothers[5] range, and I rode my hornless saddle and rope bridle on one of my good cow ponies, and surprisingly I made a pretty good hand, not much for looks but heck for stout. Even more of a surprise was the fact that at about dusk that night, a man rode into camp leading my runaway horse with saddle. It seems that the horse showed up the next morning at sunrise at a sheep camp seventy miles from where he left me. The sheep man happened to be Billie Marceles, who had held his sheep near my winter camp during the winter of 1883. He remembered my horse and knew the location of our cattle work, so he put a man on a horse and sent my horse and saddle to me. The unfortunate thing is that the horse was never any account after that incident.

We worked on up the plains to the Salt Lake Ranch owned by Jim Newman,[6] and after working his cattle we moved on to Portales Lake and worked Doak Good's[7] cattle. Good was camping in Billy the Kid's notorious house, half dugout and half rock.[8] From there we went to the Blackwater Lake[9] and worked the Carter Brothers' cattle, and thence to Tierra Blanca[10] and the T Anchor range, which joined the Frying Pan on the south. Then we were through and struck for our home ranches, each man cutting the cattle that belonged to the ranch he represented and driving them home. Our homework then was cut out for us on the Frying Pan Ranch: to round up the cattle and brand the spring calves.

A Darn, Dirty Shame!

There were fifty or sixty head of cattle in the Frying Pan range that belonged to different boys that were in the strike and couldn't get work, and their brands were termed maverick brands, meaning they had been unbranded yearlings and strays. John Grissom[11] had invited Pat Garrett's rangers to come work through the range and get these cattle, under the pretense they would be confiscated and sold and the money would go to the school fund. So the rangers got fifty-five head of cattle in the Frying Pan range in which I owned half interest, but my partner, in whose name the brand was recorded, drowned while swimming a herd of cattle across the Yellowstone River,[12] and I had no way of establishing my right to the cattle. That, however, did not excuse Grissom, who knew in his own mind that I had an interest in those cattle. It was a dirty deed on his part to take

Then we were through and struck for our home ranches, each man cutting the cattle that belonged to the ranch he represented and driving them home. Our homework then was cut out for us on the Frying Pan Ranch: to round up the cattle and brand the spring calves.

advantage of me the way he did, but I kept mum until the branding was over and we got to the headquarters ranch. I then settled up, drew my pay, saddled my private horse, and told Mr. and Mrs. Wetsel and all the other boys goodbye, leaving Grissom, the boss, for the last. The more I thought about the actions of Pat Garrett's rangers, the madder I got. When I found Grissom, I asked him to walk out to where my horse was hitched, and when out of hearing distance of anyone else I proceeded to give Grissom my thorough opinion of him, telling him that I didn't think his future in that locality was very bright, nor did I think his friends, the rangers, would thrive. I guess I told Grissom a few things that nobody should ever hear.

Having gotten my feelings off my chest, I got on my private horse and used a Frying Pan horse on which to pack my bedding and extra clothing, with the understanding that I would send that horse back at the first passing. Then I started for the LX Ranch, where I had been promised a job at thirty-five dollars per month anytime I saw fit to quit the Frying Pan outfit. This was around September 1, 1884.

Mr. and Mrs. Wetsel had been so good and kind to me during the two years and eight months I had been on the Frying Pan Ranch. It was like leaving my own home, but my pride had been hurt, and I felt that I had to go or have serious trouble.

The LX, a Familiar Place

The LX was twenty miles north, located on the south Canadian River. I got to the ranch about four o'clock in the afternoon, unpacked my pack horse and unsaddled my saddle horse, a large, dark-bay pacing horse and a splendid animal. After turning my horses into a small pasture used for saddle horses, I went to the bookkeeper's office. I found the bookkeeper, Mr. Jim Wyness, and Bill Ruth, range foreman, in the office, and I informed Mr. Ruth that I was applying for work. He was very hospitable and said, "I'm glad you've come, Jim" and told Mr. Wyness to put me on the payroll at thirty-five dollars per month.

The LX company at that time controlled twenty-five square miles of range and had about sixty thousand head of cattle, two hundred bred mares and young horse stock, five thoroughbred stallions, and four hundred cow horses. I felt somewhat at home at the LX, as I had worked on the general roundups with two of their wagon bosses, Charles A. Siringo the spring of 1883 and Charlie Spraig in 1884. So in a day or two we started rounding up the LX cattle, branding calves, and had about fifteen days to get through with the tasks.

The Case of the Jealous Widows

After the roundup work was over, the outfit I was with, bossed by
Bill Ruth, went to Tascosa for a few days recreation and that consisted
of drinking booze, playing poker and monte and dancing at the old
adobe hotel run by old man Russell. I had gotten well acquainted with
a widow that ran a restaurant and had taken her to the dance and of
course had danced the first dance with her. For the next dance that
was thrown, I had an invitation from another grass widow and walked
out on the floor with her. It seems that jealousy reared its head in the
widow I had brought to the dance, for she simply took me by the arm
and pulled me off the floor, leaving the other widow standing alone.
I took my jealous widow home and excused myself by promising to
return as soon as I got a drink to steady my nerves. I went back to
the dance and danced with the other widow and made a date to call
on her the next evening. That was my start in Tascosa society, and I
couldn't help feeling somewhat dignified to realize that two widows
were jealous of me. When I went to Tascosa after that I never lacked
for a good time if both widows didn't happen to be at the same place
at the same time.

The Beginning of a Lasting Friendship

When I first joined the LX, I met Jim Stroope, and he and I fell in
together and became pals and were together most of the time. The
boys at the LX and I got along just fine. My period of working at the
LX was to last for two and a half years.

The next spring, Stroope and I were put with Allen Thompson's
outfit. Allen was a fine man, and all of the men that worked under
him liked him. There were about eight or nine of us, and we were a
congenial bunch. We were all good cow hands, and it was generally
known that Allen Thompson's outfit could do and did do more cattle
work in less time than any one other outfit on the ranch. The other
outfits all ran from eight to fifteen men each. Each outfit would have
a boss, camp wagon, cook, and horse rustler. We were kept pretty
busy all spring and summer going to general roundups and working
our own range, branding calves, and gathering beef steers.

A Winter and a Half

About the first of October 1884 we were instructed to keep three
of our best horses and take our wagon, cook, a load of provisions, a
contingent of seven men and make a winter camp in Chalk Canyon,

an extension of the Palo Duro Canyon.[13] Allen Thompson had decided to quit for an indefinite period to spend time at his home in Alvord, Texas. He recommended me to take charge of the outfit, a big job for a twenty-year-old, but I guess I was older than that in experience. I was put in charge, though I was the youngest man in the outfit.

My pal Jim Stroope was still with me, and the two of us made a large dugout in the canyon, excavated a fireplace, and built a crude chimney. Fortunately, we had plenty of cedar wood but didn't realize at the time how important that supply of wood would become in just a few weeks. The winter was a bad one, and many a cowman remembers the winter of 1885-86 with sore regret, for it killed more cattle than ever before in the history of the Panhandle.[14]

Twenty-five miles of wire had been put up by the T Anchor and the JA[15] cattle companies, running parallel to Palo Duro Canyon, which was the south line of the LX range. It was my business to get out on that fence line after each storm and shove the cattle that had drifted against the fence during the storm back off the plains to the breaks of the Canadian River.

The LX had a few cows that were spayed when yearlings, and they were then eight years old. When we found one we would run her back to the canyon and butcher her and hang her up in a tree, where she would freeze solid as a rock. We had a large Dutch oven in which we would put some coals from the big fire and cut tallow enough to make plenty of hot grease, then take the ax and chop off thick steaks, drop them into the red hot tallow, and oh boy! What a fat bunch of cowpunchers came out of that canyon in the spring.

The seventh day of January 1886 was a nice warm day, and the boys were all restless, so I told the cook to put his cooking utensils in the wagon and provisions to last three or four days and we would go down to the plains, about fifteen miles, and camp that night. We went to Mulberry Basin,[16] a large depression in the plains that, in winter, would afford some water from melting snow or rain. The plan was to scatter out the next day and cut some of our saddle horses out from the mustangs.

We had small tepee tents and stretched them and made our beds, hobbled our horses, had supper, and, after running out of stories to tell, all crawled in our tents and went to bed. About daylight, I awoke and stuck my head out of the tent, and the snow was blowing, being driven by a stiff north wind as cold as I ever felt. I got all hands up, and we got our traps in the wagon, unhobbled our horses, hitched the

The winter was a bad one, and many a cowman remembers the winter of 1885-86 with sore regret, for it killed more cattle than ever before in the history of the Panhandle.

Cold in the Snow

four mules to the wagon, and started for our dugout in a lope. One man rode on each side of the mules to urge them along, and we got to the canyon in two hours.

Our camp was five hundred feet below the rim rock or the level of the plains. We had a crude road available to us but would always take the mules off and run the wagon down by hand. When we went to release the mules from the wagon, we found a solid sheet of ice frozen over the eyes of each mule, and they were all blind. We managed eventually to get the wagon and mules down; then we built a big log fire. A colder bunch of people never existed, and the blizzard lasted forty-eight hours before we dared to get out. We could almost walk on dead cattle the entire twenty miles of fence line.

After this destructive blizzard the winter seemed to have spent its force, and we were busy pushing the scattered cattle we had managed to bring through the storm alive back on to the plains and into the Canadian River breaks. For several days it was no unusual occurrence to find cattle with their horns frozen until just the skin held them dangling by the side of their head, and in some instances, their hoofs were frozen clear off.[17]

A Target of Opportunity

Return—The Specter of W. M. D. Lee

I had been getting fifty dollars per month since I was put in charge of Thompson's outfit, and all seemed to be going well. The men liked me as boss, and the ranch management seemed pleased with my work.

One day Mr. Ruth sent for me, and it seemed he had a concerned look on his face. "Jim, this is confidential. Mr. Hollicott,[1] the manager, has received a letter from W. M. D. Lee, and it contains allegations against you. Lee signed this letter as president of the Cattlemen's Association, giving it more weight than if it had just come from Lee of the LS Ranch.

"The allegations are that you have had a personal interest in the maverick brands of cattle and have been in sympathy with the strikers, who have also become cattle rustlers. This letter alleges further that you took part in the defense of Lem Woodruff against the murder charge for killing three LS men in Garrett's ranger service. The association further advises Hollicott to dispense with your services. Now, Mr. Hollicott thinks very highly of you, Jim, and he and I had discussed this matter, and we agreed that I would turn your outfit over to John Henry. You would work under Henry at the same wages you have been drawing, as boss. This would serve as a partial compromise with the association and preserve all the planning details that had been completed for the outfit."

I was speechless at first and incensed, but as I thought about it I could understand the position Hollicott was in. The range schedule would require me to go to Liberty, New Mexico,[2] and work back down the Canadian to our LX range and all the other association ranges, and if I were in charge, they might try to give me an unfair deal, and I might delay the work for an indefinite time by losing control of my temper.

So all was agreed, and we were off in a few days for Liberty, 150 miles west. Right then and there I made up my mind to recover my fifty-five head of cattle that Lee's rangers gambled off in Las Vegas.

The first roundup was in the Bell[3] range in New Mexico. When it was our turn to look through the herd of about five thousand cattle, they were all bunched together, with seventy-five to one hundred men circled around them. John Henry rode up to where several LX men and I were sitting on our horses and directed his remarks to me, saying, "I have instructions to not allow any of my men to cut out or drive any cattle not in the LX brand or an adjoining ranch brand." So I rode in the herd, and after I had cut out ten or twelve LX cattle, I then spotted three Mexican steers, and, since thoughts of the Alamo caused a total disregard of the rights of property between me and Mexicans, I proceeded to run out a four-year-old Mexican steer. John Henry dashed up and said, "What are you cutting that steer for?"

I said, "On my knowledge of brands of cattle and where they belong, and I have two more to cut yet." After getting the other two, I rode out and told Henry that I was through cutting cattle, but perhaps he had better look through the herd to make sure I hadn't overlooked anything.

After we finished the Bell range, which had taken four days, I had managed to acquire seven or eight strays in our herd. Then one evening when I was detailed to herd the cattle until time to corral them, I proceeded to gather a pile of mesquite roots, make a fire, and heat my branding iron, which consisted of a quarter-inch steel rod turned up at the end, called a running iron. I then ran out one steer at a time and changed the brand to my brand. This effort, which I felt very good about, went on for twenty-five days as we worked the various cattle ranges down the Canadian River.

When I branded a steer, I would run it back into the country we had already worked so it wouldn't be in the roundup the next day. I would just have to take the chance of it getting into the fall roundup.

When we got back to the LX Ranch I had branded fifty-five head of perfectly good stray cattle and considered I had just beat some other fellow to them. In any event, I had compensated myself for the original number of my cattle that Lee's rangers confiscated, and I felt justified and satisfied, and I quit that game. I never would have participated in the art of changing brands if Lee hadn't tried to get me discharged and accused of being in sympathy with rustlers.

Good Riddance of the Catfish Kid

After arriving back at the LX Ranch, some of us went to Tascosa for a few days' spree before going off to brand calves. The Catfish Kid had willfully murdered an inoffensive fellow in the bunkhouse of a wagon yard. It seems that the Kid had gone in the bunkhouse in the dark, evidently to waylay someone, and this unfortunate fellow had his team in the wagon yard and his bed in the bunkhouse and had started to bed. The Kid evidently had mistaken this man for someone else.

He was tried, convicted, and sentenced to life in the penitentiary. At the same time a Mexican was convicted of murder and sentenced to serve twenty-five years. The prison officer had come after both of them, and I saw both loaded in the stage with handcuffs and leg irons, also irons around their necks that fastened them together. I am truthful in saying that the Catfish Kid is the first human being I ever saw helpless and in trouble for whom I couldn't feel some degree of sympathy.[4]

A Close Encounter with Boot Hill

Jesse Jenkins and I had remained warm friends, and I generally made his saloon my headquarters when in Tascosa. So on this trip, I enjoyed spending the entire evening sitting behind the bar on the desk platform, talking to Jesse when he wasn't busy waiting on customers.

Just about dark, I realized that I had a date with my grass widow and mentioned the fact to Jesse as I told him I would see him the next day. Then I walked around in front of the bar, and when I asked several of the boys who happened to be sitting in the room to join me in a drink, five or six lined up with me and came up to the bar. As Jesse set out the glasses and bottles, Jim East, the sheriff, popped in, bareheaded, with an Indian blanket around his shoulders. He walked up beside and almost against me and said, "Do you know what I am going to do with you?" He hadn't more than gotten the words out until I was prepared to do him in first, if I had to. And then he said, "I am going to shoot your brains out and eat them up."

Before he had a chance to draw, I leveled my .45 on him and said, "Your appetite for brains will spoil your future if you aren't careful."

At that moment, Pierce, who was East's faithful friend, had trailed East and was behind me and put his gun against the back of my head and said, "Jim, if you kill East, I will have to kill you."

Then I heard a double click still behind Pierce, and Jesse Jenkins's keen voice rang out, "Off the kid with that gun, or I will blow your head off." I realized in a moment that he was behind East, Pierce, and me.

Jesse had a cap-and-ball shotgun with the barrel sawed off to about eighteen inches long and with a six-shooter handle on it. He kept it loaded with two inches of black powder and fifteen buckshot in each barrel, and if it had gone off, not only Pierce but East and I as well would have been headless. I am confident East and Pierce felt the same sensation as I did, and at the same instant, so all was silent for a minute. Then Pierce stepped around me and took East by the arm and led him out of the house and, fortunately, East left without resistance.

It was then that I realized that East was peeved at me on account of the interest I had taken in protecting Tom Harris and defending Lem Woodruff, and further, I came to the realization that I was marked as an undesirable by the sheriff as well as W. M. D. Lee. Then the blood began to boil in my veins, for I had done no more than a civilized human should do in each case. For the life of me, I could not understand how East could be justified in wanting to take my life.

I remained in Tascosa two days and nights, and if East had approached me again during my stay, one of us or both of us would have gone to the bone yard. But thanks to providence, we didn't meet.

The Whole World?

Everyone else had hastily vacated the saloon during the gun exhibition, and after Jesse and I had talked the matter over and had taken a few drinks by ourselves, I made another start to see my widow. She and her mother were the only ones at home, and somehow the old lady had taken a dislike for me. I realized that it was rather late, and soon after I arrived, the old lady came into the room where we were and informed me that it was no time to call on her daughter. Well, I was twenty-two, and her daughter was thirty, and I believed we were old enough to make that decision. Besides, I was still mad and worried over the escapade with East, and now I felt that the whole world was against me. So I explained to the old lady, "I'm sorry, Ma'am, but unexpected circumstances detained me, and I regret that you are offended, but I really believe that your daughter is of mature age and capable of judging her company. Since she welcomed my presence into your home, I would be pleased to remain awhile." Then I asked her, "Would you be so kind as to retire, again, to your bed?"

"Well, young man, don't make your stay long, or I will be in again."

About twelve o'clock some crashing noise woke the old lady, and I heard her bounce out of bed and cross the hallway and come to the door of her daughter's room. She tried the door, but it was locked, and then ran to the outside door of the hall and around to a window of the room where we were. It had been raised as high as it would go because the night was hot and the humidity oppressive. By the time she had climbed through the window, I had gone through a door into the kitchen where there was an outside door near the corner. It was so very dark that I missed the door and ran into the corner, and by the time I turned back, the old lady was within six feet of me. I planned to jump around the corner of the house and grab her as she came around and disarm her of the .45 she had in her hand. When I made my jump, a clothesline caught me under the chin and threw me on my back, and the old lady cocked the .45 in my stomach. I eased up on my feet while she was pouring out fiendish utterances in my face. I then grabbed her right hand and shoved the gun in another direction and gently wrenched the gun from her hand. After I had taken the cartridges out of the cylinder and had thrown them away, I told her, "I will be back tomorrow night to talk to you, and you had better make up your mind that, first, I wasn't born yesterday, and second, you'd best not be under the impression that you will make a goat of me."

The next day I went back in the middle of the afternoon, and I was met at the door by the widow. She invited me in, seated me, and told me not to pay any attention to the old lady. We were laughing and talking about the escapade of the previous night when in came Mother with her gun. The widow jumped up and took it away from her and began laying the law down. She said to the old lady, "Don't think you are going to embarrass the company of my choice, thinking that by so doing, you will force me to pay attention to your pet Jones." The widow told her mother that she had no more use for Jones than a hound dog. So I began laughing and calling the old lady "Mother" and telling her that she should be ashamed of her attempt to assassinate such a nice-looking, innocent boy as I. And besides, I told her that I was a prospect for a goodhearted son-in-law.

Finally, the old lady started crying and laughing at the same time. Soon we were shaking hands, and I bade her goodbye. Then she told me to forget it all and to come back whenever I liked. I thanked her, then went on my way but never went back anymore.

An Unpleasant Assignment

When I got back to the ranch, several outfits were prepared to start rounding up cattle and branding the calves, as it was now September 1886, and this would be the last branding for the year. I was detailed to Henry's outfit for that work. Henry had been distant toward me ever since I ignored his orders in the spring at the roundup in the Bell range, and I didn't have much respect for him because of the orders he was giving. I knew in my mind that he hadn't received any such instructions and was only giving the orders to intimidate me, so the first roundup we had, Henry sent Bud Simmons in the herd to cut out the cows with unbranded calves.

Simmons ran out a cow and two calves, and I had no way of telling which calf belonged to the cow, so I didn't make any effort to turn either back. Henry came rushing up to me and said, "I wish you would turn cattle back that are not wanted and try to help the work along." I invited him to go to a place that is supposed to be very hot and rode off to the camp wagon about one-half mile away and unsaddled my horse. My intention was to get my dinner, catch a fresh horse, get a pack horse, and then drive the balance of the seven mount horses with me as I quit the ranch.

Just as we were eating dinner, Bill Ruth, the range foreman, rode up from the headquarters ranch to see how the work was progressing. When dinner was over and I had the opportunity, I spoke to him, "Bill, I'm glad you came, and if you have no objections I will ride back to the ranch headquarters with you."

"What's wrong, Jim?"

"I'm not a good enough cowhand to get along with Henry."

Ruth laughed and said jovially, "I will take charge of you and give you a chance to learn to be an expert."

I accompanied him to the headquarters ranch, and I was then reassigned to Matt Atwood's[5] outfit. There I spliced beds with my old chum Jim Stroope and got along fine until the fall work was finished. Then we had to work through several other ranges up to the Canadian, and this took us an additional three weeks. We came back through

Tascosa and made our camp about two miles from town and stayed there three days and nights.

A Dangerous Event

Matt Atwood and Jim East were raised near each other in southern Texas and had come to the Panhandle together. The second night we were in town, East and Atwood got to quarreling while several of us were lined up at the bar, drinking. There were four or five of us that belonged to Atwood's outfit, and in a few minutes there were as many of East's friends also in the saloon. East's friends were on one side of the room and Atwood's on the other, all watching each other, strung up to high tension. It seemed that each side was waiting for the first break to be made, which would have amounted to a battle royal. East and Atwood stood right in one position and quarreled from ten PM until sunup the next morning, and outside of their low mutterings, you could have heard a pin fall.

Finally, I stepped between them and said, "Why worry over things that have past / When worrying is of no use, / Why not hope and look ahead, / And let your smile be a flag of truce. Let's go to camp, Atwood, and get some breakfast and take a nap, and you fellows can finish your quarrel this afternoon. By then, perhaps, you will feel more like fighting. Besides, both of you must be pretty well run down." I took Atwood by the arm and forced him out. It simply had been a case of each man trying to catch the other fellow's eye distracted so that he could get first draw. But they had stood all night with their eyes fixed on each other, and each one knew that even if he killed his man, the killing wasn't over as long as any two of the opposite sides were standing.

That evening we came into town again, and on the way I spoke to Atwood, saying, "Matt, I don't have any idea what your's and East's trouble is about and don't really care to know. But if it is serious enough to quarrel all night and not fight, just chew the rag and endanger eight or ten other lives, then it is too serious for me to participate in any further." I told him, "Under these conditions, I don't care to run with you if you intend to continue your rag chewing. It looks to me like you and East ought to either make peace or fight in less time than eight hours."

In an hour after we got to town, Atwood and East met, took a drink with each other, and shook hands. The war was over for the time being.

Early in the morning hours of the following day, we discovered a prairie fire across the river on the south plains. We mustered our forces and rushed our camp wagon out about ten miles, camped at the foot of the plains, and left the cook, John Temple, to get dinner.

Never a Dull Moment

The next day we pulled into the ranch and had just begun to get our minds back to the cattle business when early in the morning hours of the following day, we discovered a prairie fire across the river on the south plains. We mustered our forces and rushed our camp wagon out about ten miles, camped at the foot of the plains, and left the cook, John Temple, to get dinner.

We galloped up on top of the plains and onto the fire location. Our object was to fight it out and keep it from getting in the river breaks, which was our important winter range. We first shot down a beef, split him open, and tied a rope to each front foot, then fastened the rope to our saddle horn. Then we struck a gallop, dragging the open part of the beef over the burning grass. The balance of six or seven men strung out on foot putting out what fire the beef failed to smother. We fought the fire in this manner until eleven o'clock that night before we put it out. It had been a running battle as we had followed and fought the fire for ten miles. One man had been detailed to follow with the horses belonging to the men that were on foot fighting the fire, so that when we were finished we were all able to mount up and strike for camp.

The sky had clouded up and the weather had turned real cold. We were tired and very hungry and didn't get to camp in time for the dinner Temple had cooked. He had cooked a large camp pot full of beans and had left them set in the sun all evening, a warm fall day in the last of October of 1886. When we arrived in camp, about 1:30

81

in the morning, all were very tired and hungry, and everyone filled their tin plates with beans, got black coffee and sourdough bread. We proceeded to gulp it down like it was our last meal. When we were in the middle of the meal, my pal Stroope yelled at the cook and asked him if he put vinegar in the beans, and he said "Yes." By this time we were through eating and rolled out our camp beds.

It was raining a slow fall drizzle, but we all had heavy tarpaulins, and the rain was no bother. We were all asleep in a few minutes, but our peaceful slumber was of short duration. Men began scattering in all directions, some vomiting, some running off at the bowels, and some doing both. Some were cursing and some saying "Oh Lord," and a sicker, madder bunch of men never lived. I honestly and truly believe if we had not been so sick we would have made mincemeat out of that cook. He didn't feel very safe, so when we got to the ranch, the boss fired him and he drifted westward. I never have relished beans very well since, and that has been forty years ago.

A Deputy Out on a Limb

Trading a Lasso for a Badge

After the usual cuts in men, I was kept at headquarters and rode about ten miles of fence and back at night. We had had a sufficient amount of rain during the spring and summer to provide the range with splendid grass, and this favorable condition for the cattle caused them to go into the winter in fine shape, resulting in the winter losses from poverty being exceedingly small.

The first of April 1887 came with warm spring days, and with them came the heel flies to pester the cattle. They caused the cattle to run in on the river, resulting in the men being called in from their lonesome winter camps. They were organized into outfits to round up the cattle on the sand bars of the river. Our orders were to cut the three- and four-year steers out, and when we got a herd of from fifteen hundred to two thousand, one outfit would start them on the trail to a large pasture for spring and summer grazing. This pasture was owned by the LX and was located on Turkey Creek, near Caldwell, Kansas. The grass in the Kansas pasture was called bluestem and was of a top, cattle-fattening quality, and in the fall, the steers would already be near the Kansas City market for shipment.

By the tenth of May, we had gotten the steers all gathered and on the way to Kansas, and I was back at the headquarters. I was lying on my camp bed, which I had spread some distance from the ranch house and near the commissary, meditating on whether or not I would quit the cowboy game and go to Tascosa and work for the sheriff. Some important changes had occurred in the law enforcement picture. Jim

Tobe Robinson, Oldham County sheriff 1887-90, date unknown. Courtesy J. Evetts Haley Collection, Nita Stewart Haley Memorial Library, Midland, Texas.

East was defeated for Oldham County sheriff by Tobe Robinson[1] in the November election of '86. Tobe Robinson had been a range foreman on the LS Ranch, was about fifty years old, and had been in the Panhandle since the 1870s. For several years he was employed as a government messenger, carrying messages from Fort Elliott[2] to Fort Sill[3] and Fort Supply[4] during the years when the Kiowa, Comanche, Cheyenne, and the Arapaho Indians were leaving their reservations and taking the war path—an ideal training ground for a frontier peace officer. Tobe Robinson, whose sister married a cousin of mine, had on several occasions suggested that I work with him as a deputy.

When the spring of 1887 came, it brought the Fort Worth and Denver Railroad[5] to Amarillo Creek, four miles west of the present city of Amarillo. Little did I realize that I was about to start a long and somewhat varied career as a peace officer.

Rag Town in All of Its Glory

Where the tracks crossed the Amarillo Creek, the boarding cars of the Irish construction gang were spurred off in a beautiful little valley

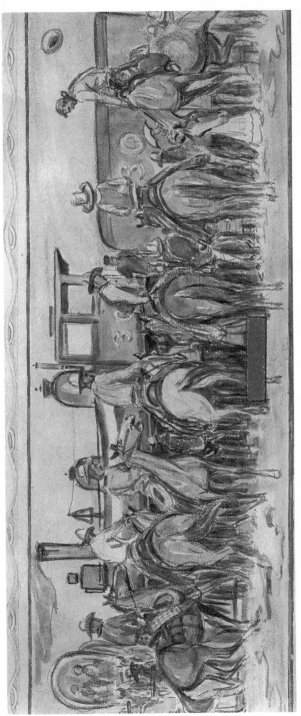

Coming of the Railroad and the Founding of Amarillo in 1888

When the spring of 1887 came, it brought the Fort Worth and Denver Railroad to Amarillo Creek. . . . Where the tracks crossed the Amarillo Creek, the boarding cars of the Irish construction gang were spurred off in a beautiful little valley decorated with huge cottonwood trees and willows.

decorated with huge cottonwood trees and willows. Overnight a tent town arose, with four saloons equipped for gambling, two restaurants, two supply tents with groceries and work clothes, and several tents of the inevitable dance hall women.[6]

Robinson had fourteen counties attached to Oldham County, and Potter was the county farthest east in his official territory. The LX Ranch lay in Potter County. Immediately upon receiving word of the new town in his official territory, Robinson put an old Negro on a horse and sent him to the LX Ranch to get me.

I had gotten into such deep thoughts of the future and of work prospects in general that I was very restless, not able to sleep. As a result, I tossed from one side of my bed to the other, and as I look back, it must have been a premonition. About midnight, old Negro Bob rode up to the hitching rack for horses, tied his horse, then hollered hello. I answered him, not knowing who he was or his reason for being there. My six-shooter lay across my lap in my right hand fully cocked as he approached. When he was within twenty feet of me, I asked who he was and what business he had. He replied, "It's me, Mr. Jim. I'm Bob, with a letter for you from Mr. Tobe Robinson." Bob had ridden from Tascosa, the county seat, a distance of thirty miles.

The letter was brief, just requesting me to come to Tascosa that night without fail. So I took old Bob's horse and rounded up the horse I wanted to ride, then woke up the general manager, Mr. Hollicott. I informed him I had decided to go to work for the sheriff; then Bob and I headed our horses toward Tascosa. As we came in sight of the little pioneer adobe cattle town, the morning sun was spreading its rays over the picturesque river valley in which Tascosa was situated. Had I realized then that it was doomed to die in so short a time, my heart would have been very sad indeed.

After eating a hearty breakfast and saddling a fresh horse, Sheriff Robinson and I started for the tent town. Robinson rode his favorite saddle horse, a pacer called Rowdy, and, like all pacing horses, Rowdy would stumble when the going was rough. Robinson had something in a gunny sack tied behind his saddle, and when Rowdy would stumble, I could hear metallic rings. So I asked Robinson what he had in the sack. He said, "Just some hobbles," and I supposed he had hobbles for our saddle horses.

We arrived at Rag Town about four o'clock in the afternoon. There were tents occupied by all forms of humanity waiting to reap their harvest off of the track layers and graders. These men from the work gangs came into Rag Town every evening, and they were all Irish.

Sheriff Robinson took me to all the places and gave me the same introduction at each place. He would say, "Gentlemen, I am the high sheriff of this and thirteen adjacent counties. This kid is Jim Gober, and my deputy sheriff. He is the man I am putting here among you to protect life and property, and prosecute such violations of the law that in his judgment is necessary, and his judgment will be mine. If you respect him as your officer, as you should, and desist from pulling rough stuff, you will find him to be a pleasant officer and a fair dealer. On the other hand, if there are any gunmen or petty larceny thieves or women beaters in the town, it will be advisable for them to move out before the kid locates them. That's three classes of undesirables he never gets along with. I can attest to this because I have known him for five years."

After making the rounds and securing a place in a tent restaurant where I could sleep, we went to our saddle horses, and Robinson untied the gunny sack from his saddle and emptied out the contents: six pair of handcuffs and three pair of leg shackles. Then he said, "Kid, these are all the dependable friends you have here. Use them when you think it necessary, and trust nobody. Do your duty, and if anyone commits an offense you think should be prosecuted, put them on the stagecoach and bring them to Tascosa. Now, goodbye and good luck. If there is any gunplay, get yours first; protect yourself, above all. *Au revoir, mi amigo y compañero.*"

A Tough Transition

The sheriff then paced away towards Tascosa. I just stood there and watched him and Rowdy as far as I could see them by moonlight. After they were out of sight, I felt this penetrating feeling of loneliness that seemed to not only disarm me emotionally as I experienced a sick feeling in the pit of my stomach but to physically paralyze me with fear. My overwhelming thought was that if those handcuffs and leg irons were all the friends I had, it was a chilly place for a civilized boy to be in.

I leaned against a hitching post for the longest time, just pondering whether the world held peace and pleasure or trouble and disappointment for my future. At last, a sweet vision of my dear lovable mother crossed my mind, and I could imagine that I heard her voice speaking the kind and loving words she used to repeat so often to me: "Son, be kind to every one you meet and you will never lack for friends, and you will never fear any man."

I went straight to the tent restaurant where I had arranged to sleep. It was hard to believe that I was so tired, but it occurred to me that I hadn't gotten much sleep the night before. I told the restaurant man, who's name was Abe Hyman, that if he heard of any trouble to wake me immediately. As destiny would have it, about midnight Abe ran to my bunk and said, "Get up; there is shooting in the saloon across the street."

I dressed myself hurriedly, slipped a pair of handcuffs in the waistband of my pants, grabbed my .45-caliber Colt, and ran into the saloon. Loud talking was coming from the back end, partitioned off for gambling rooms. I opened the door and stepped in to find a gambler called Comanche Bill with his head bleeding. He was stamping his feet, cursing, and threatening the people around him. I called his partner, a nice-looking fellow of above-average intelligence, to one side, and I asked him what was happening. He said, "Bill got what he deserved from a cowpuncher. The cowpuncher bought some drinks for Bill's girl, and the two of them were getting pretty cozy when Bill got sore and slapped the girl. Then the cowpuncher lammed Bill over the head with a .45, the gun went off, and Bill fell. The cowpuncher then ran to his horse and galloped off. It all happened before you could say 'Scat.'"

I asked him to describe the cowpuncher, and he said that he was from the Frying Pan Ranch, a heavyset man about thirty years old, with a light moustache. Then I recognized that the man he described was Jim Murry, a person with whom I had worked at the Frying Pan several years before. Comanche Bill was still cursing, bleeding, and raving, and wanting to find the cowpuncher. I asked his redheaded, freckled-face jane to get something for a bandage. She rushed out and was back in no time with something resembling a woman's panties. I made Comanche sit down on the stool chair, and freckled jane held a basin of water as I washed off the blood, got some sugar and turpentine, mixed the two, then bandaged his head with his jane's panty leg. She was kissing him and calling him "Honey," seemingly forgetting that her eye was swollen and black from the blow Comanche had given her a few minutes before.

Comanche was still cursing, grating his teeth, stamping his feet and saying how many wicked things he would do to that cowardly cowpuncher. Finally, I thought of a scheme to bring an end to this seemingly endless charade, for if I could get him shut down, I most surely could get the jane shut up. So I laid my hand on his shoulder and said, "I believe you'd better cheese and save your strength and willpower until about noon tomorrow. You will need it all. I happen to know the man you have called so many vile names and want to chew up so bad. When a man wants to fight as bad as you say you do, I believe in giving him a chance. The other man is a square guy, and I know of three fighters that he gave a fair chance for their lives. He was just lucky and won out. Now, it's only twelve miles to the Frying Pan Ranch, and I'm going to put a man on my saddle horse at daylight and send him after Murry. They can be here by twelve. Just the three of us will walk over the hill to the creek valley, and I will see that you have a square deal. Look your .45 over carefully and see that it is in working order. Keep mum; no one must know but just us three. Now, good night, Comanche and your squaw. See you at twelve sharp tomorrow."

The stagecoach came through Rag Town about sunrise going east to Wichita Falls, and when I got up the next morning, Abe said, "I lost two of my boarders; served them breakfast at five o'clock this morning. They set up all night for fear they would miss the stage. Comanche was hurt pretty bad, I guess. He didn't say a word to any of us, and he is always so windy. I know he is in bad shape when he isn't talking and telling about the fights he has had."

I said, "Well, Abe, I'm sorry to see you lose any customers, but if that pair had stayed here I couldn't have enjoyed my meals when they were in sight. I'll tell you what, Abe—I will try to get you two more customers in their place."

As long as Rag Town existed, which was about six months, no one ever knew the exact cause of Comanche Bill and his girl hastening away from Rag Town, except myself.

The Aftermath of Comanche Bill

I slept until about eight o'clock that morning, and while I was eating breakfast, Charlie Gillespie, the boss of the Frying Pan Ranch, came in and shook hands with me and asked me in a serious mood where the man was that got killed. I told him that no one got killed, and he looked astonished. Staring me in the eye for some time, he ventured to say, "Jim, Murry woke me up at the ranch at two thirty this morning and told me that he went to hit a man with his gun and pulled the gun off accidentally and shot him dead. Murry had drawn what money he had coming and left for parts unknown at three o'clock this morning."

I said, "The man he hit over the head and the jane he hit him over left here on the stage at five this morning, so that this vicinity is now rid of three damn fools, and all is for the best." We had a hearty laugh, and Gillespie returned to the ranch. Murry was never heard of again, and if he is living today, he believes he murdered a man over a red-headed, freckled-faced jane.

After getting through with Gillespie, I made a general round of all gambling tents and saloons and told them all in a nice way that those that had women that they might get jealous of had better not have them in the saloons and gambling houses. I explained to them that I was taking this time to warn them that when the cowpunchers and railroad gangs meet women in those places, they think of these women as public property. They believe that they have as much right to their company as anyone. All agreed that the cowpunchers and railroaders were absolutely right.

The Revelation of a Detective's Instinct

The last saloon that I visited was run by Tip McDowell, who had followed the Fort Worth and Denver as it was built, all the way from Fort Worth. He had four of the toughest-looking men I ever saw as helpers. I had quite a lengthy visit with Tip and had taken a drink with him and bought a round for the whole tribe.

One man in the bunch attracted my attention more than the others. He was introduced to me as Charlie Collins and was about thirty years old, six feet and two inches tall, with black eyes and a black mustache. This fellow probably weighed two hundred pounds and appeared to be an athletic person. I noticed that every time I looked at him, he dropped his eyes to the floor or looked off in another direction. Finally, I asked Tip where his place was located while he was in Fort Worth, and he said, "I run a saloon with a vaudeville show. I was located in the Acre."

I knew what "the Acre" meant. It was the red-light district commonly known as Hell's Half-Acre, and for ten years, a tougher bunch of human beings never lived than infested Hell's Half-Acre in Fort Worth.[7] Then I was satisfied that Tip and his bunch would have to be watched more than all the rest.

The next morning, while eating breakfast, an old Irishman came in with his head all bandaged up with a red bandanna. He asked the proprietor for something to eat, saying that he was slugged and robbed last night. I spoke to the proprietor and told him to feed the old Irishman, and I would pay for it. The old man thanked me heartily and ate his meal, and when he was through, I asked him to take a walk with me. When we got out of sight, we sat down under a cottonwood tree on the bank of the creek, and I began asking him questions about the robbery, and he related his story. He told me that all he knew was that he had cashed his time check at Tip's saloon and that the amount of the check was forty-five dollars. The next thing he could remember was that he woke up this morning in an old dugout under the bluff and behind Tip's, with his head peeled and not a cent in his pocket. Then I said, "Come and show me the dugout." So we walked around under the creek bank directly behind Tip's saloon and fifty yards distance from it. I immediately saw the blood where the old fellow had lain all night, but I also found the tracks in the sand of one man that went across the creek and up the hill, and I followed them straight to Tip's back entrance. I told the Irishman to come to the restaurant for supper and I would pay for it. What I never told the old man was that I was tracking anyone. He had never noticed that I was looking at the ground as we were walking towards Tip's.

Soon after he went into Tip's saloon and I went back to the old dugout, I cut three twigs from a bush and made a careful measurement of the track that had made the plainest imprint in the sand. I measured the length with one twig and cut the twig the exact length of the imprint; then I took a second twig and measured across the ball of the footprint, then cut it to the exact width. With the third twig I measured across the front part of the heel, then cut the twig.

My next move was to go to Tip's, where I found Collins and asked him to have a drink with me, and, after showing him courtesy and respect, I asked him to take a walk with me. He readily consented, evidently feeling highly honored. I said to him, "Let's walk down to the creek, where there should be an old dugout nearby where I camped in the winter of 1882. I just want to see if it looks natural." By so doing I had taken him right over the ground where I had measured the track of the man that had packed the old Irishman in the dugout, but I didn't go into the dugout, where the blood was so evident. I just remarked to him that I had spent many lonely hours in that hole, and then we walked on back toward Tip's, and Collins asked me to have a drink. He proceeded to tell Tip that I had just taken him down to the creek and showed him my old home. At this point I said, "I will see you again" as I walked out and down the street a block, across to the creek, and down to the dugout. I immediately took out my three sticks and applied them to Mr. Collins's fresh track and found an exact fit for each stick. Being satisfied that I had the king thief spotted, I was elated, and I felt confident that I would get him red handed.

From Tip's saloon, straight back from the rear fifty paces on the bank of the creek was a large cottonwood tree. The bank was ten feet above a deep, clear pool of water. This tree shaded the ground for thirty feet around it.

The weather was warm, being that it was in the middle of June, and the night flaps of the tent saloon were tied back as far as possible, day and night. So I laid my plans to go to the creek every night after it was dark and follow the creek bed around to the tree. There I would climb on top of the high bank to sit down there in the dark with my back against the tree, in the shadows, and watch what went on in Tip's saloon. The saloon was well lighted, with three large brass coal-oil swinging lamps squarely spaced the long way of the tent. From the black shadow made by the cottonwood tree I could see every man inside and every move he made.

Well satisfied with my prospect, and confident I was going to put out of business the first bunch of pickpockets and thugs I had ever come in contact with, I went leisurely around Rag Town, unconcerned, until I retired for the night. Since the next day would be payday for the construction gang, I felt sure that I would catch my man that night and resolved to stick by my cottonwood tree all night if necessary.

By noon the next day, there were about two hundred Irish track layers from different camps up and on the line, and the saloons were jammed. About the middle of the afternoon there were several fist-fights between them, but I payed very little attention to them, just dropping in to where they were congregating, from place to place. Every once in a while, I dropped in to Tip's place and watched the Irish cash their time checks. Some of them would give their checks to Tip, not taking any money but standing right at the bar and ordering drinks until Tip told them they hadn't anything left. That really meant that as soon as they got intoxicated, they were broke.

Tip's place seemed to hold the larger part of the Irish, as they were all acquainted with Tip and his four men because they had set up their tent saloon every place the boarding car had stopped, from Fort

Worth to Rag Town—a distance of 342 miles. Since the boarding car moved on the average of fifteen miles each move, you can approximate about how much dealing these Irish construction men had had with Tip and his men.

When these poor, unfortunate Irish drank until they could stand up no longer, Tip's men would take them to the rear of the tent, which was constructed by setting up six four-by-four scantlings in the ground fourteen feet apart on each side of a space eighteen feet wide and twenty feet long. These uprights were then boxed up by walls made with one-by-twelve boards about six feet long. The tent was then stretched on top of the walls. Tip had no partitions, as he didn't have any gambling. Gambling was too slow for Tip, so by dusk, there were as many as fifteen or twenty Irish dead to the world laying in the rear of Tip's saloon, where he had been merciful enough to put sawdust on the ground for the occasion.

After watching, for several hours, the most interesting show I had ever experienced in my life, I realized it was getting dark, so I leisurely walked up to Tip and asked him how long Collins had been with him. He told me that he had been with him about two years but said that he had known him from a barefoot boy, as Collins was raised on a farm near Fort Worth and was an honest, dependable fellow. When he had to go to Fort Worth, he always left Collins in charge of the saloon. I remarked that Collins understood putting these old Irish to bed. Tip replied, "Oh, yes, he takes care of them, and it wouldn't be healthy for anyone to molest them while they are asleep."

I turned and walked to the rear, where Collins had just laid one down that was protesting, and I said, "I see you are the lodging clerk. Nice job—how long have you been with Tip?"

He replied, "About six months."

I said, "You don't look to be a Texan."

And he said, "No, I was raised in Chicago; only been in Texas a year."

I had heard enough, so I said, "Well, goodnight, Collins. Take good care of these old fellows. I will see you in the morning." I went out the front entrance and turned toward the creek, then at a safe distance I made for the old cottonwood and sat down with my back against that tree, four feet across. I pulled off my hat and sat there with a full, unobstructed view of Tip's place. Tip's other two men, Red Daley and Dutch McGuire, were busy cleaning, emptying slops, and waiting on what few Irish that hadn't gotten sufficient tonnage to put them to sleep.

Collins was still trying to put his rebel down, and suddenly the old fellow got to his feet. At that display of insolence Collins grabbed him by the legs with one arm, threw the other arm around his back, and came out of the back door and right straight toward me. About halfway from the saloon to the big tree were several beer casks or barrels. Collins stopped at the barrels, laying the old fellow on the ground. I could see him plainly, as he was in line with the lights from inside the tents, and the tent, being tied back, gave the light reflection back to where he was going through the old man's pockets. I am satisfied that Collins thought he was in the dark and not observed by anyone.

After he had searched all the old man's pockets, he deliberately picked him up by the back and legs and, doubling him up like a jackknife, he stuffed him with all his might into one of those barrels, turned the barrel on its side, and gave it a kick. It was a downward slope to this high bluff, with the deep pool of water beneath. When he started the barrel, Collins ran back to the saloon, and as soon as it was safe, I got up.

When the barrel was within six feet of the bluff, I stepped in front of it and proceeded to free the old Irishman from his peril. It was clear that if the barrel had gone off that bluff it would have turned open end down, and his weight would have sunk the barrel, or most of it. Later, if anyone had seen the barrel they would have thought someone put it there to soak up the leaks. The consequences would have been that the turtles, fish, and water moccasins would have had an Irish feast for as long as he lasted.

After a few minutes of fast work I got the old man out and laid him down on a level spot covered with buffalo grass and put his cap under his head as a pillow. Then I hastened around where I could enter Tip's saloon from the front. A pair of handcuffs was under my coat, hooked over my revolver belt. I had taken them off of the belt as I walked and adjusted them in my left hand, ready for action. Then I put my left hand in my pocket and slipped my holster around on my belt in front of my left side.

When I entered the front door, Collins was handing Tip some money. Collins, Daley, and Dutch were lined up in front of the bar, and Tip was behind Collins, being the closest man from the door. Collins said, "Come on, Sheriff; you are just in time to join us in a drink. We have had a busy day, and we're all pretty tired."

I walked up close to his right side with my left hand still in my coat pocket and my right almost touching the handle of my revolver, hidden by my coat. I said, "No, Collins, I never drink when I have immediate duties to perform, but go ahead, take your drink, and take a good one. You may not get another one for a long time."

I shall never forget the expression that came over that demon's face. He seemed to be paralyzed. I said to him again, "Take your drink. I have some business with you, and I am in a hurry." He raised the glass to his mouth slowly; his hand trembled until he spilled part of his whiskey. When he had the glass to his mouth, as quick as a flash I snapped one cuff on his right wrist, drew my revolver with my right hand, and commanded the other three not to move. Then I said, "Farmer boy, put your left wrist in this bracelet, and be prompt and peaceable about it, and all will be well." After getting him handcuffed, I searched him and found a heavy pair of "knucks" and a few dollars in silver.

While the rest of the den of thieves watched, I left with Collins and took him down the street to Lee Cone's saloon. I had known Lee Cone at Tascosa and knew him to be an honorable fellow. There I asked Lee to loan me a quilt and another fellow to go to Abe's restaurant and get a pair of leg irons. I spread the quilt with one end joining a big center post that was well set in the ground. Then I made Collins lie with his feet astride the post and snapped the leg irons on his legs. I said, "Collins, I'm taking more pains with you than you take with guests at Tip's rooming house." But Collins had never said a word from the time he extended the invitation to join him in a drink at Tip's.

As soon as I had Collins safe and as comfortable as general surroundings would afford, I asked Lee Cone to look out for him and not let anyone go near him until morning. I told him I would take him off his hands by sunrise. When I had finished I went to Tip's saloon and found him, Daley, McGuire, and the fifth man of his bunch, whose name I never learned since he seemed too busy as a porter most of the time. The four of them were holding a very earnest conversation when I entered. Before they had time to ask a single question, I spoke to Daley and McGuire and said, "Come with me. I need some help." They sprang to their feet in a very obedient way; then I led the way out the back entrance to where I had left the unfortunate son of old Ireland. Then I said to Daley and McGuire, "Take this man into Tip's place and lay him to rest with his brothers."

When they had straightened him out on the sawdust, I asked them if they knew him. Dutch McGuire replied, "Sure we do. That is Mike Stone, got his identity cashed this afternoon, and he was here not longer than an hour ago."

Tip came up about that time and said, "Yes, I cashed his check for $22.50, and he would have the money, so now I guess he has been robbed; let's look in his pockets."

I said, "His pockets have already been looked through. You let me see the check you cashed for him and the one you cashed for that old fellow lying there with the bandage on his head, the one that was robbed night before last and cracked on the head with knucks. His name is Jimmie Kruger. He says you cashed his identity for forty-five dollars—yes, I believe that was the amount."

And Tip turned, went behind the bar, and reached under the counter or back shelving, pulling out a medium-size handbag. He proceeded to look through the many identification checks he had taken in for rat-gut booze, enough to put the horny-handed Irish to sleep. After ten or fifteen minutes he found the stack of checks in question. I took them from him and found the ones that matched the amount I had been told. Then I asked Tip, "How much of these checks did those old men spend over your bar?"

He said, "I should guess about half."

Then I replied, "Collins must have deposited in the neighborhood of thirty-three dollars with you. I saw him hand you what he got off of Mike Stone, and naturally I presumed it is his regular custom to bring and deposit what he gets from each victim. Anyway, I demand thirty-four dollars, or I keep the checks."

By this time the four of them were of an ashen color and their eyes blared wide, but none spoke for a minute. Finally, Daley said, "Tip, the officer is trying to do the right thing. You had better do what he asks."

Immediately, Tip opened his cash drawer and counted out to me thirty-four dollars. At that point I was just waiting to unload my craw on that band of thieves. I looked at Tip and spoke in a tone where all could not fail to hear, and I said, "Now, Mr. McDowell, I'm taking your good, honest farmer boy to Tascosa on the stage in the morning with two charges of highway robbery and one of assault with a deadly weapon. I wish to say to you that you are the first man to invade this hospitable territory as a larceny thief with four confederates. You have disgraced the reputation of this country for more than one hundred square miles. I know a number of men in this vicinity that are under assumed names, but they have that high degree of honor that they protect life and property of any American citizen."

Then I said to that collection of rats, "I'm going to give you a little confidential advice. I'm suggesting to you that you take down your licenses[8] and mail them to the county clerk at Tascosa and ask him to try to get you a refund of the money for the unused time designated on the license. Then pack your goods and get back to Hell's Half-Acre as soon as possible. When I get back here tomorrow night, if you and your gang are still here, I shall send a messenger to the Frying Pan Ranch and one to the LX Ranch asking for six cowboys from each ranch. Before those twelve cowpunchers I will state the facts and circumstances as I have found them, and I fear your saloon will go up in smoke, and that beautiful old cottonwood tree back there will be decorated with the filthy bodies of four of the dirtiest thieves that ever invaded this territory."

Care and Concern for Two Old Irishmen

I told McGuire and Daley to bring Kruger and Stone, dead or alive, to Abe's restaurant, to bring them one at a time, but not to fail to deliver the goods. After giving those instructions I went back to Lee Cone's, where I left Collins, and found him O.K. From there I went to Abe's and found that Kruger had been delivered. In a few minutes, they came in with Stone. By this time the two old fellows had partially slept off their jag, and I ordered hot coffee for them and also told Abe to give them all they wanted to eat, but not to let them leave until I came back.

I departed to make a round of the saloons, except Tip's, going first to Cone's place, where Murry and Comanche Bill ran together over the redheaded jane; from there, to Bill Rich and Rube Burrow's place. I found everything quiet, and I concluded to go to bed and get some sleep for the trip the next day with Collins to Tascosa.

When I entered the front door at Abe's, my two Irish paupers were messing over a beefsteak, eggs, and potatoes. A mess it was, for they had eggs all over their faces, and part of the time the steak would be on the counter and then in the plate, but the poor old fellows were doing the best they could. Finally, they quit, and I called Abe and handed him thirty dollars and told him to take out what they had eaten and to keep the balance until morning. Tomorrow would be Sunday, and the construction boss would be in loading them out in

Panhandle Plains Stage Coach

At eight o'clock the stage came in, and I loaded Collins on the front seat with the driver while I took a seat in the rear. We arrived at Tascosa at two thirty PM, and I turned Collins over to Sheriff Robinson.

wagons to take them out to camp so that they would be ready to go to work Monday morning. I told Abe to divide this thirty dollars equally between them in the morning, after taking out what they owed. Then I handed each one two dollars and told them that it would buy them all the booze they needed until morning, and that I was bidding them good night.

Good Riddance of Bad Actors

Next morning I arose at sunup, dressed, and went to Lee Cone's saloon. I took one leg iron off of Collins and from around the post, then put it back on his leg, as there were chain links enough between the cuffs for him to walk and take short steps. We went to Abe's and had breakfast. At eight o'clock the stage came in, and I loaded Collins on the front seat with the driver while I took a seat in the rear. We arrived at Tascosa at two thirty PM, and I turned Collins over to Sheriff Robinson. After the sheriff locked him up, I sat down and related the circumstances that caused me to arrest him. The sheriff looked back at Collins, then remarked, "He is sure a tough-looking brute. Never before have I seen any of his kind in this country. I'm sure glad you got him where he belongs." I also told Robinson about the advice I gave Tip McDowell, and he laughed and said, "Rag Town is strictly under your management, and I will stand behind anything you do. You have done well so far. Go right on, but be careful; don't let any of them get the advantage over you."

The stage went back down the line, leaving Tascosa at one AM, arriving at Rag Town at five AM. As I stepped down from the stage I thought about how good a cup of coffee would taste. After all, the happenings of the last twenty-four hours had allowed no time to just to sit, catch my breath, or even that chance to taste a leisurely cup of java. I went down the street to Abe's, and while I was enjoying that long sought-after cup, Abe said to me, "Our town is depopulating instead of growing."

"Now what has happened?" I quipped.

Abe continued, "Well, you took Tip's fellow off and he peddled his whiskey, beer, and everything he could to the other saloons. Furthermore, he hired two teams and wagons, loaded his tent and fixtures, and pulled out late last evening."

I commented to Abe, "Perhaps he will find a location more suitable for his method of doing business. While Rag Town lasts, there must be a reasonable degree of fairness and justice among its inhabitants."

That ended the first experience or, rather, preliminary start as a peace officer. As long as Rag Town existed, which was six months, I never had to make another arrest, never heard of a drunk being robbed, and every soul, every man and woman, apparently had the highest regard for me as an officer of the law and a citizen as well. A friendly state existed between everyone, and I soon came to know them all by name, men and women alike. As I cultivated the acquaintance of Mr. Rich and Rube Burrow, I became fond of Burrow. He was a man of about thirty-five and a splendid specimen in his physique, being about six feet in height and around 190 pounds in weight. His brown hair played well with his light brown eyes and his rather dark complexion. For some reason, he seemed to have taken a great fancy to me.

A County to be Formed

An Election in the Winds

I n a few days Sheriff Robinson and Jesse Jenkins came down to
Rag Town from Tascosa. Jesse now was interested, with Lee Cone,
in a Rag Town saloon. He remained a warm friend to me and was
considered to be a likable man by all the cowboys. Jesse had filed a
homestead entry on a section of land adjoining Rag Town. He and
Sheriff Robinson informed me that plans were being made by a
number of prominent men from Abilene, Texas, to have an election
to establish a county seat and elect county officers for Potter County,
as the new county was to be called, and that they were going to run
me for sheriff. I thanked them for their confidence in my ability, but
told them that because of my age, barely twenty-two, I wondered what
my chances of success would be. Nevertheless, I told them that I
would run my best, that it wasn't my nature to turn away from any
challenge. I accepted with enthusiasm, from that moment on, the
challenge of becoming the first sheriff of Potter County.

These men from Abilene, Texas, who Jesse and Tobe had mentioned, all arrived in this locality in the early spring of 1887, and they
had filed on sections of land along the railroad survey. A number of
prominent men from Henrietta, Texas, had also filed on sections of
land in the same general area. Among those from Henrietta was
Judge W. B. Plemons,[1] an able lawyer and a genteel man with the
highest degree of honor and moral character. We had become confidential friends from our first introduction.

Judge and Mrs. W. B. Plemons, ca. 1887.

The prominent figures in the Abilene bunch were Colonel Clabe Merchant,[2] Colonel James T. Berry,[3] and Jim Holland.[4] There were also several friends of Holland. These men began to visit Rag Town almost daily, and they were freely discussing the coming election and several possibilities for a town as well as a county seat. Most of the prominent men advocated Colonel Berry's section as the logical location of the new town. It was four miles east of Rag Town, just on the edge of the plains.

After a few days of discussion, and through the reasoning and suggestion of Judge Plemons, it was decided that there would be an election ordered for August 6, 1887. In the interim period, the days dragged by just about the same in Rag Town.

Campaigning, Such As It Was

As soon as the date for the election was made public, candidates for the various offices began to announce in the Tascosa paper, and my name was one of the first to appear as a candidate for sheriff, and it was a period of two weeks before I had an opponent. The opponent who announced his candidacy turned out to be my old LX Ranch boss, Bill Ruth. I was surprised and hurt at heart when I realized that Ruth was not the friend he had pretended to be, but I kept silent.

Within a few days, Charlie Gillespie, foreman of the Frying Pan Ranch, also announced.[5] Gillespie had taken charge of the Frying Pan Ranch long after I had left, coming off the T Anchor Ranch. I didn't feel that he was under any obligation as a friend, but I knew that I had two staunch friends on the Frying Pan that would stay by me and use their influence in my behalf. These friends were Mr. and Mrs. Wetsel, the bookkeeper and his wife, who, when I worked on the ranch, were almost a father and mother to me, and this relationship began when I was just sixteen years old.

I felt sure I would get more votes there than Gillespie, and I also believed that I didn't have an enemy on the LX Ranch but also knew I had several steadfast friends there. But it seemed like a hard game where I had to depend on getting men to vote against their boss. On the other hand, since I had declared candidacy first, I would stay to the finish.

It began to seem, though, that those two ranch bosses had a much greater advantage over me, as they were with their men all the time. A good tactic came to my mind: I decided not to let Jesse Jenkins and Sheriff Robinson do the electioneering with the cowboys until just a few days before the election. Then I would visit each ranch and stay long enough to have a talk with each man.

Judge Plemons was on the ticket for county judge, and I was as much enthused for his success as for my own. Jim Holland and Mack Moore[6] of the Abilene bunch were on the ticket for county commissioner. Also John Seely from the LX Ranch and Tuck Cornelius,[7] who was formerly from Colorado City, Texas, were running for that office. Billy Laird from the LX was running for county clerk. John Bain was on the ticket for treasurer. These names that I have mentioned were the prominent figures in the election, and they were running without opposition.[8] I was the only candidate to have opposition of any consequence. As the date for the election grew nearer, everyone, it seemed, had less to say, for it appeared that they had adopted my policy.

On the fourth of July, every one of the settlers and a number of the cowboys came to town. I acted just the same to all I met as when I was a cowboy with them on the ranch. If anyone mentioned the election, I would say, "Boys, you know me, and I think we are the best of friends, and I believe you know in your own heart that if I am elected sheriff of Potter County, it will not change my heart or principles. I have that degree of loyalty and respect for friendship that if any of you had announced for sheriff first, you would have my hearty support, and no inducement could have caused me to come out against you. This is the first time in my life I've had to battle against a man who I had always appreciated and respected as a loyal friend, but I realize that my confidence was misplaced, and it hurts to be disappointed in a friend. So you boys choose for yourselves in the race between Ruth and me.

"Gillespie I expect to beat on his own ranch. I also expect to get my share of the homesteaders on the plains, and I feel sure Robinson and Jenkins will carry the west end of the county for me. I think there are thirty-one votes in the Mexican Plaza[9] and the Pescado,[10] and Jesse will get them to a man. So the deciding vote is with you boys, as there are about sixty of you, besides the settlers, that vote at your ranch."

Ruth was going from place to place wherever he saw a crowd, asking everybody to have a drink and introducing himself as the winner in the sheriff's race. He had with him Matt Atwood, a wagon boss on the LX, and they claimed to be cousins.

After most of the cowboys had left for the ranches all pretty well jagged, and the settlers had departed in the same mood, I met Colonel Berry and Judge Plemons. Colonel Berry said to me, "Come on, Gober. You are going to have a drink with us, and we want to assure you of our hearty support. Your opponent, Ruth, looks to me like he has stolen a sheep."

I said, "Colonel, I assure you and the judge that I appreciate your friendship and feel more sure of my success when such men as you are supporting me. Since this is the first interest I have taken, or even had, in politics, it has looked like I have had a hard game, but I'm no quitter, and I will stay to the finish, and if I lose I won't be ruined."

After we had taken our drinks, Judge Plemons said, "Gober, we are for you because we believe you to be a square boy and our kind of people. I have a Texas-raised wife and five Texas-bred and -born children. We left a comfortable home and pleasant surroundings at Henrietta, Texas, where I had the honor of serving the people as Clay County judge. At present, we are living in a dugout five miles east on the plains, and we have come to stay and be citizens of Potter County. We want to be friends to you, and I would be glad to have you come out and meet my wife and children." I thanked the judge and shook hands with him and the colonel and bade them good night.

Final Strategy

All Rag Town was quiet, and everyone had been peaceable with all their drinking the entire day, so I felt well satisfied and went to bed. I didn't go to sleep for three hours, however, because I kept studying the election situation until I felt that I had it fully solved to my mind's satisfaction. What I had decided was that Judge Plemons, Colonel Berry, and Clabe Merchant had declared themselves for me, and they were all experienced in the political game, and therefore they would carry Rag Town most solid, with the exception of Holland and five or six of his bunch. In my solution, Mr. and Mrs. Wetsel would get the majority of the Frying Pan box, and Sheriff Robinson and Jenkins would get the Mexican vote at the Pescado Plaza. This left the LX Ranch as the place for me to do my head work, and I decided to wait until one day before the election, then to go to the ranch and spend the day and night in a social way and wait until the polls were open; then, in Ruth's presence, to ask the attention of the judges and all voters present, and then to give them a fair, sensible, and reasonable talk.

With that decision behind me, I threw all worry off my mind and felt perfectly at ease. I did, however, hear numerous reports about who on the LX was going to vote for Ruth.

In a few days, Matt Atwood's cook, old Bill Hensley, came to Rag Town and mentioned that Matt Atwood was telling all the boys on the ranch that when Ruth was elected, he, Atwood, would be in charge of the ranch, and that every man who voted for Gober would be out of a job. I said, "Well, Bill, if any of those boys think more of a thirty-dollar job than they do of their freedom to express their will at the election, Ruth is welcome to their vote, but I feel sure there are only a few of that kind." I went on to say, "I'm not surprised at Atwood, as I thoughtlessly spoiled his reputation of being Frank Jackson, as he had confided to some of the boys. Frank Jackson was one of two men that escaped alive when the Sam Bass gang was double-crossed by Jim Murphy at Round Rock, Texas, in 1880.[11] I knew Frank from the time he was fifteen years old until he was twenty-four. He killed a Negro at Denton and then joined the Bass gang.

After I went to work on the LX Ranch, the first person that confided in me about the secret of Atwood being Jackson, I laughed heartily and told them what I knew. It got to Atwood, and he never liked me after that for spoiling his reputation as being the brave and daring train robber Jackson. But I am sorry, and I swear that I wouldn't intentionally spoil any reputation a man chose to build for himself." I just crossed that one off by quipping to myself, "Just let Matt go and do his best, and Ruth too, for that matter, for they claimed to be cousins and must have about the same low principles."

I continued with Bill by saying, "So I guess that they might bear down on the boys pretty hard, but I have concluded that I would not want votes that had to be gotten that way. If a man will use such tactics on his fellow men to control votes, wouldn't it be dangerous to elect him as the sheriff? I don't call a man a square guy who will use such tactics."

Old Bill Hensley was redheaded and wore a long red mustache. He looked straight at me and said, "You are right, and I am going to put the same proposition to everyone I dare to when I get back to the ranch." So Bill and I had a farewell drink and Bill rode away, and I didn't see him again until election day. But something would come to me every day in the way of confidential news. It made me feel more confident every night when I retired. I didn't lay awake studying the situation after laying my plans. The nearer the election day came, the more certain I felt of my plans as being the right course of action.

About the fifteenth of July, things had been so quiet and peaceable in Rag Town that I became restless and lonesome. So I saddled my horse and rode to the Frying Pan Ranch and stayed all night. I told the Frying Pan boys that I had come for a social visit with them and Mr. and Mrs. Wetsel. The reason, I explained, was because things were rather lonesome over at Rag Town. I also told them that they were not to expect me to perform as an electioneer, for it would be impolite for me to come to my opponent's home and do that. Before going to bed that evening, I visited in Mr. and Mrs. Wetsel's apartment for several hours, and I told them that I was staking my hope in them to get what votes they could for me and was confident of their influence.

Next morning, I started for Tascosa to have a talk with Jenkins and Robinson and to tell them of my confidence in them to carry that area. I got to Tascosa about three PM and visited with Jenkins most of the evening until two AM the next morning. Robinson joined us occasionally, and I outlined things as I had planned them. It was agreed for Jenkins and Robinson to get to the Pescado box early the morning of the election with a sufficient size jug to give every voter an eye opener and try to get all the votes cast in time for Jenkins to join me at the LX Ranch by noon. I figured the LX boys, or most of them, would put off voting until afternoon.

After all plans were agreed on, I started back to Rag Town the morning of the seventeenth and arrived at Rag Town about four PM. After visiting all around, I found nothing unusual had happened and that my importance as a respected peace officer when away, as well as when on the ground, seemed well established. Also my visit had given me new confidence in my friends, so I went to bed early and slept sound until sunup next morning.

The County Seat—Here, or There?

By the time the track laying for the railroad had passed Rag Town, the talk was that there would be a switch and siding put in four miles west. That was to be done at a point near the beginning of a broken, rough, gully-washed country that ran for fifteen miles before striking the south Canadian River. From there they would have a stretch of fifteen miles up the river valley on the opposite side of the river from Tascosa.

When the boarding cars moved, that would mean the disappearance of Rag Town. So I figured that after the sixth of August, when the county seat would be established, whatever was left of Rag Town that didn't follow the boarding cars would go to the county seat.

I began to take an interest in and to study the different possible locations for the county seat that were to be voted on. As time was drawing near, the different parties owning or rather having homesteaded entries on the sections named on the ticket were getting more enthused every day and would discuss their advantages over the other fellows to me, while guaranteeing their support to my cause. I gave each one the same expression of my feelings—that I couldn't afford to commit myself in favor of any particular location, for two

General Merchandise Store

All of Rag Town was abandoned, and most all went to Amarillo, the new county seat. . . . Cone and Duran, from Tascosa, put up the first adobe building and put in a charge stock of general merchandise. Carter and Morton were next, with a frame building with general merchandise.

reasons: the first being that I had no choice; the second was that I needed the support of every man I could get and felt as though I wanted to be fair to all alike. In further explanation, I stated that I wasn't for or against any particular location for the county seat, that either location on the ticket would suit me.[12]

The Election, and Amarillo Takes Shape

By this time, Colonel Berry had informed me that Jim Holland, a candidate for county commissioner, had gone to New York a few years back to buy counterfeit money from a man named Tom Davis, and he had killed Davis over the deal. It had broken Holland and all the kin and friends he had to try to get him out of the New York tombs.[13] So the Abilene bunch had begun to show their true colors.

The sixth of August rolled around, and the election was held. Colonel Berry got the county seat location on section 188, four miles east of Rag Town. Judge W. B. Plemons was elected Potter County judge, and I was elected sheriff of Potter County, receiving four votes over a margin of two to one more than Ruth and Gillespie combined.[14] Jim Holland, John Seely, and Tuck Cornelius were elected commissioners of Potter County. John Bain was elected county treasurer and Billy Laird, county clerk.

All of Rag Town was abandoned, and most all went to Amarillo, the new county seat.[15] Houses went up rapidly, and a good many lived in tents with boarded-up sides for several months. Cone and Duran, from Tascosa, put up the first adobe building and put in a charge stock of general merchandise. Carter and Morton were next, with a frame building with general merchandise. Then Smith and Walker came, with the same line. These three firms and their stocks of goods would do credit to most any small city today. Garrett Johnson[16] put in the first saloon; Jack Ryan,[17] the second; and the Fort Worth and Denver Railroad built a very nice depot.[18] Also, large stock shipping yards were all hurriedly constructed to take care of cattle shipping, which was coming on immediately. Judge Plemons called the commissioners together and arranged for a temporary courthouse, which was to be a frame building. It was soon completed, and everything moved along nicely during the fall and winter of 1887.

A Matter of the Heart

In the meantime, I had gone with Garrett Johnson to Judge Plemons's house, which was plank walls covered with a tent, to get the judge to make out an application to have Johnson appointed cattle inspector. It was early in the morning, and their breakfast was just being put on the table by Mrs. Plemons and her sixteen-year-old daughter, to whom the judge introduced Johnson and me. There were four other small children, three boys and a girl. After I left, I couldn't have described anyone of the family except the older daughter, and I could have always given a perfectly accurate description of her, if we had never met again. At first glance, I felt I had known her always. She was five feet, six inches tall, with wavy brown hair and light brown eyes. I got away from Johnson as soon as possible, got off by myself, and studied whom I had known that this sweet girl resembled, but I couldn't place anyone.

In a few days, I met her and another young lady, Miss Cora Brookes in a confectionery. Miss Belle Plemons introduced me to Miss Brookes, and I immediately introduced them to the confectionery man, Frank Anglin.[19] At the same time I gave Anglin a wink and nodded to Miss Brookes. I bought some pop and, while drinking the pop, I asked Miss Plemons to escort her home. Anglin asked Miss Brookes, and all was well. They lived in different directions, so it was understood that Anglin would take Miss Brookes home within a few minutes, as soon as his partner arrived in the store.

So Miss Plemons and I bade them goodbye and started off by ourselves. I took her home, met her mother for the second time, and found in her a friendly, hospitable southern lady. She and her daughter invited me to call again, and I did very frequently. In fact, we were constant companions at all social gatherings, and I would have to have legal advice from the judge every time I got lonesome to see my sweet girl. That seemed to occur about two nights in the week, besides Sundays.

The cattle shipping was now in full blast, with hundreds coming from New Mexico, Arizona, and from the South and Southwest, from as far as the border of old Mexico. Any direction you would look from town you could see a herd of cattle. The supply of stock cars was inadequate to move the cattle as fast as they came, and consequently they had to be held until cars could arrive, which would sometimes be ten days.[20]

Cowboys, in large numbers, were in town day and night, and they were drinking and gambling. However, I got along fine with all, despite the fact that among them were some very desperate men. All seemed, for some reason, to like and respect me.

By the first of December 1887 the shipping was all over for that year, and the town was quiet through the winter months.

Just a Li'l Old Game of Chance?

In January 1888 we experienced a big snowstorm one night. I was sitting in the back room of Johnson's saloon by a big coal stove when Judge Plemons, Colonel Berry, Clabe Merchant, Mack Moore, and Tom Wallace[21] all came into the back room. They sat down to a round table and ordered hot toddies. The bartender brought the drinks in on a tray, nicely decorated with slices of lemon and with some nutmeg grated in them. When Judge Plemons pulled out his purse to pay for them, Colonel Berry stopped him and said, "We are going to play freeze-out poker to see who pays for the drinks." All agreed, and I got them a deck of cards and poker chips and gave them each a stack of twenty chips. The game was on among five old gentlemen from fifty to seventy years old, Colonel Berry being the oldest. The Colonel, the first to lose his stack, payed for the drinks and said, "Let us take a stack at five cents each, and if one gets broke he can buy more." All agreed, and each had taken another hot toddy with the understanding that the one that won the first jackpot was to pay for them.

Tom Wallace had a sore hand, and when it came his time to deal the cards, he would ask me to deal for him. They were all feeling pretty good, and I concluded to have a little fun, so I went out to the barroom and got a deck of cards and stacked them so as to give them all a four-card flush, except for one player. The flush was jack high, and to the fifth man I gave a pair of queens so he would open the pot. Wallace was the fifth man, so he opened the pot. All four called him, and Wallace drew three cards. The other four drew one, and, of course, all caught a seven to their suit, helping their flushes, and they were all slipping their buckskin pocketbooks out at the same time, and then the betting began. Wallace, of course, dropped out, as he didn't help his queens. The other four raised back and forth until they were all in. I had to get busy and keep their money separated and equalized, as I didn't want anyone to quit, a loser. Finally, they showed their hands, each one confident he had the pot won.

Now, it had taken twenty minutes to get them settled down and get them to understand that their hands were all tied together and no one would win. When they saw how it was, they were the worst plagued bunch of old aristocratic gentlemen I had ever seen. The old colonel said, "By God, I have played poker forty years and never saw anything like that before."

Then I laughed and said, "Colonel, it's a bad night and getting late, and I just made that deal so you old gentlemen could get all the play out of you on that one hand and go home and get in your warm bed." Every time I would see the colonel, for some weeks, I would say, "Let's have a little poker game, Colonel." Then he would curse me, humorously.

The town dragged on through the winter of 1887-88 in a crude way. By spring, Mr. McGregor had built a nice frame hotel, and his son-in-law, Mr. Rudolph, had started a newspaper, making the second one, the first being the *Amarillo Champion,* started by H. H. Brookes,[22] the father of Cora Brookes. By that time the town had a population of five hundred people.

A man by the name of L. B. Collins, a friend of Clabe Merchant who went broke in the cattle business in west Texas, had come to town. Clabe Merchant introduced him to me, saying, "Gober, what this man tells you I will vouch for. He is a good, honest man and a good businessman." So Mr. Collins informed me that he had saloon fixtures and a stock of goods on the road and would be short of money for his county and state license, which would amount to six hundred dollars. I told him I would give him until I made my quarterly report on tax collecting, which would be the first of May, about ninety days off. He thanked me and had a small frame building erected near the hotel. In fifteen days he was doing business and was a likable man with a splendid personality. He was a good mixer and soon had the largest patronage in town.

A Dirty Hand in the Commissioners Court

Jim Holland, chairman of the commissioners court, had begun pressing negotiations to bond the county and build a brick courthouse and jail. Judge Plemons was pleading with the commissioners that our temporary courthouse would answer for a couple of years, and by that time our county would be more able to build, and that it was his desire to keep our county script at par value. So from time to time when the commissioners court met, Holland and Judge Plemons had a heated argument over the courthouse problem until Holland realized he couldn't get the deal through as long as Judge Plemons was Potter County judge.

John Henry, from the LX Ranch, was another commissioner, as John Seely had quit and John Henry had replaced him. So Holland began to warm up to Henry and in fact made a warm friend of him. Since three commissioners was a majority, Holland now had the power to do anything within the power of the commissioners court because he (Holland) already had Mack Moore, one of his bunch, that would do anything Holland said.[23] Judge Plemons, an able lawyer holding the position of county judge, was a roadblock to Holland, so he arranged with his loyalists to cut the county judge's ex officio salary of fifty dollars per month to twenty-five dollars per month, knowing full well that it would hurt the judge's pride and he would resign. The deal worked as Holland had planned; then he had an acquaintance, a person of the same low principles from Abilene, already on the ground to accept the appointment as county judge. The dishonorable Judge Quinn,[24] who hadn't any law education, also had a man from his home nest brought in as county attorney. That man probably had all of a common high school education. So the whole commissioners court was now wholly Holland's, and he began negotiations immediately with Martin, Burns, and Johnson, whose headquarters was Abilene, Texas, Holland's home. The plans and specifications for the courthouse were furnished and approved by the commissioners, with the building to cost forty-eight thousand dollars. The brick was to be made locally, despite the fact that there wasn't any sign of clay within twenty-five miles. The building was constructed hurriedly, with the county bonded for forty-eight thousand dollars, and the bonds were accepted as pay by Martin, Burns, and Johnson.

Because of my curiosity, expert mechanics figured the actual cost of this building when it was completed, as a personal favor to me. Using the highest costs for both materials and labor, the total cost was figured at twelve thousand dollars.[25] I had taken an active part in talking against this outrage on the taxpayers, and, quite naturally, I made an enemy of Holland and his loyalists. Sadly enough, I could never have any respect for any of them after they had taken such a dirty advantage of Judge Plemons. They cleverly eliminated Judge Plemons in order to pull this treacherous robbery of the county for that unnecessary courthouse.

I kept pretty busy, as a good many herds of cattle were coming in to be shipped to Montana, the Dakotas, and Wyoming for spring and summer grazing. The Texas ranchers had learned that the steer cattle would get larger in these northern territories as they put on more flesh. So it became a custom to cut their steers as early as March and April and ship them to the north.

The Pursuit of a Desperate Man

To Separate a Lamb from a Wolf

About the time we were all settled down in our new home, I received a letter from Sheriff Sparks of Denton County with a warrant enclosed for the arrest of one Lee Fuller, accused of murdering his brother-in-law. Sheriff Sparks informed me that he would pay six hundred dollars' reward for Fuller's arrest.

In a few days I received a letter from Mrs. Grissom, the mother of Bing Grissom, the boy that camped with me in 1882 in the panther's den on the Pease River. Mrs. Grissom was almost like a mother to me. I had been at her house often, having gone home with Bing from country dances on many occasions. The youngest Grissom was a boy named Joseph. Mrs. Grissom informed me that Joseph had left, and, she thought, with Lee Fuller. She also thought they were headed for the LX Ranch, where Bing Grissom was then working. She asked me to please keep a lookout for them and to get her boy away from Fuller and send him home or get him a job where I could look out for him.

In about ten days, Joe Grissom, then seventeen years old, rode into Amarillo and came looking for me. After talking with him a few minutes, I said, "We will put your horse in the livery stable and then go to the house and see Father and Mother." We took his horse to Tuck Cornelius's livery barn, where I told Cornelius, confidentially, not to let the boy or anyone else have the horse without a written order from me. Then we went home, where it was like a reunion, for Mother and Joe's mother had been warm friends since the early settlement of Denton County, Texas. Finally, I took Joe into my room

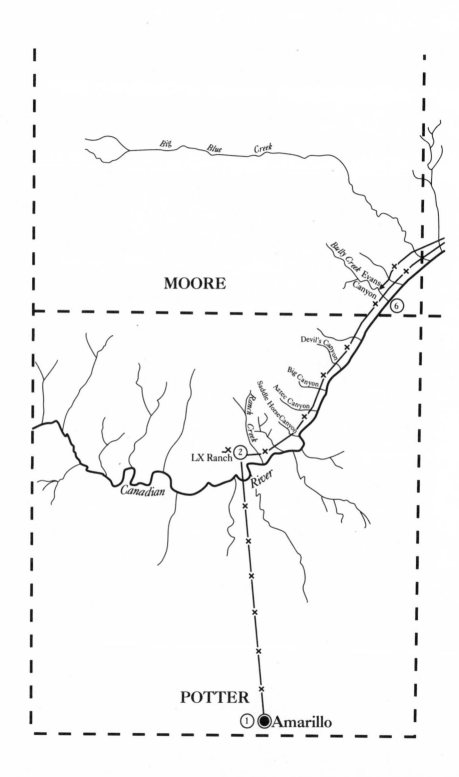

MOORE

Big *Blue* *Creek*

Belly Creek Evans
Canyon

⑥

Devil's Canyon

Big Canyon

Aztec Canyon

Saddle HorseCanyon

Ranch Creek

LX Ranch ✕② ✕

Canadian *River*

POTTER

① ●Amarillo

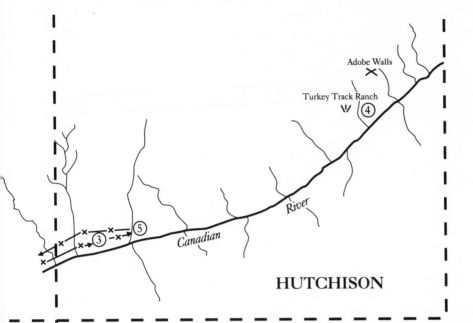

Adobe Walls ✕

Turkey Track Ranch
\/ ④

⑤ ✕—✕—➤
③ ✕—✕

Canadian   River

HUTCHISON

Down the River After a Killer:
Searching For and Capturing Lee Fuller
circa 1888-89

LEGEND

① Amarillo: Sheriff Jim Gober and Deputy Cleve McNeal
      depart for last known location of Lee Fuller, the LX Ranch

② LX Ranch: The two lawmen depart for Fuller's next reported
      location, Allen Thompson's Branding Outfit

③ Branding Outfit: The pursuers depart for Fuller's next reported
      destination, the Turkey Track Ranch

④ Turkey Track Ranch

⑤ Encounter with Bud Simmons; lawmen double back to Evans Canyon

⑥ Capture of Lee Fuller

Historic Battle Site ✕

Jim Gober's Route —✕—✕—➤
(constructive)

Statute Miles

5 4 3 2 1 0   5   10   15

© 1996 James R. Gober

and read the letter from his mother. Then I looked him straight in the eye and said to him, "Joe, if you want to go home, I will buy you a ticket. If you want a job, I will get you one but, positively, your association with Fuller is at an end." Joe shed tears freely, and when he had dried them away I asked him the whereabouts of Fuller. He informed me that he had left him at the LX Ranch.

The Search For a Fugitive

While Fuller was from my home county, and I knew of his reputation as a tough fellow, I had never met him. There was a friend of mine, however, by the name of Cleve McNeal, who was tending bar for Garrett Johnson. He was personally acquainted with Fuller, so I went to McNeal and deputized him to go with me to the LX Ranch.

It was twenty-five miles to the LX Ranch, so we saddled my splendid matched horses. These beautiful mounts were full brothers, Frank and George, light bay with white feet, a white star on their foreheads, and well-bred horses. They were strong, durable, half steel dust, and not only were good saddle horses but also made a splendid buggy team.

Cleave and I left Amarillo at twelve thirty and arrived at the LX Ranch at 3:30. Trying to avoid any premature disclosure of our presence, we approached the ranch from behind the big adobe stable and corral and put our horses in the barn, loosened the saddles, pulled off the bridle, and gave them some hay. We went into the ranch kitchen and asked the cook if Fuller was still there. "No, Sheriff. Fuller left right after the noon meal and had said he was going to Allen Thompson's branding outfit down the river."

Allen Thompson's outfit was some twenty-five miles away, so I asked the cook to fix us a five o'clock lunch. I informed McNeal that we would give our horses water and a good feed of grain, start down the river at six o'clock, and get near Thompson's camp about breakfast time, before they had started on their cattle roundup.

It was a beautiful, moonlit night, but we were restricted to narrow trails traveling over rough country, paths that were beaten out by cattle. We moved across canyons and over cliffs, and the route was very familiar to me, as I had been over it numerous times while working on the LX. I knew we would have to walk and lead the horses over many cliffs and ledges, and it would take us all night to make this twenty-five miles if we had the best of luck. McNeal was a fat, chubby fellow and not used to riding horseback or taking outdoor exercise. By one o'clock in the morning, McNeal was very tired, and we would have to rest often. Climbing each cliff or place where we had to walk and lead our horses consumed too much time, so daylight caught us with five miles yet to travel to reach the camp. As soon as daylight came I could take the river bed and travel the sand bars without getting in the quicksand, and we would then make much better time.

Good Plans and Anticipation

We came in sight of the camp in the morning as the sun was an hour high in the sky. I could see the men all had horses saddled, standing around the wagon. That meant they were ready to start out in various directions to round up the cattle in the river valley—to cut out the cows with unbranded calves and brand the calves. So I said to McNeal, "You keep up with me; I'm going to lope right up in camp and dismount. By the time my horse stops, you do likewise, keeping as close to me as possible. The boys will all be shaking hands with me, and if Fuller is there, you make right for him, shake hands, and hold on to his hand. I will put my gun on him, and we will take him without hurting him or anyone else."

We loped into camp and dismounted, and the boys all rushed up and began shaking hands with me. I kept an eye on McNeal to see if he recognized Fuller, but he never made any move, and I soon realized there were no strangers there. After drinking some black coffee and eating some bacon and sourdough bread, I took Bing Grissom aside. "How long ago since you saw Fuller?"

"Jim, it hasn't been but an hour since he went down toward the river saying that he was going to the Turkey Track Ranch."[1] He added, "You should be aware that Fuller has .45 Colts and a full belt of cartridges buckled around him, and he had said to the boys, 'I'm not gonna be taken alive!'"

The Pursuit Continues

The Turkey Track Ranch was twelve miles down the Canadian, so McNeal and I mounted our horses and struck a fast gallop down the river valley, which was bordered on one side by the river and on the other by the rim rock of the north plains. The rim rock stood five hundred feet above the level of the valley and was considered impassible without a tedious and dangerous climb.

We galloped two miles and met Bud Simmons, the only son of the old lady Simmons of Tascosa. She was the one who had cocked the .45 on my half-dressed carcass as I lay on my back from an unexpected encounter with a clothesline. I described Fuller to Bud, then asked him if he had seen such a man. He informed me that he left Fuller sitting in his remote cabin reading a book, his horse standing in front of the door saddled and with the bridle on.

I knew the cabin that Simmons was using as a campsite. It was a small rock house, one room about ten by twelve with one door and one window. The cabin sat one hundred yards up Evans Canyon,[2] from where the canyon opened out to the river valley. This canyon was very narrow, with high, rocky walls, and was only a mile long, at which point it butted against the rim rock of the plains.

"How can I get to the cabin without Fuller seeing me?" I queried Simmons.

"There's a large haystack across the level of the canyon, in front of the house and fifty paces distant from the cabin." He went on to say, "You could come in the canyon with the haystack directly in front of you and be within fifty yards before Fuller can see you. Then you will have to study some plan to get you from the haystack into the house without arousing Fuller's suspicion."

Closing in on the Prey

By the time we got to the haystack, I had my plans fixed. We dismounted, tied our horses to the fence that was around the haystack, pulled off our cartridge belts and holsters, and put some extra cartridges in our pockets. Then we concealed our revolvers in the waistbands of our trousers, and I said to McNeal, "When I go from behind the haystack, I'm going in running. You start fifty feet behind me and run like you are trying to catch me, and I will run right in the house like I am scared. When Fuller takes his eyes off of me and looks at you, I will beat him to the draw."

We made our run according to plans, but when I got inside the house I found no one there but McNeal and me. I then went outside. "Look!" I said, as I pointed down at the horse tracks and the drag marks of the bridle reins in the sand. "They're going off toward the running stream of the canyon. And there are tracks of Fuller, on foot." With my time as a horseman and a cowboy, I knew the horse had gotten thirsty and gone for water. Fuller obviously missed his horse and had gone after him. The question was, would he come back to the cabin, go over the rim rock, strike northeast for No Man's Land[3] or for a neutral strip?

Then I placed a goods box across the door of the cabin and sat McNeal on the box with instructions that if Fuller came back, I would try to get there by the time he dismounted. I advised him to shake hands and hold on to Fuller's hand, and I would throw my gun on him. I then started climbing up the side of the canyon wall to reach the rim rock so that I might be able to see for quite a distance on the level plains. If Fuller had gone that way, I probably would be able to see him. I had gotten only fifty or sixty feet up the wall when Fuller popped out of the underbrush and was in front of the house. He shook hands with McNeal before I could get back. McNeal used good sense, however, and just sat back on the box in the door. Fuller half sat and half stood on another goods box that stood on end, and when I got on the scene, McNeal introduced me to Fuller. I reached out for his hand, but he had it on the handle of his .45 and made no effort to shake hands or change his position.

He was a giant of a fellow, six feet, two inches tall, with black hair, small black eyes, and weighing some 190 pounds. I began talking to him about the country and asking him if he was hunting work. His answers were very curt, his position remaining the same, with his hand resting on the handle of his revolver and his small, bullet-looking black eyes set on me. In my conversation and movement I had gradually worked almost against him, with a view of clinching him and depending on McNeal coming to my assistance.

As I sized Fuller up as ignorant and desperate, I pulled a cigar from my vest pocket and offered it with my left hand, intending, if he reached for the cigar, to draw my gun with my right hand and take a chance of beating him on the draw. He never moved a muscle but said, "Thanks, I never smoke."

Then I conceived the idea that I could make him move his hand before he thought about it. I had a large gold watch and an elaborate gold chain with a gold horse for a charm, so I turned, facing McNeal, who still sat on his box like a statue, and said to him, "If we are to get to the Turkey Ranch by noon, then we must be riding." While in this position I slipped the guard out of the bottom hole in my vest, leaving the end sticking in the buttonhole, and turned, facing Fuller. Then I said, "What time have you?" At that same moment I pulled my watch, dropping it square in front of Fuller. He grabbed at the watch as it fell, and at the same instant, I had my .45 Colts fully cocked right in his face. He raised up and stood straight; then I told him to put up his hands, and by this time McNeal also had him covered. He still hadn't raised his hands, so I said, in a very strong voice, "I'm going to tell you a second time, put up your hands!" He raised them slowly, and I directed McNeal, "Take his revolver out of its holster and put the cuffs on him."

We tied a rope around his horse's neck and to the horn of McNeal's saddle, then helped Fuller on his horse. I tied another rope from one of his feet to the other, under the horse's belly, and started him and McNeal ahead of me, up the valley. The valley extended only two or three miles before we struck the rough gorges and pinnacles where we would only have a narrow cow trail to follow. We had gone about a mile when Fuller pulled his horse up to a stop. I rode up and asked him what he wanted, and he said, "I will take that damn cigar you offered me." We had a friendly laugh and I lighted the cigar and handed it to him. Then we continued on our way.[4]

The Disappointment at Denton County

We got to the LX Ranch about dark and fed our horses, got supper, rested two hours, and then rode into Amarillo about midnight. I had taken Fuller home with me and had slept with one handcuff on his wrist and the other on mine. The next evening we took the train to deliver him to the sheriff at Denton, Texas, a distance of 350 miles, going directly to Fort Worth, then over the Missouri Pacific to Denton. When I turned Fuller over to the sheriff, he said, "As soon as the commissioners meet and approve his bill, I will send you the six hundred dollars reward." Several months later, after I wrote Sheriff Sparks asking an explanation for his delay, he replied that the commissioners refused to allow his bill or to pay the reward.

I had only one consolation for capturing Fuller, and that was that I had consoled Mrs. Grissom by getting her baby boy away from an unscrupulous criminal and murderer and bringing the criminal to justice. But I knew that the sheriff of Denton County, my home, was a crook, and unfair with a brother sheriff, and if I ever chanced to meet that sheriff, there would have been a settlement.

Fuller was tried and acquitted. The man he had killed was his sister's husband, and she was the only witness, and she swore that her brother was not the man. Fuller was only out of jail a week until he stole a horse and saddle in Cooke County. He was caught by Sheriff Pat Ware and sent to the penitentiary.

Corruption Plans a Murder

A Shady Unrest in the Commissioners Court

On my arrival at Amarillo, I found quite a stir among the gang of Potter County commissioners from Abilene. When I chanced to meet Colonel J. T. Berry on the street, he had a look on his face that defied description. "Jim," he said with anger and disappointment in his voice, "Jim Holland has been negotiating with H. B. Sanborn. He's double-crossing me and throwing in with Sanborn to move the town from its present location to the adjoining section to the east, which would mean one mile east." This is the same Sanborn whose cattle interests brought me to this county in 1882 to help establish the Frying Pan Ranch.

The colonel had given Holland and Clabe Merchant an interest in his town site as a compromise to unite the Abilene bunch before the election in 1887. Colonel Berry had been a wealthy man but had met with financial reverses and was broke, and so was the entire Abilene bunch. Holland, in his cunning shrewdness, had met Mr. Sanborn and outlined his plan to move the town if Sanborn would purchase the land and finance the deal. He (Holland) would take a small interest in the lots in the new town.[1]

Sanborn, being an active, shrewd man and of somewhat the same unscrupulous nature as Holland, grasped the opportunity. In a few months a large frame hotel was erected in the new town site, and it was called the Amarillo Hotel.[2] Soon the business houses began to move to the new town, and things were at welding heat between Holland and Colonel Berry.

Hotel Amarillo, Amarillo, Texas, ca. 1889. Courtesy *Amarillo, Texas: The First Hundred Years, 1887-1987, a Picture Postcard History* (Amarillo: Ray Franks Publishing Ranch).

Conspiracy to Commit Murder

Clabe Merchant had known my father in the early settlement of Denton County, and Merchant was an honorable man that stood for square dealing. He had been in the cattle business all of his life, and his word was as good as gold.

Merchant came to see me at the courthouse a few days after my conversation with Colonel Berry. I could tell that something was really bothering him as he stepped up close to me and said in a rather low voice, "Jim, can we talk privately?" I ushered him quietly into the sheriff's office and closed the door. He leaned over my desk, still not totally comfortable with our privacy, saying, "Jim, this is serious business. You know I've been mixed up with Holland in the town site with Colonel Berry, not because I have any use for men of Holland's nature. But Jim, I look on you and feel toward you just like I believe your father would feel by one of my boys if his life was in danger. I'm going to warn you, as a friend, to keep what I'm going to tell you strictly to yourself. It is this Holland and his commissioners that are going to appoint a man named Givens as constable, and when they appoint him, you watch that man at all times. I know of him, and you can have your own ideas, but don't forget to watch your step. Jim, Givens is a hired gun, a killer."

I thanked Clabe Merchant for his interest and concern, and as I opened the door to my office and he departed, I must admit a form of shock came over me. The shock that I felt was not brought on by fear of this supposed hired gun, Givens. Instead, it was a shock to contemplate what kind of future I would have dealing with elected county commissioners whose moral values were so low they'd have to improve to be on the same plane with the devil.

In a few days the commissioners met in private, and as I sat on the hotel porch and watched them go into the courthouse, I wondered if they really believed they had a big enough man to do the mischief that undoubtedly they were planning. It was interesting to note that there was a man with them I'd never seen, a stranger in these parts. After the group had been in the courthouse about an hour, they all came out and went in different directions. The stranger made straight for the hotel, where I was sitting on the front porch. He came up within eight feet of the edge of the porch, and I noticed that he had a large, new belt and holster, with a new .44 Colt revolver and a belt filled with cartridges.

He was a big man, with a craggy, weatherbeaten face, a long nose, and piercing steel-gray eyes. I could just see and feel the meanness in this man as he said in an unfriendly tone of voice, "Is your name Jim Gober?" I answered that it was, and he said, "Are you the man that is supposed to be the sheriff of this town?"

I replied very forcefully, "There isn't any supposition, Mister. I am the sheriff." At the same time I stepped off the hotel porch and right in touching distance with him. Then I said, "What can I do for you?"

"I have just been appointed the constable of Amarillo, and I understand the law hasn't been properly enforced in this town, and I'm going to enforce the law, and if you want to work with me, all right, and if you don't, I don't care a damn."

I said to him calmly, "Mister, you have come a long way to accept a position as constable, and apparently Jim Holland has full confidence in you to carry out any detail he gives you. And Holland is chairman of the commissioners. As long as you are enforcing the law, you will not have any trouble from me or need any assistance." Just as I finished, he wheeled around with his back to me and threw his hand on the handle of his gun; then, turning back around, he faced me squarely. To his big surprise, he was looking into the muzzles of two short .45 Colts. I had my hands on these twins under my coat the whole time since I had seen him approaching me. Then I just smiled and said, "You tell Holland that you had to put off this job for the present, and if he's in a special hurry, he had better do it himself." I told him further, "I wish you could toss the job off to him, for I'm sorry for you or any other man that is weak enough to commit murder for money, but in case you make the second attempt, my sympathy will cease." He turned and went towards the courthouse, and I stepped up on the hotel porch and sat down in the same chair I had left.

I was heartsick to think that a man had been sent for and armed and clothed with the authority of a peace officer for the sole purpose of assassinating me. And still, it was so cunningly done that I had no proof, and I dreaded another meeting with that man. It seemed, however, that I could not count on any relief from the sickening pressure on my heart.

You Reap What You Sow

I was insulted and hurt to the core. After sitting in the same spot and in the same mood for two hours, Mr. John Hollicott, the manager of the LX Ranch and one of my bondsmen, drove up in his buggy with one of his magnificent teams. Mr. Cornelius had seen him and came across the street from the livery barn. Hollicott turned and shook hands with me and said, "Let's go get a drink."

I said, "No, John. I have taken a pledge with a friend not to drink over the bar for six months."

He looked me square in the eyes and I think realized I had been shedding tears. He laid his hand on my shoulder and said, "We will go in the back room of L. B. Collins's saloon and have a cold bottle of beer."

I could not resist further for fear Hollicott would think I was disrespectful of his friendship, so we walked about ten steps to Collins's saloon. We went in past the bar and went through a door into the back room, which was, in reality, the gambling room. As we entered, we realized there was a disturbance in progress, and we stopped instinctively just inside the door. I had instantly placed my right hand on my short .45, which I always carried in the waistband of my trousers, in front and to the left side, so that my coat would hide it from public view.

Givens apparently had gone into the gambling house and tried to collect seventeen dollars from each of the ten or twelve gamblers. When he saw John Hollicott and me standing by the entrance, he shook his fist in the face of the gambler with whom he was fussing and said, "If you damn sons of bitches don't pay me before sundown, I will make you leave town, and if there is any son of a bitch here that don't like it, I will put him in the bunch." While making these last remarks he wheeled, facing me, and reached for his gun. I threw my left hand in a pointing position toward his gun and told him to take his hand off his gun. Instead, he drew it and brought it out over-handed. As he drew it, my .45 bullet pierced his left side, missing his heart but cutting into his spine. He dropped to the floor with his gun still clutched in his right hand. I was near enough that instantly I jumped and stomped on his arm and wrenched the gun from his hand, laying it on a table, half cocked. I then raised him to his feet and got one arm over my shoulder and mostly carried him into the hotel.[3]

The funeral was put off for a day or two until his wife and child, whom he had deserted several years before, could come from Decatur, Texas.

The Aftermath of a Nightmare

When Givens was buried, I drove out to the funeral and stayed until he was put away. His wife had stopped with Mrs. Wetsel, and she had sent word for me to come over. When I arrived, she introduced me to Mrs. Givens and told me that the lady didn't have money to get home, so I gave her money to pay her way home. She explained to me that she had come through respect and indicated it was no surprise when she heard of his death, for he had led such a reckless life that she couldn't live with him.

The Givens funeral was part of the early history of Amarillo, since it brought on the need for a burying ground for the settlement. I grieved over the incident and was full of sorrow for some time but realized that it was either Givens or me.

The next day after Givens was buried, I called for an examining trial before the justice of the peace that Holland had appointed as the running mate for Givens. His name was Cap Andrews, and he was a man about fifty years old. Andrews wore a long, black beard and was a fiend on Faro Bank Whiskey and lewd women. If he had any relatives, he never let it be known.

At the examining trial, after as many as fifteen witnesses had corroborated the facts I have related, the county attorney, who was a Holland loyalist, made the captain a glowing speech and asked that I be placed under five-thousand-dollar bond to await the action of the grand jury. The captain began stroking his whiskers nervously. His jaw shook, and his knees as well. Really, I felt sorry for him, because he was yet another victim of a mastermind in criminal cunning. After ten minutes of this miserable feeling that had seized Andrews, he braced himself and said, "Your bond is five thousand dollars."

I replied in great anger, "Your answer is not for me, Andrews, but for you and the balance of your cutthroats to reap your reward in hell, where all of you belong." Fuming mad, I then stomped out and went to Garrett Johnson's saloon.[4]

A Baring of the Soul

Garrett Johnson was a fine young fellow, coolheaded and fearless, and, while he drank to some extent, he always controlled himself so as to be capable of acting with good judgment. For these reasons, I had made Garrett Johnson a special deputy. A boy twenty-five years old, redheaded and of athletic build, by the name of Tom Higgins worked for Johnson as bartender. Tom Higgins had been well-raised in Pennsylvania by wealthy parents but had disagreed with his father and left home at the age of sixteen years and had come to Texas. Understandably, he had seen rough times. I called Johnson and Higgins to one side and told them what had taken place at the trial. "I am the last man on earth to ask a friend to share my trouble," I stated. "However, the gangsterism of Holland and his cohorts has brought me to the point where I cannot stand further imposition, because I see nothing in the cards but a sellout for me with any and all of the Holland bunch. I'm gonna sit in the back room with the door open. If any of them come looking for me, just direct them to the back room."

Johnson spoke, "We are with you, Jim, and rest assured that if the Holland bunch start it, there will be a general house cleaning." Higgins spoke by himself, insisting, "We have got to go to the court-house right now and kill at least one of the Holland bunch. We've got to show them they can't do these things and get away with it."

Johnson pointed a finger at Higgins, saying, "Listen, Higgins, let them start it, and we'll finish it."

"Higgins," I said, looking him straight in the eye, "sit down and listen to me. Let Holland and his bunch be the aggressors; then we will be in a much better position to bring about change. If we take brutal action now, we will be blamed, and they will be in a much better position to continue their dirty work." Johnson and I had a hard job just keeping Higgins from starting out to do the job singlehanded. But Higgins liked me, and I finally convinced him that we must not be the initiators of violence.

The Beginning of a Legal Avalanche

We three sat in the saloon until midnight while the Holland bunch and their followers were still in the courthouse. Suddenly, the silence of the early morning and the air of tension in the saloon were broken by the screech of the braking wheels of a freight train pulling in from the east. In a few minutes, W. H. Woodman,[5] who was district attorney and a warm friend of mine, came into the saloon. He had heard the news of the incident while at Clarendon,[6] sixty-eight miles east of Amarillo on the Fort Worth and Denver Railroad, where district court was then in session. He had slipped on the freight train and come to my assistance under the pretense of aiding the one justice of the peace. Woodman shook hands with me and said, "Judge Wallace[7] is preparing a habeas corpus proceeding to present to Judge Willis[8] at Clarendon tomorrow to hear written testimony given at your examining trial and to fix your bond." Woodman continued, "I will go over to the courthouse and ask where the prisoner is, and when they inform me that they haven't arrested you, I will ball hell out of them and ask for a gun and tell them that I will arrest you and take you before Judge Willis at Clarendon." All was agreed, and Woodman was off for the courthouse, where about sixteen wolves of no human principles were congregated. Woodman, who wore his raven-black hair long and hanging in thick curls to his shoulders, was brave as a lion and forceful as a moccasin.

When this bunch of serpents told Woodman they hadn't yet attempted to arrest me, he raved at them for ten minutes, and Tom Higgins, who had gone with him to see the show, wasn't disappointed. Then Woodman demanded a gun and told them Higgins was the only man who had permission to move in his direction. He cautioned them not to come near him while he was waiting for the train at the depot. Then he and Higgins came back to the saloon and joined Johnson and me. Woodman's good sense and sense of humor had gotten me in better spirits, and after a couple of hours' visit, the train came, and Woodman and I were off for Clarendon.

The next day, Judge Wallace presented the habeas corpus to Judge Willis, and after Willis looked over the written testimony given before Andrews at Amarillo, he said confidently, "From the written testimony, I don't see that you should be required to give bond, but as the justice who held your examining trial demanded five thousand dollars bail, I shall cut it to twenty-five hundred. Have you anyone in the courtroom that will stand with you in recognizance for your appearance?" At that instant John Hollicott and his bookkeeper rose to their feet and came and faced Judge Willis. He told us to raise our right hands; then he proceeded to swear us to appear before the next session of the Potter County district court. I was then at liberty to resume my duties as sheriff of Potter County and to await the next assault of the villains.

A Feeling of Spiritual Exoneration

On my arrival home, and after eating supper with my father and mother, I went to Judge Plemons under the pretense of seeing the judge, but in reality I wanted to see my dearest and most loved little friend, his daughter. My duties as sheriff had kept me so busy that I had not the opportunity to see her for several months. I was eager to see her sweet, smiling face, and I wanted to console her if she was grieving over my unfortunate affair.

To my heart's delight, Belle saw me coming and met me at the front yard gate. She shook my hand and held on to it until we were in the house. When I expressed my grief and sorrow over the shooting of Givens, she spoke up in earnest tones and said, "I'm glad to know you have the moral courage to successfully defend your manhood and your life, and I realize if you hadn't used the best of judgment, you would be in the grave the other fellow is in." She went on to say, "I earnestly hope you will be successful in the future, under similar circumstances."

We were alone, and I rose to my feet, and she rose also and met me halfway. "Belle," I said in almost a whisper, "I wasn't ready, after so long, to see how beautiful you really are." At that moment we embraced and we kissed, and I received the happiest thrill of my life. All doubt of Belle's love, future happiness, and confidence in me was wiped away, and my heart dismissed the heaviest burden it had carried.

After a two-hour visit, I returned home and felt exonerated from my unfortunate affair by God and at least one angel. I had no immediate concern and felt none for the future disposition of my criminal case. In fact, I felt so little concern that I refused to employ counsel. Things in general were quiet for some time, and no one spoke of the tragedy.

An Unexpected Setback

I had a new pair of boots made of kangaroo leather and had worn them only a day or two when I walked into Johnson's saloon about dusk one evening. The bar was lined up with section men of the Fort Worth and Denver Railroad. In front of the bar was an iron foot rail that stood sixteen inches from the bottom of the bar. The floor in front of the bar was wet from beer being slopped on it. As soon as I entered the saloon, one Irishman that had known me at Rag Town grabbed me and evidently intended to pick me up bodily and set me on the bar. He thought the world of me, and we had had several good, friendly scuffles at Rag Town. When I resisted him and we clinched like two playful schoolboys, my left foot slipped under the iron rail, and his weight snapped my leg just above the ankle. I said to myself audibly, "Oh, no! With the other problems I'm having, I surely didn't need a broken leg." Two or three of them helped me to the back room to a cot and cut my boot off. By that time I was gasping with pain, and a couple of the men went and got a doctor to set my leg and brace it with crude splints. Four men then carried me to a room in the hotel.

The next day the doctor put my leg in a plaster of paris cast and told me it would be four weeks before I could get up on crutches. With the prospects of hobbling around on crutches for weeks, I knew that I was going to need some help, so I deputized E. F. True,[9] a good friend. True was manager of the breeding and caring for stallions and brood mares on the LX Ranch when I worked there. He was an eastern-raised boy but had been in the West ten to twelve years and was a likable young man. True would report to me as often as three times a day and give me any attention necessary. No real brother could have been more attentive or interested in my welfare than True. He was also just as interested in my official business being conducted properly.

My sweet little girl, Belle Plemons, came to see me most every day at the noon hour, brought something nice to eat, and visited with me for an hour.

After being in bed eighteen days, I sent for a carpenter to arrange for him to make a pair of good, strong crutches and to deliver them to my room by six o'clock the next evening. I asked him to say nothing to anyone about what he was doing. The evening of the nineteenth, about dark, the old carpenter came up the stairs and into my room with a real nice pair of crutches. They had spikes in the end and were well braced in every respect. I congratulated the old man and tried to pay him, but he refused to accept any pay for his work, just saying, "I'm glad I had the chance to do something for you, Jimmie."

I thanked him profusely and said, "I will practice with them a few days here in the room so I won't be so awkward when I get out."

More Chicanery from the Outlaw Officials

About eight o'clock I could hear loud talking in Collins's saloon, which was only ten steps from the hotel. I recognized True's voice and knew something was wrong. I quickly dressed myself as best I could, having to split the left pants leg clear above the knee to get it over the plaster of paris cast. When I was dressed, or partly so, I got down on the floor with my crutches by my side so I could drag them along. Then I slid myself to the stairway and down one step at a time on my hips and hands, dragging my crutches as I went. When I got to the sidewalk, I got up straight on my well foot, got my crutches set under my arms, and started for the saloon. Just as I entered, I saw Holland, Mack Moore, and True all scuffling. I hollered at them, "All right, break it up, now!" but True had already fallen to the floor by the time he heard me.

They turned True loose, and Mack Moore ran to the end of the bar and jumped up on a small icebox. As he did, I saw the handle of a .45 in the waistband of his trousers. I hopped over almost against him, where I could drop my crutches, and I braced myself by putting my left hand on the bar. Then I directed, "Moore, put up your hands," and as I said it he drew his gun. I forgot to hold on to the bar, and instead I grabbed at his gun and caught it with my third finger under the hammer just as he pulled the trigger. The pain from my leg increased my anger, and I hit Moore square in the forehead with my .45.

As he fell, the hammer of his gun cut off half of my finger. The pain from the finger injury was bothering me, as there was blood everywhere, but I had his gun and mine too and managed to get a crutch under my left arm. Moore finally got up and ran out of the saloon while Jim Holland started toward me. I threw both guns on him and he screamed, "For God's sake, don't murder me!" Then I handed Moore's gun to the bartender and held the other on Holland while I

130

searched him. He was unarmed, but then I noticed something shocking. My loyal deputy, True, was stabbed in the left side of the back and was bleeding badly. It then occurred to me that some of the blood I had thought had come from my finger had apparently been coming from True.[10]

By this time some allies had come in, among them Jim McIntyre, a very dependable friend. I asked him and Collins to assist True to his room. The saloon was soon cleared. Moore and Mel Thompson had disappeared first, and I was sure that Moore was the man that had stabbed True, as I had seen him at True's back when I had hollered at them.

After a doctor had dressed True's wound and found it to be of a dangerous nature, I asked McIntyre to go with me. Before we left, I got the doctor to put a dressing on my finger. We sent for the cab man, old Barney, the only name I had ever known. I dragged myself into the cab, with McIntyre helping me; then McIntyre got in and told Barney to drive us to Mel Thompson's house, a one-room house three-quarters of a mile from the main town. It was dark, and there was two or three inches of snow on the ground. When we got within one hundred yards of the house, Barney stopped and said, "There is a man running away from the house." I told him to drive after him and to catch him. Barney ran the horses right up by the side of Mel Thompson. I instructed McIntyre to get out and search him and throw him in the cab; then we proceeded to the house.

We all got out and told Thompson to unlock his door. Then he said, "Moore is in there, but I don't intend to get my head shot off by opening this door."

I felt in my pocket and found a half-dozen sulfur matches, took them in my left hand, and evened them so that the heads would be in a position to catch fire at the same time. Then I braced myself on my crutches with my gun in my right hand. I gave the matches to Barney, telling him, "When the door is thrown open, strike the matches and throw them gently up toward the ceiling of the room." Turning to McIntyre, I directed, "Back off ten feet and take a run at the door and kick it in as close to the lock as possible with all your might." McIntyre was six feet tall, weighed two hundred pounds, and was a cool, level-headed man. When he hit the door running at full speed, it flew wide open, and Barney tossed the matches up inside the room.

We located Moore lying on a wall bunk. Near him on a small table near his head was a large, pearl-handled .45. I hopped in at the door, warning Moore that if he moved so much as a muscle, it would be his last move. At that instant, McIntyre was at my side with another match blazing in one hand and his gun cocked fully in the other. I picked up the gun from the table, totally amazed that Moore never made a move to raise up off his cot until I handcuffed him and told him to get on his feet.

Moore was put in the cab, and I told Thompson he'd be safer at home than he would be trying to assist his brother assassin any further. We then took Moore to town and turned him over to Garrett Johnson and instructed Garrett to slip him on the first train and take him to Tascosa. I told Garrett to tell Sheriff Robinson to keep Moore until I came after him, as I was afraid to keep him in Amarillo until the excitement died down.

All through this escapade, from the moment I entered Collins's saloon and saw Holland and Moore holding True, it was a mental strain and an internal battle with my impulses to keep from killing Holland and Moore. I realized, at different intervals of time, that I was as justified killing them as I would have been in destroying two rattlesnakes. They were my arch enemies and the masterminds that were constantly weaving trouble for me and the county, but my heart was set on not putting another burden on it, since I had experienced enough recently.

It was forty days before True could leave his bed, and for the first ten days, it was an even bet whether he would live or die.

The Bitter and the Sweet

Jurisprudence

Our district court was to convene on the first of January, and I was anxious to go to trial so I could marry my only hope of happiness, Belle Plemons. When the court finally convened, I began to scheme to make the grand jury indict me so I could stand trial and forever be exonerated.

There had been a new judicial district created, the forty-seventh judicial district, and our county was in it. Judge Plemons had been made district judge, and it was a constant worry to me whether it would be an injustice to him sitting on the bench as presiding judge for my trial. I realized that the Holland bunch would criticize Judge Plemons and say I was cleared because I was going to marry his daughter. If I mentioned anything to the judge, it might hurt him. This issue left me out on a limb.

The grand jury reached an indictment charging me with manslaughter. The district attorney for the new district was L. G. Wilson, who lived at Plainview, eighty-five miles south. I had never met him until he came to this session of the court. However, I approached him and asked if he would try my case during the present term and explained to him that I was anxious to get the trial over with because I wanted to get married. He seemed to be a nice fellow, but he said he was sorry, but it was impossible in such a short period for him to do justice to his responsibilities as prosecuting attorney.

I could not dismiss the constant burden on my mind and the haunting dread of the possibility that Judge Plemons would have the responsibility of being trial judge. Also, it was of great concern that the district attorney might put the trial off from term to term and keep it hanging over me a year, or probably two. After careful study, I decide to dismiss the most important one in my mind, that of taking any chances of embarrassing Judge Plemons.

Do You, Belle, Take Jim To Be . . . ?

January and February had passed, and the first of March found Mr. Hank Siders traveling on business to the T Anchor Ranch. Mr. Siders had been ranch foreman of the T Anchor Ranch for several years before quitting to accept an appointment as cattle inspector at Amarillo. The Siderses were warm friends of mine and of Judge Plemons, and Mrs. Siders, a beautiful young woman, was very fond of Belle Plemons and had decided to accompany her husband to the ranch. She had invited Belle to go with them, and Belle told her she would ask her mother and let her know. Belle came to me and outlined the invitation and asked my advice. I smiled and said, "I hate to be selfish, but I will have to insist on joining the party, as I always liked the surroundings over at the T Anchor Ranch, and the boys over there are all nice boys and friends of mine. So you tell Mr. Siders to get a two-seated rig, and we will drive my buggy team, Frank and George." So all went well, and we were off right after the noon hour. The T Anchor Ranch was sixteen miles south of Amarillo near the Palo Duro Canyon.

We were welcomed heartily on our arrival at the ranch, and old Heb Smith, the cook, spread a delicious supper. Afterwards we visited until eleven o'clock; then Mrs. Siders and Belle were given a nice room, and Mr. Siders and I were given a camp bed on the floor.

The next day we left the ranch for home at ten o'clock in the morning. I had decided to ask Belle if she felt she would be doing herself justice if we were to marry before I had my trial. When we were about five miles from Amarillo, I asked her in just those words. She took me by the hand and looked straight at me with her beautiful, soft, light-brown eyes and said, "I have exonerated you and am willing to stand by my decision until death." Then I said, "I am going to Fort Worth day after tomorrow, and if agreeable with you we will have a preacher and a few of our nearest friends and get married tomorrow night, at ten o'clock, at your home. After the ceremony, we will come to the hotel and remain until the morning train." All was agreed, and I said, "I know that I am not fair with you to give you such little time, but I feel that elaborate preparations are unnecessary. I have studied

Belle Helen Plemons
Gober, ca. 1890.

day and night to come to a conclusion best suited for our peace of mind and for our future happiness. Also, it will take the burden off of your father's shoulders of being the trial judge when I do have my trial. When we are married, that will disqualify him from sitting on my trial and require a special judge. Then, when it is over, no one can say 'Judge Plemons freed Gober because he was going to marry his daughter.'"

Belle said, "That is a noble spirit of loyalty to Father as a friend, but Father has never thought of that, and, if he had, it would make no difference to him, for he has a higher regard for you than any other man in this county. Your plans are fine, however, and suit me. I will be ready to go with you to Fort Worth as Mrs. Gober, and it will be a happy moment when I am your wife."[1]

Now this was 1889, and I had experienced three years of a strenuous and stormy life as the youngest elected sheriff in the United States, and the prospect of having my idealized girl for a wife and companion gave me such encouragement that it seemed the clouds of trouble would blow over. My prayer was that in the future I would have peace and happiness and a record as a good and capable sheriff. I realized that in November of next year there would be an election again, and I would either be reelected or defeated, as the case might be. Also, I would have my trial in the fall, during September, and either be exonerated or it wouldn't be good policy to run for reelection in 1890. I believed I would be both exonerated and reelected in 1890.

Belle and I had a nice three-day visit in Fort Worth. We stopped at the Pickwick Hotel and immediately called Miss Cora Brooks, Belle's girl chum from Amarillo, who was staying with some friends. Cora came to the hotel, and we had a nice visit with her during our stay.

We returned home and took up our abode with my father and mother in the four-room house that I had built for them. Most of the town by this time had moved to the new town. The large hotel was completed and operating with W. P. Hardwick as manager, and it seemed that it was necessary for me to be in the new town most of the time. Usually I kept a horse saddled all the time, day and night.

More Trouble From the Ruthless Few

My sister Sallie and her husband,[2] married earlier in Denton County, had moved to Amarillo. One Sunday evening, I had my wife and sister in my buggy, and we had been to the new town and were returning home. Just as we got opposite Sam Finley's saloon in the old town, Judge Plemons and Judge Quinn were standing outside the back door of the saloon, and they hailed me. Quinn, being the spokesman, said, "John Beavers is in the saloon with a large knife opened and making trouble with Finley." I handed the lines to Belle and told her to drive on home, and I went in and took the knife from Beavers and took him to jail in an intoxicated condition.

Two hours later his brother brought me a note from Quinn to "turn Beavers out." I told the brother it was Sunday evening and his brother was intoxicated and to inform Judge Quinn that jail was the best place for Beavers until morning. By that time he would be sober. For some unknown reason, it seems that this incident gave a signal to the villains, who began to stir and caucus. They kept it up until two o'clock Monday morning, talking confidentially, and Holland, Moore, and the judge were taking drinks at short intervals. At eight o'clock, I turned Beavers out.

That evening Judge Quinn, Jim Holland, Moore, and the county attorney, their high school buddy, all being from Abilene, went to the

Captain S. A. McMurray, Company B, Frontier Battalion, Texas Rangers, date unknown. Copyright, 1996, The Texas Ranger Hall of Fame and Museum #80-318.

depot secretly and wired the attorney general of the state at Austin, Texas, telling him that they had a sheriff who was a desperado and had refused to obey the orders of the county court. They requested a company of rangers to protect life and property and to maintain efficiency in the court. The wire was signed Judge Quinn, County Judge; Coney Henderson, County Attorney; Jim Holland, County Commissioner; Mack Moore, County Commissioner.

In a few days, Captain S. A. McMurray[3] and five rangers arrived in Amarillo. Captain McMurray came to me and introduced himself and said, "Gober, I have been sent here under the instructions of the attorney general and by request to him from the county judge, county attorney, and two county commissioners to keep peace and assist in enforcing the law when my services are necessary. I want you to understand that I am here with no malice or prejudice against you, for I think I understand the situation, and I sympathize with you, for you have quite a burden for a kid. And any time day or night that you need me or any of my men or all of them, call on me, and we will be glad to assist you." That was the first I knew what had brought the ranger company to Amarillo. Then it dawned on me what the result of the all-night caucus between Holland, Moore, and Quinn had been. I thanked Captain McMurray and found him to be a gentleman in every respect. There were two or three young fellows that were a little on the bad-man order, but McMurray, being a man about fifty years of age and of broad experience, was well capable of controlling his men, and we got along fine.

The new hotel in the new town had a barroom that did a thriving business. Jim Holland could be seen in this barroom at most any hour, and my friend and bondsman, John Hollicott, was staying at the hotel about half the time. Holland was consistently cultivating Hollicott's acquaintance by accompanying him around town and sticking with him until he returned to the hotel. He would even go to the ranch with Hollicott and stay a couple of days, and Hollicott would come back to town with him.

Holland could drink more and still stand up than any one man I ever knew. Hollicott, being his constant companion, was drinking to excess, and it kept growing on him. I knew Holland would break him before he turned him loose, and it grieved me to see the serpent coiling around him, as good a heart as John Hollicott possessed. But Hollicott was a Scotsman and considerably on the reserved, independent side, so I knew it would hurt his feelings if I tried to warn him. All I could do, it seemed, was to grieve over seeing my staunch old Scottish friend slaughtered, financially and physically. Hollicott was worth, at that time, fifty thousand dollars and commanded a salary of thirty-six hundred dollars a year as manager of the LX Ranch. He was a bachelor, fifty years of age.

I finally decided to get an apartment in the new hotel so I would be more handy to my work and would be nearer to Belle. We got the apartment and moved into the hotel, and I could see every day that Holland absolutely had Hollicott's confidence. I never spoke to Holland but never came in contact with him and Hollicott without showing my respects by saying, "How are you, John?"

Finally, the Trial
Now it was September 1889, and the district court had convened, and I went to the district attorney and asked him if he was ready to

try me during this term. He said, "Yes, Gober. I am going to try you, but I haven't any case. I haven't been able to find any evidence that is sufficient to hope for a conviction, and I'm glad. We will go to trial, and when it is over, we will never be bothered with it again." I grabbed him by the hand and shook it heartily and thanked him.

The next morning, after the usual preliminaries preceding court, my case was called and set for hearing the next day, with Judge Willis presiding as special judge. Judge Willis had examined all the testimony given at my examining trial and had cut my bond in half from what the justice of the peace required, so I felt sure I would have another burden off my mind the next day. My heart was very light, and I went to the hotel and told Belle the news. She spoke confidently when she said, "I have never been worried one moment about the outcome, but of course I am pleased to know the district attorney is honest and won't try to make things disagreeable."

That evening and night I never left our room. I felt so relieved that I just felt tired and wanted to rest until the next day, but I was so anxious for the next day to come that I couldn't sleep. About two o'clock in the morning I got up, lighted a cigar, and smoked for half an hour. Belle begged me to lie down and try to sleep, saying, "You will be worn out before the day is over."

I was at the courthouse early the next morning, and when court convened, a jury was impaneled in an hour, as I had taken only two challenges and the district attorney didn't take any. Judge Wallace had volunteered to defend me, and a lawyer by the name of Crutchfield, who had come from Tennessee, also asked to assist Wallace. The trial proceeded rapidly, and the case was closed and in the hands of the jury by four PM. The jury was out in deliberations just long enough to take the first ballot, and they came in with the sweet verdict of not guilty.[4]

Now it is useless to try to put into words how happy I felt. I shook hands with all the jury men and thanked them; then I shook hands with Judge Willis, telling him that I appreciated the fact that my case had been tried before a fair and able jurist that had done his duty fairly and impartially. The Judge said, "You, in reality, should have never been tried, although it may be best, as you are now exonerated by the law as well as the general public. I hope you will never be unfortunate enough to be placed in a similar position again. However, a sheriff has dangerous responsibilities, especially in the western counties."

War with County Authorities Continues

Moore had made a five-hundred-dollar bond to await the grand jury for stabbing True. No one had actually seen him do it, and the unfortunate consequences were that the grand jury failed to indict him.

It was quiet in the county for two weeks after the court was over. Finally, one Monday morning I rode down to the courthouse, and on the front door was a written instrument tacked on the door. The document had been done with straight strokes of the pen or in printed form to disguise the handwriting. It read, "We the best citizens of Amarillo being afraid of Jim Gober and feeling that our lives are in danger have organized ourselves into a body as a vigilant committee to deal justice to the said Jim Gober." The minute I read the infernal lies, I knew Moore was the perpetrator, and this dirty insult, done in such a cowardly way, was more than I could stand. The rotten bunch had appointed an ex-policeman from Kansas City, Kansas, in Givens's place. His name was Jake Lowmiller.[5]

I got on my horse, Frank, and rode to the harness shop and stood by while the harness maker made a whip according to my instructions: half the length of a black snake whip, with two pounds of small birdshot in the butt end. When it was finished, I got on Frank and rode down the main street to try and locate Moore. Then suddenly I saw him come out of Henry Ortman's saloon and start across the street to Smith and Walker General Merchandise Store. I rode up in front of him and dismounted and lit in on him with my half mule whip. He ran into the store, with me after him laying the whip on his back and shoulders.

The new constable happened to be in the store, and he rushed up and drew a long, .44-caliber, nickel-plated gun, the same gun I had stomped out of Givens's hand. As Lowmiller drew his gun, I grabbed it by the barrel with my left hand, dropped my whip, and drew my gun with my right hand. At the same time Lowmiller grabbed my gun by the barrel with his left hand. Then the tug-of-war started, and it was a foregone conclusion that the one that got his gun loose first would kill the other.

Lowmiller was a fat, chunky-built man, and I was six feet and with an athletic build. He outweighed me by about twenty pounds, but I was quicker on my feet and had longer arms. We scuffled without uttering a sound for five minutes, and I could detect that Lowmiller was weakening. Then my old chum Jim Stroopes and Lige Lynch came in through the front door. Lowmiller hollered at them to help him disarm me, and Stroopes yelled, "You must think I'm a fool to mix with two guns, and them fully cocked!"

There were several looking on from different points of view, and Lowmiller yelled in a trembling, broken voice, "If you put your gun up, I will put mine up."

I said, "You drew yours first; put yours up first. I don't want to hurt you unless I have to." At that instant Lowmiller turned loose of my gun, and I of his, and each of us put our guns away.[6]

I went straight to the printing office, having to pass through the old town of Amarillo to get there. When I arrived, I wrote an answer to the anonymous bluff I had found on the courthouse door and asked the editor, Mr. Rudolph, to publish it, which he did.

Confronting Desperate Baby Killers

I had received a letter from Breckenridge, Texas, from the sheriff of Stephens County enclosing a warrant for the arrest of a man and two women, sisters. He provided a full description of each of them, stating that they were wanted for two charges of murder. He further stated that at least one of the women was a dangerous character and went armed at all times.

They had left a rented farm mysteriously, departing in a two-horse wagon. The sheriff also gave a description of the wagon and team and stated that after it was discovered that they had left, the neighbors and the owners of the premises, while investigating to ascertain the circumstances of the mysterious disappearance, had found two infant children buried in the orchard. They were supposed to have been killed at birth.

When I left the printing office, which was a block from the rear of the new Amarillo Hotel, I had to pass down the back street running parallel with the hotel. Before I was even with the hotel, I noticed a man who was a stranger to me loading scraps of lumber and trash in a wagon with loose planks for a bed. When I looked at the team, it filled the description of the one the sheriff of Stephens County had provided.

He had cautioned me that if I ran into the man, not to take any chances, because he was a bad, desperate man, and dangerous. I realized that I must surprise this man if I was to take him without trouble, so I rode by without stopping but kept in the street in front of the hotel, following it one block south. Then I turned at a cross street and rode until I came to the alley leading to my man and the team. I rode up within six feet of him and just a little past him; then I stopped, turned, and said, "Good afternoon, sir. Are you in the business of doing public hauling?"

He replied, "Yes, I am."

"I need some cleaning up around a residence I have just completed."

"I will be glad to take care of that as soon as I am through with the job I'm on."

I told him, "Fine. I believe I can show you my house from where we stand." At the same time I spoke, I dismounted my horse on the left while the man was on the right side of the horse. I gave the bridle reins on the left a yank that made my horse run backwards, causing my man to step and grab at the reins I had released on purpose. When he turned from the horse to look at me, he looked down the barrel of a Colt .45, fully cocked, with the demand to "Throw up your hands!" He stood like a statue, and I told him a second time and added, "Put up your hands, or I will kill you in a second." He shot his hands up, and I took the .45 from the waistband of his trousers. I handcuffed him and, after tying my horse by the side of his team, got into the wagon and told him to drive the team.

Knowing that my next move must be to locate the two women, I said to him, "I suppose you want to inform your family as to what has happened." He said that he did. I asked where they lived, and he pointed to a small, unpainted house about a quarter of a mile down the street. When we arrived at the turn off to the house, he started to turn the team in the direction of the house, and I grabbed the reins and turned the team back into the main road leading to the jail. I informed him that his place was considerably out of the way to the jail and that I would come back and break the news to his family.

After locking my prisoner in jail, I engaged a closed cab, which in those days was drawn by horses. I instructed the driver where to go and also told him that as soon as I got into the house to come to the door and be ready to come to my assistance if so notified. He drove up near the front door, as there was no yard fence or sidewalk. I went to the front door and knocked. A tall, coarse-featured woman with long, yellow hair hanging loosely down her back opened the door, and a younger woman of better appearance stood behind her. I told them that I had an important message for them, and I said, "Permit me to read it, and I will read it to you."

While I spoke I was entering without invitation and, once inside, was surveying the interior of the room to see if there were any guns handy. When I was satisfied, I told them to be seated while I read their message. I took a seat in front of them and took out the sheriff's letter and warrant from my inside coat pocket and began reading the letter.

The young woman began to cry, and the older woman, who was a degenerate, uncivilized personality, began to curse. She had a freckled face and dead-looking eyes of a peculiar color, and about halfway through the reading of the warrant, she sprang at me like a panther. I seized her wrist, and the commotion brought the cab man running to my assistance.

When he entered, I had my victim on the floor with one knee on her stomach. The other woman was crying bitterly and begging me not to hurt her sister. I instructed the cab driver to put the crying woman in the cab; all the time I was bearing down on my victim's stomach with more force. She finally relaxed, and I drew my handcuffs and fastened them on her wrists. I put her in the cab and told both women that they would have to go to jail until the sheriff from Breckenridge arrived to take them back to Stephens County.

After locking up the sisters in separate cells, I went to the depot and wired the sheriff to come and get his prisoners. When he arrived, he gave me a complete explanation of the crime they had committed. It seems that the two sisters had both been living with a man and had both given birth to a child. The babies had been killed and had been buried in an orchard, and the trio had left under cover of night. Neighbors had gone to the small farm from which this beast had deserted, and, finding two small areas of loose dirt under a peach tree, had dug in and found the two infants. It was my understanding that the man got a prison sentence of twenty-five years and the women some lesser sentence.

This sudden change had served to relax my mind from the recent escapade with Moore and the constable. It had served to cool my temper down to almost normal, and I feel to this day that discovering this man and the two women and making the successful capture saved bloodshed, for I was so mad, I was approaching the state of irresponsibility. I know that I was ready to commit any degree of chastisement necessary against my enemies, had I come in contact with them.

I had begun to get concerned about Belle staying in the Amarillo Hotel. Since I was coming in contact with my enemies every day and

143

night and might have trouble at any hour, I realized that it was not the place for Belle to be, since I didn't ever want her to see me in trouble.

I owned a business lot two blocks from the hotel, so I had a frame building, sixteen by twenty-eight, built on the lot and had it suitably partitioned for a home, with the idea that when I decided to build a home, I could use this building as a small business place. When the frame building was completed and nicely furnished on the inside, we moved in and set up housekeeping. I was well pleased with it, and so was Belle, for she was a splendid cook and had taken great pride in her cooking and her housekeeping. The place was close in to the central town area, and I could spend more time with her.

A New Election and Its Aftermath

A Calm before the Storm

It was now April 1890, and the November election would soon be a reality; the voting population would also be much greater. Jim Holland had made considerable money out of the new town by having H. B. Sanborn's backing, and the town of Amarillo was growing and had achieved the reputation of having more cattle shipped from it than any other one point in the world. The courthouse that was built at the old town stood almost alone and a mile from the business part of the new town, but the courthouse building had cracked badly, as the bricks were not fit, to begin with, to be put in a building. So Holland got his allies together at a special meeting of the commissioners and declared the building unsafe, condemned it as a county courthouse, and had it wrecked. They took what brick that didn't crumble to alkali dust and built a one-story building at the new town for a temporary courthouse. This was the final act of Holland moving Colonel Berry's town site. The task was now finished, and Holland had gotten all the cream of being chairman of the commissioners court.

As the time drew near for the November election, Jake Lowmiller, the constable, announced as a candidate for sheriff and tax collector; and a man named Kinney, a very nice fellow who had been in the well-drilling business, declared his candidacy. Sixty days before the election, I announced for reelection, and that was all the electioneering I did. The Holland bunch was supporting Kinney, and Lowmiller hadn't any support, so I let them do all the talking.

Man standing at the center of the present-day courthouse square, Amarillo, ca. 1890. Courtesy Amarillo Public Library.

When the election was held, I got two-thirds of the votes. My enemies were stalled once more for a while, but not for long.[1]

The Rat Pack Strikes a Mortal Blow

My old bondsman signed my bond, with one additional, that of H. T. Cornelius. Mr. Cornelius had come to Rag Town before the organization of the county, and while he had known all the Holland bunch and was friendly with them, he and I were congenial friends. Cornelius had moved to Amarillo among the first settlers, put up a livery barn, and enjoyed a liberal patronage. He and his wife had the honor of having a baby girl born to them, the first baby born in Amarillo. Both he and his wife seemed to think the world of Belle.

Things started off nicely for the new term, and everything moved along so peaceably that I felt my worries were over until November. However, Holland got his bloodhounds in a session cloaked in the guise of a commissioners meeting and declared my bonds insufficient, as state tax collector, and made an order requiring that a more sufficient bond be secured by real estate owned by residents of the county. What they did was to create an impossible set of conditions to meet, since the land was all state school land or owned by nonresidents, which I'm sure they realized in advance.[2]

I offered as good a caliber of bonds as it was possible to make, and he rejected them and declared the sheriff's office to be vacant, proceeding to appoint a man named Criswell[3] as sheriff. Criswell, who had come from Vernon, Texas, had been deputy sheriff there.

The commissioners served notice on me to turn over to Criswell my office and all the books and records pertaining to the sheriff's office. I refused and maintained possession of my office and books. Then the commissioners brought suit against me for possession, and when

City Hotel, Ed Conrad's Feed Store, Amarillo, ca. 1890. Courtesy Panhandle-Plains Museum, Research Center, Canyon, Texas.

Amarillo, Texas. Street scene in Amarillo showing the 66 Saloon, the Crescent Hotel, a liquor store, and a hardware store, ca. 1890. Courtesy Panhandle-Plains Museum, Research Center, Canyon, Texas.

district court convened, the four commissioners, Judge Quinn, and another man named Hamlin[4] that converted to their nest all swore that the citizens of Potter County were biased and partial in favor of James R. Gober, and it would be impossible to get a fair and impartial decision in Potter County. They asked for a change in venue to Donley County, with Clarendon the county seat. Judge Plemons, as district judge, was disqualified in the case, and some special judge from Fort

147

Captain W. J. McDonald,
Company B, Frontier Battalion,
Texas Rangers, date unknown.
Copyright, 1996, The Texas
Ranger Hall of Fame and
Museum #82-8.

Worth sat on the bench and granted the change of venue. The district court would not convene again for four months, and that would make it April 1891.[5]

Intimidation with Retribution

Criswell came to me and said, "Gober, this matter will have to be settled in the courts, and there is no reason for us to have any hard feelings. We can be just as good friends as we ever were, and when the court decides if the decision is in your favor, you will receive the salary and the fees of the office. If they decide for the commissioners, I will receive the sheriff's benefits. It is not me that is making this fight but the commissioners, and they were going to appoint someone, and I had just as well accept it as anyone."

Then I said, "Mr. Criswell, I'm glad you have a sensible view of this matter. Your spirit is the same as mine, and there is no good reason for us not to be good friends." All continued to be fine for two weeks.

S. A. McMurray had resigned as captain of Company B, Ranger Force, and Bill McDonald[6] had assumed the charge. McDonald was altogether a different character than McMurray. McDonald was seeking a reputation as a notorious general and hero and was somewhat boastful of his adventures in capturing or killing outlaws, but he seemed to be friendly with me. However, I noticed that he and Criswell were together often, and it was not unusual to see them playing faro or monte at the same table.

I met McDonald one afternoon in front of L. B. Collins's saloon, which had been moved from the old town and now located near the new Amarillo Hotel. McDonald asked me to have a drink, so we went into the saloon and found John Merchant, who was visiting his brother Clabe. Ace Henson[7] was also there, and each of these men was past fifty years of age, and McDonald about forty.

After a social drink, McDonald proposed to have a poker game, and all agreed. We went in the back room, and L. B. Collins began issuing the poker chips. He had locked the door between the barroom and the back room where we were. Before we had played one hand, there was a knock on the door. Collins opened the door, and Criswell came in and stood behind McDonald a few minutes, watching. Then he touched me on the shoulder and said, "I want to speak to you privately." He started to a small room in the rear, and I followed him.

When we got inside, McDonald had followed, unnoticed by me. Criswell handed me a paper, and, as I took the paper in both hands to read it, he drew his gun and said, "I will have to disarm you." At the same time McDonald grabbed my gun, and then I realized why McDonald had organized the poker game. Criswell then spoke, "Gober, we don't want to hurt you, but I think you will agree that it would be in the best interests of all concerned if you volunteered to resign your position as sheriff of Potter County and to do so as soon as possible, but certainly before the convening of the district court in Clarendon." He went on to tell me to give a lot of thought to his suggestion. Although I was burning with rage inside at this cowardly insult, I also realized that an unarmed man could exercise little force against two armed snakes, so I nodded and left the saloon.

I went home and stayed until after supper. Then I kissed my wife and told her that I might be late getting home. Before leaving, I grabbed my short Winchester shotgun, then went down the back street and into a friend's place of business. I called to him in his back room and told him I would remain there, and for him to go to all the saloons and see if he could locate Criswell, and to let me know where he was. In a few minutes my friend returned and informed me that Criswell was in Jack Ryans's saloon, talking to the bartender. I went to the front door with my shotgun cocked, and I saw that Criswell was standing at the far end of the bar and behind it. My eyes met his as I said, "Put up your hands, you cowardly cur," and he raised his hands, to my disappointment, as I hoped he would draw for his gun. I am honest enough to acknowledge that I intended to blow his head off.

Just then, a ranger who had apparently seen me go into the saloon threw his gun on me from behind. From behind the ranger I heard the voice of my kid brother[8] say to the ranger, "Take that gun off my brother, or I will blow you into eternity." Then I knew I was safe from behind, but I had never taken my gun off of Criswell, and he had never lowered his hands.

I spoke to the bartender and told him to take Criswell's gun, so he raised it from the holster and asked me what I wanted done with it. I lowered my gun and told the bartender to lay Criswell's gun on the bar; then I said, "You dirty old cur, take your gun. I want you to have it at all times, but you must not expect to trap me again. If you make another gun play on me, you'll be pushing up bluebonnets in the new cemetery."

Criswell wouldn't pick up his gun until I left. By this time my brother and the ranger had reached an understanding, and so the confrontation ended with no one hurt, for which I thank God.[9]

You Can't Trust Anyone

A man by the name of Baker, about sixty years old, was introduced to me as a lawyer who had just arrived in Amarillo to establish himself in the practice of law. I was told that he would be glad to represent me in the county suit against me, so I agreed and was favorably impressed with Mr. Baker as an intelligent old gentleman. I gave him one hundred dollars as a retainer fee. Mr. Baker had some useful information to give me every day and was quite attentive in working with me as his client.

About a month prior to the coming court date at Clarendon, Mr. Baker came to me and said, "Gober, I have to make a trip to Hamilton County on special business, and I would like to go in a rig, camp out at night, and cook my own meals on a campfire. If you could furnish a rig and let your old bachelor brother[10] go with me, I would really appreciate that. I think a great deal of your brother, and it would be a great trip for him as well as recreation for me before the case is tried at Clarendon." Baker stated, "I have had all my papers for the case completed and ready for the trial."

I told him, "Certainly, I will let you and Brother drive my buggy team hitched to a light wagon. Just go and get yourself a camping outfit together, and you can start tomorrow morning." He figured fifteen days for the trip to Hamilton County and return, and the next day they were off.

In about ten days my brother returned with the wagon team and informed me that my lawyer gave him the slip at San Angelo. Then it dawned on me that Baker was rung in on me by the Holland bunch and had duped me for about three hundred dollars, and not only that, it was only twenty days until the trial at Clarendon.

So with my back to the wall once again, I called on my friend, Temple Houston, to represent me and also asked W. H. Woodman, who had retired as district attorney and was practicing, to join my legal team.

When the court convened, Judge G. A. Brown[11] was on the bench. Houston started to read his answer to the commissioners' petition, and Brown stopped him and informed him that the action of a commissioners court was final and that no court had the jurisdiction to undo the action of a commissioners court. He added that it seemed absurd and unfair, but such was the law in the state of Texas.

At that moment I realized for the first time what odds I had had stacked against me from the very beginning, even as far back as August 1887. The sad thing is that I had to acknowledge defeat not only for myself but for two-thirds of the voters of Potter County and that this defeat was brought about by one individual of the most unscrupulous and selfish spirit of any human I had ever known.

I had left Belle with her mother, and she was in a delicate condition. About six PM, I received a wire to "come home on the first train . . . wife very sick." I got a train at seven o'clock and arrived in Amarillo at ten o'clock. Judge Plemons's buggy was at the depot to meet me, but it was then four miles from town to his home on Amarillo Creek.

When I got there, I found Dr. McGee[12] trying to help my wife give birth to a child, and it was five o'clock the next morning before the baby girl was born.[13] I believe the last six hours before our first baby was born was the most strenuous time of my life up to that time.

A Time of Stress and Strain

I had been at Clarendon for six days and I had drunk whiskey freely every day and part of the night as everyone drank whiskey during those days. As I had been under a continual nervous strain for three years while I was sheriff, naturally I drank more than if my mind had been at peace. It never had any bad effect on me until the night after our baby was born. I hadn't taken a drink from the time I left Clarendon the night before and was as sober as I ever was in my life.

When I was sitting by the bed talking to my wife, about ten o'clock, all of a sudden I heard talking outside, and as I listened, I could recognize the voices of my enemies—from time to time different ones, about eight in all, that I had spotted as being the ones implicated in the vigilante committee. I had a Winchester shotgun of short length and kept the magazine full of buckshot cartridges at all times. Never did I step out of doors at night without having it in my hands. This particular evening, I never let on to Belle that I heard anything, but soon I decided to slip out and shoot it out with them as long as I lasted, for I knew that I just couldn't have them coming to the house. I knew Belle wouldn't think anything about me taking my gun out with me, for it was my regular custom. So I kissed her and said, "I have to step out."

When I got outside, I located the voices about seventy yards away in a railroad cut, where the Fort Worth and Denver ran parallel with the premises. About halfway to the railroad was a chicken house and outhouse. I walked out to the chicken house and stood there waiting, my gun in hand. After I had been in one position for half an hour, Judge Plemons came out in his night clothes and asked me what was wrong. I said, "Please, go back in the house and say nothing. Can't you hear them talking?"

The Judge listened for a moment and said, "Son, you have been drinking pretty heavy, and your pride wouldn't permit you to bring some whiskey with you, and your nerves have given way. That is what is wrong. Come on in the house."

My old friend Jim Stroopes was staying at Judge Plemons's ranch at the time. He had retired for the night, and so had the judge and the balance of the family before the Judge had appeared on the scene a few minutes earlier. By this time Jim Stroopes had come out and had his .45, so I said to Stroopes, "You come with me." Then we walked out to the railroad cut, and I satisfied myself that there was no one there and also that there were no tracks to be seen. Then and there I decided that there was something seriously wrong.

Poisoned Like a Rat

The next morning, I sent Stroopes to town to get a quart of whiskey. I took several toddies during the day, and when night came, the same talking began, and the next day I could hear those voices at a distance. Then I suspected that it was not the booze but that I had been poisoned at Clarendon.

This annoyance seemed to get worse, right along, so in about a week, Belle was out of danger and I decided to go to Dr. Bell in Fort Worth. He had the reputation of being the best doctor in the West. When Dr. Bell examined me by placing tubes in my ears that enabled him to see inside my head, he really turned pale and said, "Boy, your iron nerve has saved your life. You have been given poison enough to kill three men, and it will take some time for this to wear off. You will just simply have to wear it out of you. I will give you some medicine, and you must take it according to directions. Don't fail to do that. If you don't get along all right, you had better come back and stay here until you are all right."

A Final Blow from the Gang

When I went back home, I felt very little relief but realized I needed all the exercise I could stand. I straightened up my business and turned the keys to my office over to Criswell.

After Holland and his commissioners got full possession they claimed a four-hundred-dollar shortage in the tax collections. C. B. Vivian[14] had been my office manager and bookkeeper, and he claimed someone had stolen a tax warrant and removed the stub. The next day, Cornelius and John Hollicott came to me. Cornelius was the spokesman and said, "Hollicott and I will have to pay this shortage unless you can pay it." Now there had been a time when I could have explained to John Hollicott that this was the last dirty trick that Holland had a chance to play on me, but that time and confidence had systematically vanished, as Holland had duped him and had his confidence. I still felt loyal to John Hollicott for his friendship and had rather suffer my right arm to be cut off than to have him think I was dishonest or disloyal to my friends.

Cornelius had wanted to buy my buggy team, Frank and George, several times, and I had never offered them for sale at any price, so

Typical businesses of Amarillo: P. H. Seewald, jeweler, and Martin & Russell law firm, ca. 1892. Courtesy Amarillo Public Library.

after a few minutes I said, "Cornelius, my accounts are not, in reality, short, and you know it. But I'm powerless to show John Hollicott who the crook is; therefore, release John Hollicott from any obligation. I will give you my buggy team and buggy, which I consider to be worth much more than four hundred dollars." Cornelius agreed instantly, and the team and buggy were in his stable in an hour.

This ended my controversy and left no chance for my enemies to accuse me of dishonesty but left me flat broke with my pride trampled under the feet of a half dozen of the most unscrupulous petty larceny crooks that had ever invaded the Panhandle of Texas. As young as I was, I realized that if I ran for sheriff in 1892, which would be the next election, and if I happened to be elected, it would be the same fight all over again. I realized that I must do something to make a living, so I bought a saloon, on time, and ran it until the spring of 1892. Then I sold it, just breaking even on my purchase.

Beginning a Life without a Badge

A New Mexico Opportunity

During that spring of 1892, I received a letter from an old friend, John Blakewood, at Roswell, New Mexico, asking me to come to Roswell and open a bar in his wholesale liquor establishment. I felt that this was an opportunity to get away from the trouble and worry that I had gone through in Amarillo. My kid brother, who was then twenty-two years old and in good health, agreed to go with me on the deal. I left my wife and baby with her father and mother with the understanding that when the bar was opened up and in business, I would come back after them.

Brother and I rigged up a wagon team and camping outfit and started for Roswell, 250 miles southwest. We were eight days on the road, and it was a lonesome time for me going farther from my wife and baby each day. When we arrived in Roswell, we met Blakewood, and he took us to his wholesale house, an adobe building thirty by sixty feet and filled to capacity with liquors, wine, and cigars, and everything that goes with the liquor business.

Blakewood told us to put in a bar and to take out a retail license. He said that he would turn over all his invoices and bills of lading, and we could help ourselves, keep our own books and charge ourselves at wholesale prices, then settle with him every month. All was agreed, and the next day we set carpenters to work, and five days later we had a real nice bar and fixtures in the front part, and we had started off nicely with a liberal patronage.

During that spring of 1892, I received a letter from an old friend, John Blakewood, at Roswell, New Mexico, asking me to come to Roswell and open a bar in his wholesale liquor establishment.

We had been running about thirteen weeks and getting along nicely and I was planning on starting back to Amarillo in another week to pick up my wife and baby. Then, one Saturday evening, John Preston, who was in the saloon and wholesale beer business, came in and asked, "Would you like to take a ride tomorrow out in the country, among the farms?" John was a likable man who I had known at Canadian, Texas,[1] and he continued by saying, "I have a good team and a light rig that I only use to deliver beer. I like to give them a good drive on Sunday, for the exercise."

I eagerly said, "Yes, I would like to see the old John Chisum ranch,[2] as I was raised and went to school with his nephews, the children of his brother, Jim Chisum."

All was agreed, and next morning Preston drove up to our saloon about nine o'clock. I had taken a quart bottle of whiskey, and we were off down a beautiful lane with huge cottonwood trees lining each side of the road, a place which was called Lover's Lane. Preston and I had several drinks, and when we got to the ranch it was twelve o'clock.

Typical street scene, Second and Main Streets, Roswell, New Mexico Territory, date unknown. Courtesy Southwest Collection, Texas Tech University, Lubbock.

Being Sunday, no one was at the ranch but the man cook, so we gave him the remains of the whiskey. We had a nice dinner and walked around over the improvements for about two hours, then started back to town.

Preston and I enjoyed each other's company immensely, reviving former days in the Panhandle. We got to town just at sundown, and as I got out of the buggy Preston said, "If you don't mind, I would like for you to go with me down to the dance hall. I have a couple of cases of beer to deliver, and when I delivered last night, there was a tough bunch in, and I thought three of them were going to clean up on me."

Escape from Injustice

Now what could I say after accepting his kind, hospitable favor? I could not refuse, so we drove to the dance hall, about one-half mile on the bank of the Rio Hondo. We unloaded the beer at the back door and started through an eight-foot-long hallway to the front. There were rooms on each side of the hallway that the women occupied. Just as we were about to enter the barroom and dance hall, we met three cowpunchers, apparently the same ones Preston had trouble with the night before. One of them made a rush for Preston, and he and Preston clinched. The other two started for him, and I drew my gun and told them, "Hands off!" Preston had gotten a hold on his man's throat and had his tongue protruding several inches out of his mouth.

He was boxing the cowpoke's jaws with the other hand. When I thought it was too one-sided, I spoke to Preston and told him to stop. He stopped like the decent man he was. The two I threw my gun on ran out the front door toward town.

Preston and I got in our rig and drove to his saloon, and he asked me to have a drink. There were several others that were in the place at that time, and when we were all lined up at the bar pouring out our drinks, the city marshal, Henry Wright, came in unnoticed by me and came up and slipped my gun from my hip pocket and said, "You are under arrest."

I said, "All right. What is the charge?"

He replied quickly, "One is for carrying concealed weapons, and the other will be displaying a deadly weapon with intent to do bodily harm."

I asked him, "How much cash bond do you want for my appearance?"

He said, "I have no right to accept cash bonds."

Preston spoke up and said, "You can take a cash bond, or you can't take him out of the house!" Preston was a determined man, and so was Wright, and both had killed one or more men. Preston had his hand on his gun under the bar, on the work or drain board, and Wright, of course, would have to reach for his, and that meant Preston would shoot first. So they eyed each other for five minutes like two mad tigers.

Finally, Wright said, "I suppose one hundred dollars would be sufficient for Gober's appearance." I gave him fifty and Preston gave him fifty, and he requested that my gun be left with him.

Now, the least fine for gun toting in New Mexico at that time was fifty dollars and cost and thirty days in jail. The other charge would be more serious. It was obvious that the two men I threw the gun down on to stop them from doubling up on Preston had run to town and complained to the marshal and would swear hard against me. Two charges would mean probably six months in jail besides the two fines. It didn't take me very long to decide that my future in Roswell was history.

My brother had heard the news and had come just as Wright was leaving. I called him into Preston's back room and told him to go back to our place and bring my Winchester shotgun back with him. When he returned with my gun, I told him to go back to our saloon, invoice our stock to Blakewood, and load our trunks, bedding, and camp fittings into our wagon. I instructed him to come on towards the Pecos River and that I would walk until he had overtaken me.

When I had walked about ten miles, he overtook me about midnight, and we drove until we crossed the Pecos River, were in another county and in the roughest part of the river. There we camped, staked our team, and made our camp beds. Brother slept until daybreak while I sat up watching down the road, expecting the marshal would follow us and appear on the horizon most any minute. I had made up my mind not to be taken back to Roswell.

When day began to break, I gathered a few mesquite roots and made coffee and some bacon. We fed the team, then ate our breakfast while the horses were eating. When we had finished, we harnessed the team and hitched them to the wagon, and we then drove forty miles that day and camped at a small cattle ranch owned by a man I knew by the name of Taylor. That night, I suffered from a bad spell of colic. I'm sure that Mr. Taylor saved my life during the night, for during my spell he got a quart bottle and put in it a teacup of vinegar and made it almost thick with cayenne pepper. It was hot stuff, but I drank it, and in half an hour I went to sleep.

It appeared that all danger of being followed had past, and therefore we took our time the balance of the way to Amarillo. However, I was very grieved that I had lost the splendid opportunity John Blakewood had given us to make money, and I was heartsick, for I knew that I had no opportunity in Amarillo except to get into trouble. Nevertheless, I was homesick to see my wife and baby, and that is all that caused me to want to live. When we arrived back in Amarillo we found that all was well.

The Changing Seat of the Law

About the first news I heard was that Sheriff Criswell had been found short in his accounts and was put out of office. He lost his section of land and left the country. An ex-ranger by the name of Grude Britton had been appointed sheriff. Britton was a nice fellow and made a good sheriff until he was beaten by R. M. Warden in the first election after his appointment, which was November 1892. Mr. Warden also made a good a sheriff and served his two-year term and was defeated by Rome Wheatley in 1894. Wheatley served two terms and was defeated by a man named J. E. Hughes, who held office for eight years.[3]

Now I will drop back to March 1893. We had a baby boy[4] born that month and were very happy that we then had a boy and a girl. But I was still in a mental strain over being unjustly disgraced by the

Holland clan. If I had been older and more experienced, I would have gone to some other locality and started in anew, but it seemed I couldn't leave the place where all my friends were and go among strangers. I guess that was the childish spirit in my heart that still remains. If I appreciate anyone as a friend, I will stand by them, right or wrong, even with the last dollar I have, or will even stake my life on them. That spirit has cost me lots of money and considerable trouble, but still, to this very day, it is a great pleasure to me.

An Oklahoma Invitation

We received notice that the Cheyenne and Arapaho Indian territory in Oklahoma was to be opened in June,[5] and my kid brother concluded that he would go and make the run. He wanted me to go with him, but I didn't feel I could leave my wife and babies just then, so my brother made the run, and he staked a valuable quarter section four miles up the Washita River from where the county seat of Cheyenne[6] was established. He got in with a man by the name of Jim Colburn, and they set up a saloon in Cheyenne. Cheyenne was located in a valley near where the Sergeant Major Creek[7] runs into the Washita River.

The next summer I went to Cheyenne to see what prospects there might be for me in that town. Cheyenne is 150 miles from Amarillo, and in order to get to Cheyenne, I had to go to Canadian, Texas, and there take the mail stage to Cheyenne. I arrived in Cheyenne about five PM and found the town in a high state of excitement. The sheriff, who was a brother of my friend Garrett Johnson, and a deputy named Bill Banks had killed a man by the name of Charley Wilson while trying to recover some Indian ponies that had been stolen from a Cheyenne chief. The ponies had been found in Wilson's possession, and the killing had taken place two or three miles from town. News of the killing had reached town at the same time the stage arrived. Wilson had made friends in the country while working on the YL cattle ranch.[8] He was considered a likable fellow but in reality was living under an assumed name and was a desperate man, according to the information that the sheriff had in his possession.

The Indian chief had been notified to come and identify his horses, and he came in a few days and brought several other Indians with him. Some of the parties in possession of certain of the ponies refused to give up the ponies, so the Indians had to identify and sequester them. The justice of the peace lived on his claim one mile from town, up the Sergeant Major Creek. He had his office and held court at home, which was a dugout in the bank off the creek.

I went to see the procedure and found three of the Indians at the justice of the peace proceedings carrying Winchester rifles. When we got to the judge's house, most of us had to stay outside under the shade of some large cottonwood trees. After sitting in the shade for an hour, I became sleepy and stretched out on the grass and went to sleep with those Indians sitting in a half-circle around me. Something occurred in the procedure that displeased the Indians, and, without warning, they all gave a war whoop and shot off their guns at the same time. Now, I've been awakened many times in my life, but never before or since have I been as wide awake in so short a time and up on my feet so quickly. There was quite a stir for a few minutes, but the sheriff soon got the Indians pacified, and the court proceeded. Soon the ponies were all turned over to the Indians, and they went on their way rejoicing.

An old Frenchman that had lived with me at Amarillo for several years had gone over to Cheyenne with my brother, John, and had filed in a nice quarter section just one mile from Cheyenne on the main road to Canadian. He had told me and also told my brother that he intended to give the land to my wife and me as soon as he improved it. The old fellow had died a few weeks before I got over to Cheyenne, and he had left a relinquishment on his claim for me. So I filed on the land and camped in a dugout on my brother's place and used his team. I cut and hauled logs and built a large dugout, half in the ground and half of logs. Then I cut posts and fenced the land. It had taken me until late in the fall to do all this work alone.

About the first of November, I went to Amarillo to join my wife and babies. By that time we had three: the oldest, five, a girl; the second, three, a boy; and the third, one, a boy.[9]

We began arrangements that would lead to us trying our luck in the Cheyenne country. My oldest brother, Tom, was at Amarillo from Cripple Creek, Colorado. He had spent several years prospecting for gold, and he had agreed to go with us. We rigged a four-horse team to a wagon, loaded what household goods we absolutely needed, and pulled out about the fifteenth of November, with the blessings of good weather. The fourth day we passed through Mobeetie in the afternoon, and the sky had become cloudy and the wind had changed to the north. We had driven about six miles out of Mobeetie when it began to snow, so we stopped and camped at a ranch situated on a

Tom Gober in Colorado mining town, ca. 1887. Courtesy Paul Tolbert, Upland, California.

small creek. The ranch was owned by two old bachelors, and they had just a one-room house, but they also had a log corn crib and offered us the use of the crib. My wife stayed in the wagon with the babies most of the time, and Brother and I tended to the feeding of our teams. We would make coffee and cook what we could behind the crib, doing our best to remain sheltered from the wind and snow. Fortunately, we had plenty of bedding and a good cover on the wagon, but the only time we could be comfortable and warm was when we were covered in our bedding.

We remained there two days and nights, and on the third morning, the sun came out. Since it looked as though the storm was over, we harnessed our four horses and pulled out towards Cheyenne, forty-five miles away. The sky soon clouded over again, and it was very cold, with eight inches of snowfall on the ground. There were drifts two feet deep in places on the road.

By three o'clock in the afternoon our teams were tired, so we camped, tied them on the opposite side of the wagon, and gave them grain. We rested them for two hours, then drove on. Since there was no water until we reached Rush Creek,[10] twelve miles from Cheyenne, we knew there could be no overnight rest stops until we reached that area. That made the trip twenty-eight miles of travel that day, with a loaded wagon, fighting the weather over the snow-packed road.

My brother would try to follow the snow-hidden road in front of the team while I drove. When he would get fagged out, I would walk in front of the team and try to find the road while he drove the wagon. Finally, it became so dark that we couldn't keep on the road, and we lost it entirely. There was the danger of going into a gulch or canyon at any moment, so I would go forty or fifty steps ahead of the team and holler, and then my brother would come to me and stop until I hollered again.

We kept up this disagreeable method until midnight, when suddenly I heard a gunshot. I immediately went to the wagon and asked my wife to hand to me my .45-caliber Colt, and I answered the shot. Then my shot was answered, and after answering each other's shots four or five times, a man by the name of Frank Turner rode up to us and said, "Your younger brother had gotten uneasy about you, and he sent me to hunt for you." He told us that when he didn't find us at Rush Creek, he presumed we were off the road. That's when he fired his gun, in the hope we would hear it and answer. Then he said, "Follow me. and I will get you back on the road," from which we had drifted a mile away.

We made it to Rush Creek, where we watered our teams. It was there we decided that, by Turner riding in front, it would be better for us to travel the twelve final miles than it would be to camp in the cold and snow. Weary but undaunted, we trudged on the rest of the night and arrived at our new home at sunup the next morning.

An old-time cowboy friend of mine, Al McKinney, had a claim just across the road and cornering with mine. He had a nice two-story frame building and invited me to bring my wife and children to his house to stay until I was able to get my belongings unloaded and set up. I was very grateful, for it provided a chance for my little frozen family to get thawed out and rested up. The weather moderated, and the second day after our arrival I had the dugout dried out, our things all in shape, and my family at home.

Across the Oklahoma Border

Sorrow, Too Much to Bear

I had to find something to do to make money with which to live, so I went to town and got a job hauling lumber from Canadian, Texas, to Cheyenne, a distance of sixty miles. When I had made my third trip and had gotten my lumber unloaded, I went home and found out from my wife that our little girl had been suffering from the croup for several nights. That night she was taken with a severe attack, and we sent for Dr. Miller. When he came, he pronounced her illness as membranous croup. By midnight that same night, she was dead.

Once again, it seemed the world was against me, insofar as having any lasting peace and happiness was concerned. My spirit and heart were broken beyond repair.

We immediately notified Judge Plemons by mail, but it would take the letter thirty-six hours to reach Amarillo. Consequently, we had to bury our darling baby, named for him, before he arrived. When the judge reached Cheyenne, he was heartbroken, as were Belle and I. The next morning after he arrived, we talked over the situation, and he suggested that Belle and the other two babies go home with him for awhile. While I knew it was for the best and readily agreed with him, it only served to add more sorrow to my misery-laden heart. I had lost one forever, and now that I must give up the others was more than it seemed I could bear. There was nothing else I could do, so I harnessed my best team to a light rig, and we drove to Canadian that night. The train soon came after we arrived, and I bade goodbye to my father-in-law and kissed my heartbroken wife and two baby boys goodbye. Honestly, I felt that it was goodbye forever, for I didn't feel I could survive the shock it all had caused me.

I put my team in a wagon yard and went to a saloon and got a drink of whiskey. Afterwards, I went to a restaurant and tried to eat, but the food would swell in my mouth till I couldn't swallow a bite. I went back to the wagon yard and spread down a pallet and lay down, but I couldn't sleep.

By daybreak, I was on my way back to Cheyenne and hadn't the least idea what to do or how to start to better my condition. It seemed as though my brain was paralyzed and my heart was breaking from despair. I was in such agony from grief and loneliness that I really believe that if I had had my .45 with me, I would have ended it all. The future was so dark, and I had no one to say a kind word to me or share my burden. It seemed useless to live.

When I arrived back at my lonesome home, I unhitched my team, fed the horses, then walked a mile to the town of Cheyenne, arriving at my brother's saloon. I learned from him that one of the horses I had left at home had strayed off, had gotten itself into a corner of a wire fence, and burned to death in a prairie fire. That was of little consequence to me, for my heart was taxed to its fullest capacity with burdens of misfortune, grief, and disappointment, and nothing could have caused more sadness than I already had.

Fond Hopes that fade and die,
Bring grief and sorrow and many a sigh,
That makes life and spirit wilt and die.
Each sorrow kills a cheer,
Each sigh kills some pleasure that may be near,
Sorrow and sighs kill the sense of care.
And then we have no soul to save,
And cannot walk in God's light as a soldier pure and brave.
So let us hope and bravely try
To pass our grief and troubles by
And journey on with hope and care,
And every weeping heart try our best to cheer
And peace and joy will always seem near.

Jim Gober

In a Dire Physical Condition

I was nervous and broken in spirit and strength, and I was suffering from a strain in my lower intestines, caused by handling the heavy lumber I had been hauling from Canadian and unloading alone. I was passing blood freely every few hours, and the next day I was so weak I didn't leave the dugout but spent all day and night in bed. The second evening my brother sent an old Negro, Ben Evans, to see about me. Ben was an old Tennessee Negro, a mulatto about sixty years old. He had a claim two miles from Cheyenne on the Sergeant Major Creek. It contained a one-room log cabin located in a grove of large cottonwood and walnut trees and included a spring in the bank of the creek, near the cabin. I had known old Ben at Mobeetie, Texas, ten years previous, when he was a porter in Joe Mason's saloon. Ben was polite and kind to everybody, and all that knew him liked him. They would have fought for him, had anyone tried to impose on him.

Ben talked to me, with tears in his eyes, and sympathized with me. He begged me to go home with him so he could take care of me, saying he would go home and hitch his team to his spring wagon, make a pallet in the wagon, and come back after me. He pleaded with me over and over again, for half an hour, explaining that he could make a good bed out of my bedding in his wagon and run it under one of the large trees in his yard. There, he said, he would be near to look after me. I finally consented, concluding a Negro friend was much better than no friend at all.

For several days, Ben would make chicken soup and coffee and bring it to the wagon, insisting on my eating. I would try and force down a few swallows, more to please Ben than to satisfy any appetite. In four or five days, I felt well enough to go to town but was still suffering from the strain and couldn't have a normal functioning of the bowels.

I met John Read, who had a small bunch of cattle and horses and was always ready to trade or speculate in a small way. After we had talked for a few minutes, I told him I wanted to leave the country and would like to dispose of my claim. He said, "I haven't any money, but I'll trade you horses for it." The next day I closed a deal with Read by relinquishing my claim rights to him for a consideration of forty dollars and five horses. When the deal was concluded, I turned the horses over to my brother to dispose of as he could and to send the money to Kansas City, where I planned to be. Then I went as a cowpoke with a small herd of beef cattle to Woodward, Oklahoma,[1] whence they were to be shipped to Kansas City. I was given a pass to go with the cattle to Kansas City.

On my arrival there, I went to a friend and explained to him my condition. He directed me to a Dr. S. G. Gant, supposed to be the best surgeon in the city, and, after making a thorough examination, we had a long talk. "Mr. Gober, your trouble is a bad strain that has caused a stricture of the rectum. The problem has also caused a paralytic condition of the main bowels from the rectum to the opening of the stomach." He told me further, "An operation is all that can prolong your life for any reasonable time."

I told him of my financial condition and of the resources I expected to get: a few hundred dollars at best from horses I left in Oklahoma for my brother to sell, but that horses were cheap, with not much demand. "However, Doctor," I emphasized, "if I live and am able to get work, I will pay you, even if the horses all die. I expect my brother will send me a reasonable amount of money anyway, whether he disposes of the horses or not," and I told him that I had forty dollars to pay on hospital fees. As a personal reference, I gave George Berry, the manager of the West End Hotel in Kansas City, whom I had known in the Panhandle in the eighties.[2]

Dr. Gant happened to know Berry personally and called him on the phone. After a short conversation, Gant hung up the receiver and said, "Mr. Gober, I will take care of your case, and at a most reasonable fee. I will charge you one $150, and your hospital fee will be $25 a week, and if I kill you, the bill is settled. You don't have to go to the hospital[3] until I get you ready to operate on, but you must take the medicine I'm going to fix for you, according to directions. Then report to me in the morning at nine o'clock. Eat nothing except what I dictate." He explained further, "It will be forty-eight hours before I get you ready for the operation."

From the doctor's office, I went to the West End Hotel and met George Berry and thanked him for the recommendation he had given over the phone to Gant. My strength was then exhausted, so I registered for a room and went to bed. About six PM, I arose and went down and ate a light meal. When I finished eating, I came out into the lobby and sat down to smoke a cigar. George Berry came over, and we had a real nice visit, talking over the early days in the Panhandle. I related some of my recent experiences and my affliction and its cause, and Berry said, "Jim, you are worth a dozen dead men, and Gant will fix you up all right; he is a personal friend of mine, and I have asked him to give you special attention. Besides, I have guaranteed his pay, so you cheer up, and the world will look brighter when you get well." I thanked Berry, bade him goodnight, and went to bed, feeling some hope for the future. It was encouraging to realize that I had at least one friend near me in this time of need.

That evening, before I turned in for the night I met John Holman from Woodward, Oklahoma, who had brought a trainload of cattle to market. Holman had known my father-in-law at Henrietta, Texas, before he came to Amarillo, and I had also met Holman several times. I asked him to be at the hospital the next evening at four o'clock and see the operation, and I gave him confidential instructions in case I kicked off.

The next morning I reported to Dr. Gant, and he informed me he would operate on me at four PM that afternoon. That afternoon, Holman was at St. Francis in time to see me go under anesthetic. When I was able to sit up in bed and was getting along nicely, Dr. Gant told me he removed 157 hard tumors from inside of the main bowel, from the size of a pinhead to as large as a common-sized bead. After cutting them off the bowel, he seared the scars with an iron at white heat. He also informed me that some of the tumors hadn't come through the surface, and it would be necessary for another operation when they did, which might be a year or five years, but they would, in time, give me more trouble.

A Physical Wreck in the Badlands

I was in the St. Francis Hospital sixty days before I could walk with a cane. It was then that I realized that I was a mere shadow of the man that I had been. Through all the suffering with this ailment, I had fallen off from 185 pounds to a mere 145 pounds.

As soon as the doctor told me I could leave, I went and bought a cheap suit of clothes costing just eight dollars and several sizes smaller than normal. I then went to the station, purchased a ticket to Woodward, Oklahoma Territory, and, after paying for the ticket, I had $1.50 left in my pocket.

There was one man in Woodward that I knew, and that was L. B. Collins. I had given him three months' time on his saloon license in Amarillo when the town was young and I was sheriff and tax collector of Potter County. I hoped to get a job with Collins until I could gain my strength sufficiently to do any kind of work.

It was a twenty-four hour ride on the train to Woodward, then a wild and woolly little town on the Santa Fe Railroad and in the Cherokee Strip.[4] I arrived in Woodward before noon, February 5 or 6, 1894. The railroad depot was three-fourths of a mile from the main town, but my suitcase was very light; and I walked, using a cane, although tired, weak, and hungry. I had only $.75 remaining of my $1.50, so I walked to town in preference to giving up $.50 for a buggy ride, for I intended to eat a square meal at the first place that I found.

A Friend with a Difficult Proposition

I went only one-half block into Woodward when I saw a sign reading Dolly's Dew Drop Inn, Saloon, and Restaurant.[5] Starved by this time, I dropped in, and when I got through with my meal and asked what I owed, Dolly said very pleasantly, "Seventy-five cents." I gave her my precious last seventy-five cents and asked her some questions about Mr. Collins, the name of his place, and how to find it. She told me what I had asked, and I departed and made straight for the Turf Saloon, his place of business.[6]

When I arrived at the saloon and stepped inside, I found Collins standing on the customers' side of the bar, taking a drink with some men. He looked over at me, and by the expression on his face, you'd have thought he'd seen a dead man, as he almost dropped his glass and did partially drop it and set it on the bar. He ran over to me, grasped my hand, and screamed in a high-pitched voice, " Jim! I heard you were dead! But I'm sure glad it wasn't so, and I'm glad you're here. I'll talk to you in a few minutes. Just step into the back room and sit down." The back room was the gambling room, but it was vacant at this time. Collins came back in a few minutes and took a seat facing me squarely. "I would have known you regardless, but I can't believe how you look, Jim, and the condition you're in, what with the cane and all." He had always seen me only as a giant of a fellow.

After talking to him for twenty minutes, explaining what had happened to me, Collins confided in me, saying, "Jim, we've got some tough birds here that have been causing me to close my place quite often or get it shot up. Now I have a man that is a little overdrawn. He'll work until Saturday night, which will be only three days; then I'll put you on. In the meantime, when we close in a little while, you go with me to the Cattle King Hotel,[7] and I will get you a meal ticket. My wife is away on a visit to her folks in Kiowa, Kansas, and you can

Collins confided in me, saying, "Jim, we've got some tough birds here that have been causing me to close my place quite often or get it shot up."

occupy our room until she returns. Then we will get one at the hotel for you."

While Collins was talking, my mind was wandering as I thought about the "tough birds" he had mentioned. I knew at that time there were twelve saloons in Woodward; Woodward was in a county that adjoined the outlaw strip known as "No Man's Land." But I had no fear of trouble with the outlaws, for I had had plenty of experience with them, and most of them knew me by reputation and knew that I would demand a square deal.

Collins's mind predictably wandered back to the subject of the "tough birds," for understandably the issue weighed heavily upon his mind, and he wanted to discuss the subject in more detail. He began again by saying, "As I mentioned, there are some tough characters in and around Woodward, and they frequently make the rounds and shoot up the saloons, sparing none. I've usually been lucky enough to hear the shooting, close this place up, and get in the hotel and stay until they calmed down. Sometimes, however, I have had to keep the saloon closed all day or all night and have lost considerable trade as a result of these incidents."

At this point I could see his expression change. I knew he had some type of a proposition to put to me, so I braced myself as he said, "Jim, now that you are here I'm not afraid to stay open, if you'll stay with me." I responded, "Collins, perhaps I had better move on to some of the Western towns where I've lived, like Tascosa, or Clayton, New Mexico, or even back to Amarillo, as I was in these places in the early eighties and never saw any bad men. I got along with all alike. Now, to stop here where you tell me the bad men cut up so desperately might cause me to get nervous and possibly spoil my good, even temper." I went on to tell him, "Perhaps you need one or more of those super-gunmen, the well-advertised conquerors of wicked men, the eternal saviors of Western towns who have promoted their own images as heroes without fault. Most of these characters have either contributed personally to enlarging their own fictitious images or at the least they never bothered to deny the veracity of the tales of their exaggerated performance. I firmly believe, when it is all said and done, history will show that some considered now to be heroes were in fact cold-blooded murderers." I continued to beat Collins's ear, saying, "When a man gets the right kind of advertising agents, they can do wonders, even miracles, to an otherwise despicable image. You'd better send for Bill Hickok,"[8] I quipped. "He was such a slick lawman, it seems, that most of his time he spent at the gambling tables and didn't need to patrol the streets of Abilene or elsewhere in search of criminals, the dangerous drunks, or other lawbreakers. Maybe Wyatt Earp[9] would do, for he had the reputation of shooting men when they were either unarmed, or had their hands high up in the air.

"Bill Tilghman[10] might be just the man for the dangerous streets of Woodward. He is used to killing them cowpunchers when they get drunk enough that they'd shoot all their cartridges away into space, or, like I said, some of these famous lawmen shoot first and ask questions later. Luke Short,[11] on the other hand, was never a lawman, if that makes any difference, but he was quite a gambler, wherever he was, in Kansas, Texas, or Arizona. He knew how to kill, for we know that he polished off one man in Arizona and another in Texas.

Those fellows like to get their names in the papers. In some instances they get paid well, and besides, someday they will enjoy reading about themselves in the magazines. As for me, I prefer to meet every man on a level and look on him as a human, and if I can't swap stock with him on a fifty-fifty basis, then I have confidence in my ability to outmanage him and take his gun until he is rational and sober." Then I asked Collins, "Who is your sheriff?"

He replied, "Tobe Odem,[12] my old partner in the cattle business." At that point Collins seemed not to want to comment any further about Odem and what to me was an obvious inconsistency between Odem and his questionable performance as sheriff.

I had known Tobe Odem since I was sixteen years old, and I knew him to be a fearless and dangerous man, so that prompted me to say, "Mr. Collins, there is something terribly wrong here, or Odem would control the situation differently. I think enough of you and Odem that I will stay with you until I analyze this problem." L. B. Collins then suggested that we break momentarily, go over to the hotel, and purchase my meal ticket. While we were walking back from the hotel to the saloon, Collins said, "By the way, Allen Thompson is here with me. He runs the gambling and will probably be at the saloon when we get there." We entered the saloon and walked back to the back room. No sooner had we gotten inside than Allen Thompson came in with four other cowboys to start a two-dollar poker game. I had worked with Allen Thompson on the LX Ranch during the years of 1884-86, and we were real friends. He was also amazed to see the condition that I was in.

With the poker game about to begin, five-handed, Allen pitched me two dollars' worth of checks, which he asked me to play as well as tending to the take off. The other players ordered drinks freely, but I ordered manatau lemonade and cigars. The game lasted about five hours and grew in the number of players and amount of money changed. When the game was over, for lack of players, I cashed in forty dollars, giving Allen his two-dollar stake and twenty dollars as half of the winnings, and then bade all goodnight and went to bed.

I lay awake and thought about a conversation I had heard between two fellows during the poker game. These men were from the Cherokee Strip, or No Man's Land, and they were talking about a dance that was to be held at the Higgins Hotel at Higgins, Texas,[13] the next night. Higgins was nineteen miles up the Santa Fe, just over the Texas line, and known as a wild old cattle town. Before I went to sleep,

I decided to go to that dance, as I felt sure there would be a bunch of Strip fellows there and, most importantly, there would be a big poker game. If I could be lucky as well as a good manager, I might win enough money to do me some good.

A Costly Game of Chance

About noon the next day I told Collins I was going to Higgins to the dance and what I was really up to. He advised me not to go, saying, "If you win any money, you will have trouble." He told me that several of the Woodward boys had gone to Higgins and made good winnings, only to have the money taken away and themselves knocked around.

I commented, "I will not give anyone cause to make trouble with me, but if anyone picks me out to make trouble, I will try to take care of myself." My mind was made up, and I went to the station and found a freight making up, so I rode it, with my twenty dollars, to Higgins Landing, soon after six PM that evening. On arriving at Higgins, I met several old-time cowpunchers I knew, and everyone seemed glad to see me and surprised both at my being so thin and my relying on a cane.

I wasn't sure where I might find the size of poker game that would serve to whet my appetite, but after a short while, a crowd of men began gathering in Scotty Rickerd's saloon. Twenty dollars was the least you could get in the game with, so I changed my winnings from the night before in Woodward, and that was all that I had. I sat down at a poker table, making the seventh player, being very careful from the start and playing close, for I knew if I lost that twenty, I had no more. Most of the players had spread large sums of bills behind their checks, so I knew if I could have any luck, I could win a small stake.

Every one of the six players besides myself was drinking every few minutes. I would take a cigar or mineral water, for I hadn't touched whiskey for over sixty days, and besides, it was important for me to keep a clear head. After half an hour's play, I picked up a hand that held a double ace heart flush. There was $37.50 in the jackpot, and the hands had been passed several times, and each time we threw in $.50 and called it "sweetening the pot."

I opened the jackpot for something like thirty dollars. As I had won several small pots and had about ninety dollars, three men to my left called my open, and Scotty Rickerd was the fourth. He called and raised back fifty dollars. The three players between Scotty and me passed, and I put in all I had, around eighty dollars, raising Scotty's bet ten dollars. I commented, "I'll have to draw like hell," then said to the dealer, "Turn them over." The dealer sat next to me on my right, and I, of course, was watching his every move. There were only seventeen cards left in the deck, but to my disgust, a pair of queens lay on the top for Scotty. When he drew two cards to three aces, he caught the two queens, beating my double ace heart flush and leaving me flat broke. But I smiled and complimented Scotty on his good luck and just sat still for a few minutes listening to comments about the unusual luck of Scotty drawing out on such a hand, with the slim chance of catching a pair out of only seventeen cards. When I recovered my balance after the shock, I rose from my seat and walked out the front door of the saloon.

An Act of Kindness Repaid

I had just stepped on to the sidewalk when I saw a big fellow with several weeks' growth of beard on his face. He was wearing a blue flannel shirt with a red silk scarf and a pair of brown corduroy trousers with the legs stuffed inside his high-topped, high-heeled boots. His eyes sparkled as he lunged at me and grabbed me around the neck and waist and held me like a vise, saying, "Mr. Gober, I thought you were dead! I'm glad to see you. You don't remember me, I know, but I never have forgotten the kindness you did me when I was a boy, fifteen. Do you remember me now?"

I really didn't know what to say to this fellow, but I replied, "I've always been kind to boys and helped many of them, and perhaps if you would tell me who you are, I might remember the kindness I had shown you."

He said, "I'm Pat Murphy, the kid you caught with the stolen mare in Amarillo during the big snowstorm."

I said, "You are not surprised at me not recognizing you, a two-hundred-pound athlete that you are now. When I last saw you, I lifted you off Conrad's black mare you had swiped to make your getaway from your parents. At that time you would have weighed scarcely sixty-five pounds. The snow was a foot deep, and you were barefooted, the knees out of your pants, one sleeve gone from your tattered coat, and no socks or underclothes. Yes, Pat, I can still see you, as pathetic a sight as I ever saw. You know, I'd been warned to look out for you and arrest you. After catching you and looking you over, I had taken you to Wood and Dickson's Tent Store and got you warm clothes, nothing costly, mind you, but warm and comfortable. I sent Mr. Conrad word to come after his mare, and as I remember, you stayed with me a couple of days before your father came after you, and I had some notion of not letting him take you when he did come."

After Pat got through loving me, he asked me if I had any money. I looked at him and saw tears rolling down his cheeks. I said, "Why do you ask? Are you broke?"

"No," he replied, "I thought perhaps I could do you some small favor."

I said, "Pat, you are not under the smallest obligation to me. As for the favor I did you, it was no more than justice to humanity, and I would do the same by any boy under the same circumstances. But I will make a business proposition to you." I went on to relate to him my special circumstances, then said, "I have just lost twenty dollars in that poker game, and it was all I had, but I have a job at Woodward and was starting to the depot to catch the first freight going that way when I ran into you. However, if you feel able to take a chance on losing fifty dollars, I'll sit back in that game. If I win, you'll get back your fifty and half the winnings."

Murphy simply rammed his hand into his high-pocketed corduroys and placed the other hand on the same pocket and began working his roll of bills out. When he finally succeeded in bringing it in sight, he peeled off five twenty-dollar bills and handed them to me, saying, "If you lose that, hunt me up and get more."

Good Fortune at Higgins

When I went back to the poker game, the same six men I had left were still playing. I sat in and asked for one hundred dollars' worth of checks. By this time, they were anteing $1.25 and made the blue checks that value. I played my hands carefully and was lucky in calling bluffs and beating good hands. My eyes never strayed from watching Scotty and the man that dealt him the two queens that had broken me. I discerned that they were signaling to each other but were very cautious about it.

Then I picked up a straight and opened the pot, and Scotty, who was pretty well jagged, played back at me and carelessly dropped the ace of clubs face up. The dealer's gaze was fixed on it as I called Scotty's raise and bet him fifty dollars more, which was all I had. I then commanded the dealer to set the deck on the table, knowing all the while that he had placed on top of the deck the club that would make Scotty's flush. Scotty hesitated for two minutes, then called my fifty. As soon as his money was in the pot, I reached out and cut the deck square in the middle. Scotty raised a protest and said he would take his money out. He had always had his way and had beat up many men in his fits of rage.

I said, "Scotty, you must be fair with me. A square deal is all I ask. I shall not expect you to be unfair. As this is your place of business, it should be your honorable duty to see that your customers are treated on the square. Instead, you are trying to cheat. You and your friend broke me once by his finding you a pair of queens. Don't expect to put any more rough stuff over me tonight. It's my intention that we leave this room friends, but if you insist on making a goat of me, one of us will not be well when we are carried out of here."

Scotty was a giant of a man with a brutal disposition, but I never intended for him to get on his feet if he attempted to raise up. He gazed steadily for some minutes, then said, "How many cards are you drawing?"

I said, "None." He showed his hand, face up—four clubs—and called for one card. He caught the ace of diamonds and tossed his hand in the center of the table. Then he went behind the bar, took a drink, and came back and sat down again. He had several stacks of yellow poker checks valued at $12.50. The game went on peacefully until dawn, when it finally broke up. I cashed in $590.

When I went to Murphy's room at the Higgins Hotel, I waked him and threw my roll on his bed. I told him to take out one hundred dollars and to divide the balance and that I must catch a train for Woodward, and it was due any minute. Murphy reached under his pillow and pulled out his huge roll of bills. He gazed at mine and then at his. Then he took out one hundred from mine and said, "You take your winnings. It may do you some good. If I lose all I have, I can get more quicker than you." I bade Murphy goodbye and advised him to stay away from the wild bunch and get on the right side of the law, but I learned a few years later that he was killed somewhere in Arizona.

Secrets of the Oklahoma Territory

An Oklahoma Saloon Adventure

Fortunately, I just made the train for Woodward, only fifty miles from Higgins, and soon I was telling Collins of my night's experience in that wild Texas town. As I had finished all I cared to tell, a fellow named Harry Hern came by, and Mr. Collins introduced him to me. Collins went behind the bar, and Hern invited me to join him in a drink. I told him that I wasn't drinking, so he insisted that I take a cigar. After lighting the cigar and he and Collins had taken their drink, Hern asked me to walk down to his place. I had heard him tell Collins that he wanted to sell his business, that his partner wanted to leave town.

Hern and I walked to his saloon, a block from the Turf, and on entering, Hern introduced me to Dave Spears, his partner. Spears was a keen-eyed, sharp-faced man about thirty years of age. Hern was probably thirty-six, and both of them were bachelors and products of Dodge City, Kansas. In reality, they were gamblers, Spears a faro bank dealer and Hern a monte dealer. Gambling in Woodward had become quiet for them. They had come to Woodward with the opening of the Cherokee Strip for settlement and figured they had seen the best of the gambling season and wanted to move on west.

After discussing their business for several hours, looking over the facilities in great detail, inventorying stock and fixtures and figuring what their license was worth, they made me a price. I told them I would talk to them further the next morning. I went to my room and figured everything closely and found they were offering me a bargain, but I lacked one hundred dollars of having money enough. They had very little stock, the license was half used, and they were renting the building. The license and stock invoiced $600, and they offered it to me for $550. I observed, however, that one of them seemed over-anxious to sell, and he confided that he had been there as long as it appeared safe for his liberty and health.

The next morning, about eight, I went to their place, called the Shamrock. I walked in, and, after the usual "good mornings" I said, "Boys, your proposition is fair and reasonable, and I'm sorry I haven't enough money to deal with you, as I have only $450, but if it will do you more good than this joint, then maybe we can do business."

They went into the back room and talked for ten minutes, then came out. Hern said, "Gober, you look like a real man, and we must be away from here, so we had just as well give you $150 as to take a chance of losing all and then some." The deal was verbally concluded, and they sent for a lawyer, A. G. Cunningham, and had him draw a transfer of license and a bill of sale for the stock and fixtures. In an hour all was concluded. As I thought back about what had transpired, it was quite interesting that I had landed in Woodward, broke after eating one meal; had been there less than seventy-two hours; and had become the owner and proprietor of a saloon, the Shamrock Saloon to be specific.

Trouble on the Horizon

The evening that followed my acquiring the saloon, I took a walk up Main Street to exercise and take a general survey of the town. As I was passing a small office I noticed four men congregated in front and heard cursing. I stopped and soon discovered that three men with six-shooters belted on their hips were abusing an elderly man. When I glanced up at the sign in front of the office I noticed that it read "B. B. Smith, County Attorney." Then I guessed that the old man was the county attorney and the gunmen had some grievance against him. Sensing a terrible injustice about to happen, I stepped in reach of the fellow that was making some wicked threats, just in time to catch his right hand as he threw it on his gun. I said to him calmly but forcefully, "My friend, you would be a terrible coward to hit or shoot a man that is old enough to be your father, and besides, this seems to be a three-pluck-one game which shows, on the face of it, you have no spirit of justice or fairness in your heart."

Oil painting by Bruce Marshall of Tobe Odem, cowboy, rancher, and sheriff of
Woodward County, Oklahoma Territory, 1895-97. Courtesy Carole Dean, Studio
Film and Tape, Hollywood.

The men all turned, facing me, and the old gentleman stepped
inside his office and closed the door. The mad gunman asked, "Who
are you, and what in the hell business is the affair to you?"

"I'm Jim Gober, and I am an American citizen who believes in
square dealing." Just then, Tobe Odem appeared on the scene and
asked what they were trying to start. I spoke to Odem and grasped
his hand, as it was the first opportunity I had had to meet him since
I had been in Woodward. Then I smiled and said, "Odem, these boys
had rung up a three-pluck-one game on Mr. Smith, and I didn't think
it fair. You know, that's downright cheating in Texas. A man that
would play that game would be hung."

Odem smiled and introduced the three and informed me that they
were his deputies. I have had shocking statements made to me before,
so I was not overwhelmed with surprise, but then and there I knew
the cause of the lawlessness in this town. A bunch of cowardly thieves
were law officers, and they had gotten Odem's confidence, or else. The
"else" I will leave to the reader to guess.

About nine PM, after the escapade with the deputies, Odem and the same three deputies, joined by two additional deputies, came into my saloon and greeted me in the friendliest manner possible. The five deputies and their superior officer had several rounds of drinks and remained possibly thirty minutes. These deputies, by name, were John and Ben Gholston, brothers; Billie Arnold; Bob Norwell; and Ben Prior, who was a brother-in-law to Odem. They all wore cowboy clothes, boots, and spurs, convincing me they had been driving cattle. Ben Gholston seemed to be the leader, and he and Odem did about all the talking.

When they had left, I closed my saloon and went to the Turf Saloon and took Mr. Collins in the back room and said, "Collins, I have just had a visit from the sheriff and his five deputies, and the cause of the lawlessness in this vicinity is solved to my complete satisfaction. You have no peace officers; instead, you have a band of thieves pretending to be officers. I am greatly surprised to find Tobe Odem entangled with crooks."

Collins calmly and earnestly said, "I am not only surprised but mortified, but I am even afraid to talk to Odem on this subject, and I advise you to keep your own counsel. These men don't care for human life and will murder anyone that gets in their way. Such situations will run their course and always come to an abrupt end when such men least expect it. I feel confident they will not bother you or your business, for Odem will post them as to who you are and what you are, and they are not taking such chances as to start a roughhouse in your place."

While I understood what Collins meant, he had not completely understood my innermost thoughts, so I responded, "I am not thinking of myself or my business, but I'm worrying over Odem's part in this gang, and I'm wondering how they got him tangled in with them. I aim to have a heart-to-heart talk with Odem and find out what strings they have on him, and I mean more! I mean to free him from their grasp."

Collins replied, "If any man can, I know you are the man to do it!"

A Sheriff's Sad Revelation

Now I learned that these five deputy sheriffs were operating mostly in Beaver County and would be out of Woodward ten or fifteen days at a time. Ben Gholston owned or maintained a ranch in Beaver County, and three other boys besides the ones I've already mentioned

All the time I was speaking, Odem sat with his eyes fixed on the floor. Finally he raised his head and told me to proceed. I did proceed by saying, "I want to know just what this bunch of thieves has on you that you are supporting them with commissions as deputy sheriffs?"

worked under Ben's supervision. They were Billie and Johnnie Hill and Tom Waddell. The Hill boys' parents lived in Beaver County, which had been known as No Man's Land or Neutral Strip, and these Hill boys also had been raised there.

I waited patiently for my opportunity to catch Odem strictly sober and this bad bunch out of town. Finally my chance came, and I met Odem and shook his hand and looked straight in his gray eyes and said, "Tobe, you have known me from when I was a sixteen-year-old boy, and you no doubt know my record as a man and as sheriff of Potter County. I likewise have known your activities for the past twenty-five years, and I have always appreciated you as being a square man and a man that was true and loyal to any trust or obligation entrusted to you. As man to man, I want to ask you a question with the intention that your answer will solve a mystery in my mind. I assure you it is only the high regard and respect I have for you that concerns me." All the time that I was speaking, Odem sat with his eyes fixed on the floor. Finally he raised his head and told me to proceed. I did proceed by saying, "I want to know just what this bunch of thieves has on you that you are supporting them with commissions as deputy sheriffs?"

After a few minutes of silent meditation, Odem looked me square in the eye and said, "Jim, carelessness and whiskey has gotten me in a mess, but I'm going to cut loose at any cost!" I grasped him by the hand and laid my left hand on his shoulder and assured him I would come to his aid day or night, at his request.

Epilog to an Untenable Situation

Soon after this, the grand jury met and found true bill for theft of cattle against Ben Gholston, Johnnie and Billie Hill, and Tom Waddell. Gholston gave bond, and the other three were locked up in the Woodward County Jail. Bob Norwell and Johnnie Gholston were the jail deputies, and a few days before court was convened, some Winchesters were left outside the jail cells. Johnnie Gholston pretended to go to dinner and left the jail door unlocked, and, instead of dinner, he spread the alarm that the prisoners had broken out of jail.

Poor old John L. Sullivan,[1] of Texas Ranger bull and some fame, was in Woodward and joined a posse to capture the prisoners. Besides Sullivan, there was Gene Hall,[2] Ben Wolforth,[3] Constable Funkhouser, and several others.

The fugitives were sighted in the sand hills near the north Canadian River, where a battle started and Johnnie Hill was killed, Tom Waddell feigned death, and Ben Wolforth lost an arm. The plot was to get the Hill boys and Waddell killed to keep them from squealing, also to lay the cattle stealing on the dead men and clear Ben Gholston. Unfortunately for them, they only succeeded in killing one, leaving two to testify. This dirty deal was so plain that the two witnesses, with vengeance in their hearts, told it all when the court convened.

Ben Gholston, a Woodward County deputy sheriff, was sentenced to serve seven years in the penitentiary at Leavenworth, Kansas. After receiving sentence, Tobe Odem started to take him to jail but lost him on the way, and then the Gholstons left for parts unknown.

Just a few years ago, Johnnie Hill's brother, who was only a twelve-year-old lad when his brother was murdered, shot Ben Goldston dead in a saloon in El Paso. Arnold died in Wyoming, and Norwell

Elsie Moody Byler, secretary to Temple Houston, posing on a sandy, deserted Main Street, Woodward, Oklahoma Territory, ca. 1896-98. Courtesy Plains Indians and Pioneer Museum, Woodward, Oklahoma.

in Arkansas. Thus the Woodward County lawless went the route that all crooks and thieves must go, either by the hand and brain of man or providence.

The Continuing Saga of Temple Houston

About January 1895, Temple Houston came to Woodward and opened a law office. I was glad indeed to have him locate in Woodward, and still, deep down in my heart, I was grieved that he had left Texas, where he could have had any place of honor and distinction as a gift of the people.

I once questioned Houston as to why he had sacrificed his beautiful home in that old home state where we were both born and raised. In his case, it appeared to me that such a compelling case existed for him to feel a part of that legacy and remain in Texas. After all, wasn't the name of his father, General Sam Houston, the hero of San Jacinto, on the lips of all Texans and permanently in their memory?

Temple Houston at Beaver,
Oklahoma Territory, ca. 1894.
Courtesy Plains Indians and
Pioneer Museum, Woodward,
Oklahoma.

My questioning of Houston, however, seemed to strike a bad chord with him. His face flushed, and his brow wrinkled from the passion of anger, and his sharp gray eyes were fixed in a stare as though he was looking at the past through a pair of field glasses. Then he shook his head until his long, curly, auburn hair waved like dry leaves trembling from the breeze. He slammed his clenched fist on the table where we were sitting and said, "By the eternal God, I told my friends before the last fall election that if Judge B. M. Baker was reelected district judge, I would leave the state of Texas, for I refused to practice law where as unscrupulous and unfair a man is allowed to preside as judge. He was elected, and I have made my word good." This act of Houston's is only one of many instances where he allowed his temper and disposition he had so thoroughly inherited from his father cause far-reaching disaster to his future welfare and success.

I had had contact with Houston in 1888, while I was serving as sheriff of Potter County, Texas. The business of the sheriff's office had taken me to Austin, Texas, and while I was there I was able to watch an interstate drill competition, featuring a drill company from each state in the union. While I am not positive which company Temple Houston was with, I believe it was the one from Houston that had won the Texas competition that year. Temple wore an officer's uniform and seemed to be not only the sharpest dressed officer but also the best performer. He impressed me as being the most mild-tempered young fellow I had ever met. I was to learn more about his temper as time went on.

At the fall term of the county court in Amarillo in 1888, I was once again to be involved with Temple Houston, for he and W. H. Woodman were the most distinguished lawyers and by far the most conspicuous. The three of us were inseparable and could be seen together, except when court was in session. Woodman, like Houston, wore his hair long, and it was raven black, while Houston's was auburn. Both men had taken a special liking to me, and I want to say at this juncture that I had learned a great deal about law from them. Being in their company quite a bit of the time, hearing them discuss cases and telling what they expected to prove by certain witnesses, and then being in the courtroom and hearing them argue cases before the juries was a wonderful educational opportunity for me. These two men, Houston and Woodman, were and remained my staunch friends during their lifetimes.

Temple Houston had made a great sacrifice when he left Texas on account of an unfair judge, only to come to Woodward, where the probate judge had three sons practicing law. That judge was old man Jennings;[4] his sons were Ed, John, and Al,[5] and whichever side of the case any one of these boys was on was the side that won.

Houston tried three cases in Judge Jennings's court. They were all decided against Houston's client, and after the decision in the third case, Houston addressed the judge and Ed Jennings in a mild but positive manner. He read the law and repeated the evidence he had introduced on behalf of his client and said, "Gentlemen, I beg of you not to pass me any more deals from a cold deck." In a few days there came up another case in which Houston represented one side and Ed and John Jennings the other. Houston calmly left the courtroom, went home, got his long .45-caliber Colts, and came back on the trail of the Jenningses. He found them in Jack Garvey's saloon. Houston shot Ed Jennings through the heart, killing him instantly. John Jennings ran, but Houston shot his arm off as he went out the front door.

The Jenningses left Woodward in a few days and moved to eastern Oklahoma. Soon afterwards, Al Jennings and Morris O'Malley organized a band of train robbers and safe crackers before their gang was killed or captured. Al Jennings went to the penitentiary for a long term but was shrewd enough to get very religious and preached to the prisoners. Finally, he received a pardon, came back home, and ran for governor and came close to being elected. Just five or six years ago he made a tour of California, lecturing, and large audiences attended.

Houston stood trial for killing Ed and was fined one thousand dollars and court costs. The costs were paid and the fine remitted. About two years later, Houston's oldest boy, then fourteen years of age, had a saddle pony, and Houston made him put the pony in a pasture belonging to a man named Jenkins. He was from Tennessee and had not been in Oklahoma long. Jenkins was a tall, raw-boned man, slow talking and slow moving. Houston's son concluded he wanted the pony and had taken his bridle and had walked three miles to Jenkins's house without any money to pay pasturage. Jenkins refused to let him take the pony.

The boy walked back to town, and I saw him approach his father, standing in front of Charlie Cutter's saloon. While they were still talking, Jenkins rode up on a very tall horse. Quick as lightning, Houston drew his .45 and fired two shots in quick succession. Jenkins fell from his horse; the shots had struck him just above the heart and ranged upward, lodging behind the shoulders. By the time the court convened, Jenkins was gone. Houston stood trial and was fined one thousand dollars for aggravated assault. The cost was finally paid and the fine remitted.[6]

Several times while Al Jennings was an outlaw, it was reported that he was in hiding in Woodward. Each time, Houston would visit every place he thought Jennings might hang out. However, I felt sure that these reports were only a hoax, for I knew well enough Al Jennings did not want to meet Houston.

The Jennings Epilog

Ten years after the Jennings left Woodward, I had occasion to go from Kenton, Oklahoma,[7] an old cow town on the Cimarron River, fifty miles northeast of Clayton, New Mexico, thence to Springfield, Colorado. Just as I left the breaks of the North Carrizo[8] and topped the level plains in Baca County, Colorado, I noticed some rocks laid as though they had been foundations for houses in years past. When I returned from my trip several days later, I asked an old man by the name of Arnold, who had been in the country forty years, if there ever was a ranch at this locality. He replied laughingly, "No, those rocks are all that was left of a glowing city, mostly on paper." He informed me that "about 1889, one Judge Jennings and his four sons had squatted on land there and had put up a shack sufficient to comply with the homestead law. The land cornering made it convenient for them to put their five shacks near each other. Then they proceeded to plot a town. They had a blueprint made showing a railroad, courthouse, schoolhouse and various business houses. The judge went east and sold the vacant lots to people in Kansas City, Saint Louis, and Chicago. After a month, the judge was still selling lots and thoroughly and extensively advertising the young city of New Boston, situated on the fertile plains of Baca County, Colorado."

Arnold continued with the story, "All of a sudden, about twenty men arrived to inspect their purchase. Upon their arrival, Jennings disappeared under the cover of night." With that story, I learned more of the character of Woodward's first probate judge and his four sons, Frank, Ed, John, and Al.

Back in Woodward, business was rather quiet. It was now the latter part of February 1896, and as time dragged along, my business picked up slowly, but I felt good to have a business of my own with the prospect of doing better. Now I could send my wife and babies a little money each month. My plans were that when I was able and the town became more civilized, I could have them with me once more. All these bright hopes gave me courage and ambition to help me regain my health and strength.

I began to feel more cheerful, and the world began to look brighter, but I realized soon that I had a poor business location. By the first of June, a man had closed out a small stock of dry goods in a building that he owned, and it was in a desirable location, so I rented his building and moved in. My business doubled the first week, and soon I had to have another bartender and was taking in from thirty to fifty dollars per day. The problem with lawlessness, however, seemed to continue. Every few nights some saloon, or perhaps two or three, would get shot up, but I was lucky and never had that misfortune.

The government land office employed twelve men, all appointees, and most all of them were from Kentucky and Tennessee. They were all well-bred men and gentlemen, but all drank to some extent and liked to have a poker game among themselves. They quickly learned of my code of honor and fair play, so soon I had their patronage exclusively.

My business was growing nicely, and by the first of January I had bought out a man in the restaurant business that joined the place I was renting. I remodeled the building and moved my saloon into my own building, on my own land. At the same time, I bought another lot with a two-room house on it to use as a temporary dwelling.[9]

About July, my father-in-law had some law business in Taloga, Oklahoma.[10] He had to come to Woodward and took the mail hack to Taloga, a distance of sixty-five miles. He spent one day and night with me, and we were both elated over my recovery of health and also my prosperity. We talked over the town being rough and wild, and I asked his advice about bringing my wife and babies to Woodward. The judge answered by saying, "I realize your feelings, Jim, and also Belle's, and know that you would be more contented being together. I feel you are capable of taking care of yourselves in any place where people have a chance of making a go of it."

At this time, I knew that my father, eighty-four years old, had been sick for four months in Amarillo. In a few days I got a wire to come at once, and when I arrived in Amarillo, my father had already died.

After the funeral, my wife and I remained with Mother a few days, and during this time she packed her and the babies' belongings. We departed Amarillo to start a new life together in Woodward. Once more, I was happy, and so was my faithful little wife. I soon bought a choice location for a residence and moved the contents of our two-room house into it. We built onto it two more rooms, making a cozy little home.

My business was still increasing, so I moved the building occupied by my saloon back thirty feet, built a front section for the saloon, and used the back building for a gambling house. I set up two poker games, a monte game, a crap game, and a roulette wheel and had a four-piece orchestra to play music two hours each evening.

In 1897, we had a baby girl born, and we were both elated. My business kept me so busy on the job that it didn't allow me much time to be at home—only at mealtime, and from twelve at night until six in the morning.

My presence on the job was the only assurance of having no disturbances. I never took a drink of intoxicating liquor, was always sober and watching all activities. If a man showed signs of causing a disturbance, I took him by the arm in a friendly way and led him to one side and told him that if he wanted me to treat him nice and be his friend, he must show me and my establishment the same respect. I explained further that I was under bond to keep an orderly house and intended to do so to the extent of my physical and mental abilities, and absolutely, there must not be any trouble in my place of business. In a few instances I would have to lead one to the door and tell him not to come back until he could come peaceably and act like a gentleman.

There was no doubt in my mind that my reputation as a Texas Panhandle cowboy and lawman had followed me here to the badlands of the Oklahoma Territory, a reputation not only of dealing fairly and squarely with all men and expecting the same in return but also of a total lack of fear of any man or any situation in which I might become involved according to my code of fair play. It was well known that I wasn't gun- or bad-man shy.

Briefly, a Lawman in Woodward County

The way I conducted my business and my personal life made me many friends, and I had the patronage of most of the business and professional men of the town. In 1898, when the Populist[11] wave struck Oklahoma, Woodward elected a Populist sheriff by the name of Bob Benn. Ben didn't have any education, and it seemed the popular feeling was that the only spirit of action recognizable in him was that of laughing.

Tobe Odem had decided not to run, and the businessmen got together and insisted that I should accept the under sheriff position to make things more efficient and to guarantee protection. So I, a Texas Democrat, was chosen under sheriff,[12] and, since I had remained concerned about the rough and wild nature of that area and the lawlessness that still existed, I accepted. In the following months I did what I saw that needed to be done, and I got along fine with Benn. I commanded the respect of all classes, and soon men's lives and property were considered safe. For this I claim no honor or credit except that of using good, cool judgment and meeting every man on the same level and favoring and fearing none.

In about a year, a man named Jeff Mynatt,[13] who I had known as a deputy marshal that had gone to Montana in the early eighties, arrived back in the Woodward area. In Montana, Mynatt had a special contingent of man killers to kill cowpunchers at five dollars a head

189

Jeff Mynatt, deputy sheriff of
Woodward County 1897-99, ca.
1899. Courtesy Plains Indians
and Pioneer Museum,
Woodward, Oklahoma.

during what was termed the "Rustlers War."[14] In reality, this was the
big cattle companies trying to run the little cattlemen and sheep men
out of business. This Mynatt was on a drunk and had been wallowing
around in the back rooms of saloons for a week. It was known
generally that he was a capable fellow when sober. Tobe Odem, who
had been sheriff of Woodward before Benn, knew Mynatt and recommended him highly to Benn. So Benn picked Mynatt up out of the
gutter, bought him a new suit of clothes, and took him to his house.

After a few days, Benn asked me if I wouldn't let Mynatt have my
place as under sheriff and explained that my running a saloon and
performing as under sheriff was not popular with some of the people.
My reply to Benn was, "Certainly. I only accepted the position for your
best interests and the interests of the citizens, but I warn you now,
you may regret picking up Mynatt."

In three months, Mynatt had shown the sheriff up short in his accounts with the county. The sheriff had left the state, and Mynatt was acting sheriff until the next election. He was elected sheriff of Woodward, and during his two-year term he got in debt to the Gerlach Bank[15] and to several merchants and was beaten in the following election. When this happened, Mynatt got on a drunk, cussed all his creditors out, and left the country. He went to Houston, Texas, got a job as a railroad bull and later was killed by a Negro.

A man named Woods[16] beat Mynatt on the Republican ticket for sheriff. As soon as Woods had taken office, he visited me and stuck a commission as deputy in my pocket without mentioning it to me. Woods, however, served well as sheriff.

A Return to the Cowboy Life

Beginning a Major Ranching Adventure

The saloon business was beginning to wear on me, so I traded it for cattle and fell back to my old calling, that of being a cowboy. I had acquired title to six hundred acres of land—well-watered, fine grazing land—and one hundred of the acres could be farmed. The land was located four miles west of Woodward, lying parallel with the Santa Fe Railroad. About 640 acres of additional grazing land also adjoined my land, and I could use and control it and have a nice little farm and ranch.

So I had a four-room house built, and I fenced all the land. Since the Santa Fe Railroad was fenced on both sides, that gave me the advantage of joining the two properties and saving one mile of fence. As soon as my house was completed, we moved from Woodward to our new ranch.

When all preparations had been made, I went to March Sandiford's ranch, twenty-five miles from Panhandle City, Texas, on Antelope Creek,[1] and purchased twenty-one hand-picked mares that were of the old LX Ranch stock, well-bred thoroughbreds. I took them to my ranch, where they joined two hundred head of cattle. With this little ranch, necessarily, I would have to have more range or dispose of some the cattle.

About this time, A. J. Chapman, who had joint ownership with C. R. Smith of an undivided interest of a large pasture in Woods County,[2] came to see me. This property was twelve miles square and located thirty-five miles east of Woodward. He proposed that, if I would take charge of his and Smith's interests, they would stock the range with not less than three thousand head of yearling steers and give me one-third of the profit when the steers were three years old and put on the market. Besides, I could run my cattle free.

After a careful study, I told Mr. Chapman that if he and Smith would divide the pasture with the other owners, who were Cap Ed Morris and Will Maxwell, and have his (Chapman's) and Smith's part of the pasture cut off to themselves by a partitioning fence, I would accept his offer. Mr. Chapman agreed and went back to the Chapman and Morris Ranch, as it was known, to get an agreement from all three of the other parties concerned. All parties agreed, and they divided the range, agreeing on specified meets and bounds. Chapman and Smith put men to work at once building the partition fence.

I gave much thought to the major adventure I was about to undertake. As my mind flashed back to my cowboy past, in some ways it seemed as though it had been decades since I had begun my life as a cowboy: a pink-cheeked kid of fifteen, enthusiastic on the one hand about the adventure that lay up the trail with Lock Forester and yet on the other hand scared stiff about the prospects of having to climb on a bronc and ride him until he was tame. I thought about the hard lessons I had learned under Crow Wright, but I had learned them, all right, and I had become a knowledgeable, seasoned cowboy from those experiences. Where I earned the cowboy leather was on the Frying Pan Ranch. There wasn't a single job as a cowpoke that I didn't have, and I certainly knew the thrills and the pains of moving cattle hundreds of miles, establishing a new ranch in a place where none had been before, and the painstaking involvement in every part of making that new ranch work. Later, my experiences on the LX Ranch served to qualify me as a senior cowboy and a trail boss.

What a great feeling it was, having gotten my earlier, practical knowledge of the cowboy trade, as I was about to jump headlong into this major undertaking. It was now up to me as a new ranch manager to apply what the good Lord had led me to learn, and to apply it well.

This range lay in rough country between the Cimarron and the Canadian Rivers, and it had a tough set scattered around in the canyons. That locality had the reputation of being the rendezvous for train robbers and other outlaws, such as the Daltons,[3] Red Buck,[4] George Miller,[5] and the Al Jennings gang. They had all been known to make themselves at home in this particular locality.

Cap Morris's nephew, who had run the ranch for several years, was said to show the outlaws special favors. I knew him personally, and I knew he was so crooked that he couldn't follow a straight road anyplace, and Cap Morris had finally discharged him. After that, he had jumped on one of the headquarters ranch locations and was becoming an annoyance and a nuisance to the whole outfit. I knew all these things, and that is why I didn't care to have the responsibility of protecting Morris's and Maxwell's interests when I was officially interested only in my connection with Smith and Chapman.

Establishing a Ranch Headquarters

At this time, my older brother was with me again, and I had also hired a boy, twenty years old, by the name of Wade Bowie. I knew his father in the Panhandle, and I had also known when this boy's mother had died and remembered hearing when Mr. Bowie married the second time. The boy told me that he had left home shortly after his father married the second wife. I had a lot of sympathy and concern about this boy, so I decided to take him on as a hired hand.

With much to be done, I left my brother on our ranch with my family, four miles from Woodward, and took Wade and a Negro boy that I had raised to age seventeen years to establish a headquarters ranch for the new adventure I had undertaken.

I picked out a location for our camp on Main Creek. On the ranch a boiling spring broke out at the foot of a large, rocky bluff and drained off through a valley to Main Creek. We leveled off a place close to the bluff which would shelter our improvements from the north. We made a space about twelve by eighteen feet, and we dug it about four feet in the ground. Then we cut nice, straight cottonwood poles, ten feet long; took the bark off of them; and set them up on end against each other all the way around, making the walls of our house. We left space for one door and two windows, and a larger cottonwood was placed in the center, at each end, with a fork in the end. Then still a larger one that reached from one fork to the other was placed, making the center brace for the dirt roof. We then laid smaller poles from the outside walls to the center log, called the ridge pole. Then we cut willow brush and laid it crossways on the small poles to make a bed for the dirt. Next, we mixed the first layer like mortar and spread it over the willow brush. Then we put on dry dirt to a depth of six inches, and we had a perfectly dry, comfortable, ranch headquarters house.

I had been corresponding with an old friend that I had known in the Panhandle in the early eighties, Jim Dobbs, . . . and he informed me that his neighbor had two hundred steers, two years old, for sale, and gave me the price, and it was reasonable. So I outfitted a camp wagon, took three men and a cook, and hit the trail for my old friend's home on the Washita.

With the ranch headquarters now constructed, we then went to Woodward and moved my cattle to the Woods County Ranch and moved my wife and babies back to our home in Woodward, as it would be much more convenient for me during the coming fall and winter. Then I would be able to ride ten miles to a railroad station and get to Woodward in an hour from the station. I expected to spend about half of my time with my wife and babies during the winter.

I was able to notify Mr. A. J. Chapman that I was ready to receive cattle to stock our pasture. He went to Kansas City and made arrangements with the Drumm-Flato Commission Company[6] to cash my draft for any cattle I might buy but advised me not to buy too heavily, as cattle were high at present and would get cheap by the next spring.

I had been corresponding with an old friend that I had known in the Panhandle in the early eighties, Jim Dobbs, and he was an experienced cowman, well posted as to who had cattle for sale, and the price. He was now living in Custer County, Oklahoma, on the

Washita River, and he informed me that his neighbor had two hundred steers, two years old, for sale and gave me the price, and it was reasonable. So I outfitted a camp wagon, took three men and a cook, and hit the trail for my old friend's home on the Washita.

The next day, after arriving at the Dobbses' house, we went and looked at the two hundred head. We found that the owners were two brothers named Gibson that I had known when we were small children in Denton County, Texas. After looking over the cattle, I bought them at one dollar less on the head than the quoted price. I also bought several small bunches of cattle and one bunch of 250 head of mixed cattle. We returned to Woods County with five hundred head of cattle purchased at a very reasonable price for our new company, Smith, Chapman, and Gober.

Mr. Chapman and Mr. Smith both lived at Gainesville, Texas, twenty-two miles from Bolivar, my childhood home. Both Smith and Chapman corresponded with me regularly, and we decided not to buy any more cattle until the next spring. That left me with five hundred head of company cattle and two hundred head of my own personal cattle. We had plenty of grass and water for them and enough for more cattle, if I had had them.

Dealing with a Rustling Mind Set

That summer, a man by the name of R. C. Edmanson had leased range from Cap Morris and Will Maxwell and moved twelve hundred head of cattle from near Chickisha, Oklahoma. Later he had discovered some watered land in the range that was subject to homestead entry, and he filed on one quarter section. He built a house and took possession of a choice part of Cap Morris's and Maxwell's range. His quarter section claim adjoined our area on the west, so he had no fence to build.

Not long after he got himself located, the Drumm-Flato Commission Company sent out a man by the name of Jim Brison to count Edmanson's cattle. It seems that they had loaned him a large sum of money on the cattle that were represented to be a certain quantity as well as designated classes. John Mosely had thrown in with Edmanson, pretending to be helping gather and count the cattle. Brison was an expert cowman and caught them counting the same cattle twice, and he made a report by wire to the Drumm-Flato Commission Company that the cattle were short by four hundred head and that Edmanson was crooked. The company immediately sent Brison the notes and mortgages secured by the cattle, with instructions to gather and ship in all he could find.

Edmanson would pretend to help Brison gather the cattle in the daytime and have some of his men driving off small bunches at night. After Brison gathered all he could find, the commission company sent me the mortgage and notes with instructions to gather the balance, if a balance could be found. The commission was, of course, carrying my new cattle deal and impressed the fact on my mind that they expected me to protect them, especially in my locality.

I immediately wrote Mr. R. C. Edmanson a friendly but at the same time strictly plain business letter and put Wade Bowie on a horse and sent him to Edmanson's ranch to deliver it. The letter explained to Mr. Edmanson my instructions and that I was obliged to protect any legitimate interest of the Drumm-Flato Commission Company, but at the same time, in this particular deal, I wished to treat him fair and just and would like to have his assistance and his goodwill. I also mentioned the fact that it was then late in November, and the cattle had been handled roughly and should be put on rough feed, at least if they were to go through the winter. He was also advised as to what location I would round up the next day.

I didn't get any reply, so the next day I rounded up in the extreme western part of the range and got sixteen head, and the brand had been burned into another brand. These cattle were taken to our new headquarters ranch, and they were put in a small pasture we had fenced off as a horse pasture for our saddle horses.

That evening, I rode to a little country store and post office. There I met Edmanson, and he shook hands with me and said, "I am glad you are going to gather those cattle. I couldn't get out to help you today but will be with you tomorrow. Where will you work tomorrow?" Then I told him the part of the pasture I would work the next day, but when next day came, once again Edmanson didn't show up. We got fifteen more head of cattle over-marked, the same as those of the previous day, and we took them to the same small pasture where we had left the ones from the previous day. When we got to the ranch area with the second bunch, we discovered that the first bunch was gone.

It was almost dark, and I knew it would be morning before I could do any good trailing, so I went to a wire gate leading out in the direction of Edmanson's ranch. Sure enough, I found tracks indicating that the cattle had gone through that gate. Also, there were tracks of two horses indicating that two men had been involved in driving the cattle away.

Next morning I sent John Jones and Jim Barclay to pick up the trail of the stolen cattle and stay on it if possible. I was to strike south to the Canadian River and ride a line ten or twelve miles up the river and see if the cattle had crossed. John Jones was an ex-sheriff of Clayton, New Mexico, that I had known for years as a cowboy before he had served as sheriff. I had hired him to work for me on the new pool ranch with a view of having a dependable man to leave in charge during any of my future absences. Jim Barclay was also a friend of long standing and was representing the Texas Cattle Raisers' Association as an inspector and agent for stray cattle.

I met Barclay at the Canadian River, and he informed me that he and John had found twenty head of Edmanson cattle about ten miles up the river near Dock Black's ranch. These cattle had the brands fresh burned into and over an older brand. The new brand was B, and the old brand on the cattle was 5, a brand easy to convert into a B.

Jones had taken the cattle back to our ranch. Apparently, the stolen bunch had crossed the river and was supposed to be near Seiling,[7] in the possession of a butcher by the name of Allbright. It was ten miles south of the river to Seiling, and the sun was just setting, so we decided to ride on into Seiling that night and put our horses in the livery barn and go to bed at the hotel. Our plan was to get up in time to get to Allbright's by sunup the next morning and to catch the cattle before he had them out of the feedlot.

We were up by daybreak the next morning, went to the livery barn, woke up the stable man, and saddled our ponies and struck for Allbright's. When we arrived, we found the cattle, as we had expected, in the feedlot. We dismounted and went to the front door, where Barclay knocked loud enough that I believe it could have been heard in the next county. In a few minutes, a woman opened the door, just enough to see us, and started to close it, but Barclay shoved his foot in between the door and the jamb. He held the small open space and told her we were after those cattle and asked her to tell Mr. Allbright to come out. She replied, "Mr. Allbright isn't at home."

Then I asked her where Mr. Allbright had gotten the cattle, and she replied that she didn't know. I said, "Lady, you tell your husband that Jim Gober got the cattle, and he will understand that he and Edmanson have failed at stealing one bunch."

We went to the corral and turned the cattle out and hit the trail for home. That night, we stayed overnight and corraled our cattle at Mr. Hoogs, which was about halfway to our ranch. The next day we got home, and the following day I took Barclay, Jones, Wade Bowie, and Fred Wagoner and went to Edmanson's ranch and rounded up his home pasture. We took about fifteen cows and calves that he had been weaning, and it was obvious that he had intended putting a different brand on them once they were weaned. From that time on until February 1899, I gathered 336 head of cattle scattered over three counties, and 16 head was the most I found in any one place.

Edmanson, his nephew, and Otis Guthrie, who worked for Edmanson, had driven these cattle to different thieves they happened to know and left them to be disposed of as they could. When I would locate a bunch and asked the man that had them in his possession where he got them, every man gave me the same answer, "A man left them with me to feed them." I would ask each one what that man's name was, and the fellow would study a minute and say, "I can't remember."

Then I would say, "Well, you are in a rather awkward position, for I am taking the cattle."

After I had worked the country thoroughly, and had gotten all the cattle I could find, I bought feed, such as Kaffir corn[8] and hay, from the farmers along the Cimarron River and cut the cattle in bunches sufficient to consume the amount of feed at each farm. I had it in each contract that the farmer would distribute the feed to the cattle and care for them each day. Once or twice a week I would ride through the cattle and see that they were being cared for according to contract. Although the cattle were poor, I got them through the winter with only a loss of six head.

The Incident at Griener Canyon

Late in the fall I rented a place on the Cimarron River valley, a small farm with a two-room log house, a log barn, and a good corral. I rented it from an old bachelor by the name of Mason, and I moved our camp there for the winter. South of our camp, about eight miles, was rough, broken country and a large canyon called Griener Canyon.[9] In the canyon was a scattered settlement, and during this winter they often had dances.

While I was in Kansas City on business, Jones, Wade Bowie, Fred Wagoner, and one of Cap Morris's men went to Griener to a dance,

Courtesy Private Collection

While I was in Kansas City on business, Jones, Wade Bowie, Fred Wagoner and one of Cap Morris's men went to Griener to a dance, and after they had danced for an hour, they went out to see if their horses were all right. They found that Jones's and Lee Stallings's horses and saddles were gone.

and after they had danced for an hour, they went out to see if their horses were all right. They found that Jones's and Lee Stallings's horses and saddles were gone. Then they went back in the house and checked up on the crowd and found that two suspicious characters by the name of Loppin were missing. Lee Stallings knew where they had been camping, in a dugout about six miles from the dance. He and Jones got on Bowie and Wagoner's horses and made a straight ride for Loppin's camp. When they got there, they tied their horses under a bluff and went into the dugout to wait for the Loppins to return. In half an hour they rode up and came in, not suspecting that anyone was in the dugout. When they walked in, Jones and Stallings threw their guns on them, disarmed them, and then Jones asked them what they had done with the horses and saddles. They denied any knowledge of them. Then Jones told Stallings to get a rope off Bowie's saddle and bring it to him. When Stallings came in with the rope, Jones told him to cut off enough to tie these fellows' feet and hands and that he proposed hanging them. Stallings cut one piece of the rope off, and one of the Loppins squawked, saying, "We turned your horses loose and hid the saddles and bridles in a cave, and we will show you where they are." So Jones and Stallings went with them to a cave that the opening was not more than four feet in diameter but widened out and ran several hundred yards under the earth. Jones sent one of them into the cave after the saddles, bridles, and also Mexican blankets. It took the fellow some thirty minutes to bring them out.

After getting the saddles, bridles and blankets out, Jones made the Loppin brothers take their saddles off their ponies, which were a pair of nice little mares, and they started riding for our camp. The ground was covered with snow when they got to our camp about noon. Negro Sam made them dinner, and after they ate, Jones told the Loppins that Gober would be in sometime that evening and would take them to Alva,[10] the county seat, and put them in jail, but if they would give him their ponies and agree to never be in our pasture again, they might depart free men. They thanked Jones and lit out on foot in the snow and never were heard of in our part of the country.

I got in the next evening, and Jones told what he had done and all the circumstances leading up to the end of the episode. The tale was both amusing and disgusting, and I told Jones that by all means he should have held the fellows until I came and that he should get the ponies off his hands as soon as possible. However, we had so far caught every thief that attempted any depredation on us, and they would probably turn the tables on us sooner or later.

Now the winter of 1898 was over, and it had been a mild winter, and the effects of it were over by April 1899. All my cattle had wintered fairly well, and I was insisting with Mr. Chapman and Mr. Smith for an understanding as to stocking the range to a reasonable capacity, and they were putting me off from time to time.

I had made personal friends with Major Drumm[11] and Billy Flato,[12] the president and vice-president of the Drumm-Flato Commission Company, and they put me on a regular salary of five dollars per day and expenses as an outside man and kept me investigating bad deals. Where a man was found short on a number of cattle or was mismanaging his cattle, I would have to go and take charge and ship what he owed to the company or dispose of them to the best advantage, according to my judgment.

On June 14, 1899, we had another baby girl born. Everyone thought she resembled me so distinctly that we named her Jimmye. We now had two boys and two girls, and we were as happy as it was possible for us to be. My oldest sister, who was a widow with two

Polk Street, Amarillo, ca. 1900. Courtesy *Amarillo, Texas: The First Hundred Years 1887-1987*, a Picture Postcard History (Amarillo: Ray Franks Publishing Ranch).

children, had come to live with us for awhile, and she was of a nature to give cheer to all around her. She was of immeasurable help and made life more pleasant for my wife when I would be away, which was quite often.

The Ranch Undergoes a Change

By the first of July, my cattle and the Edmanson cattle were in good flesh, and I shipped all the steers to the Kansas City market. Also shipped were the cows that were fat and barren.

I was satisfied that there was some split between Smith and Chapman and that they weren't going to invest any of their capital. Therefore, I thought it best to close out what I had bought with their interests, close up the deal, and turn their range back to them. After shipping in all the fat stuff, I went to Gainesville, Texas, where Smith, Chapman, and I had a final settlement and dissolved our partnership. I took over what cattle we had on hand and assumed the indebtedness to the Drumm-Flato Commission Company, then went to Kansas City and bought the cows and heifers of the Edmanson cattle from the commission company.

By fall, I had made another shipment of calves and fat cows and only kept back the well-bred cows. I had taken them and all my belongings to my ranch near Woodward and had also moved my family there. It was soon apparent that I had more cattle than I could handle on that ranch through the winter, so I rented a range twelve miles south of Woodward, where my youngest brother was then living. I got him to look after the cattle through the winter of 1899. The cattle wintered well, and it was now April 1900, and another reasonably mild winter had passed.

Becoming a Cattle Sleuth

Passive Resistance and Active Cheating

Mr. J. H. Nations[1] had come to Woodward to close out some bad cattle deals on which he had been holding the financial papers. Billy Flato had instructed me to assist Mr. Nations, and I found him set up in an office building joining the Central Hotel. Since the completion of these deals would take him two months, Nations had two wagons with bosses and crews of men, and they worked the ranges and gathered the cattle and kept them under herd.

Of the cattle deals that Mr. Nations was attempting to settle, Nick Hudson had the largest one, and he had come up short. Hudson had cut out one hundred of the best cows and turned them over to his brother-in-law, and he had had the brother-in-law put in a bill for feed that was equivalent to the value of the cows. The last roundup of these cattle was to be held at the ranch where Combs, the brother-in-law, was holding the cows. The one hundred cows were all in one brand, called the Circle Bar brand.

Nations told me to attend this last roundup and gave me a list of brands to cut. He remarked, "Those fellows are trying to steal one hundred cows from me, but I will have to reclaim those, so you needn't cut the Circle Bar cows. There will be some men at the roundup from one of my wagons to take what cattle you find to the herd we are holding several miles up the river. Also, my bookkeeper, Mr. Moss, will be there to count what you cut out."

When I arrived at the roundup I noticed that there were men from several miles around present for the sole purpose of retrieving their cattle. It was customary for the men whose range a cattle roundup was being held on to send men in the roundup, by turns, to look for their cattle. It was also a discourtesy for a man to go in a roundup of cattle without being invited.

Hudson and Combs had sent all the other men into the roundup, three or four at a time, and they had all gotten their cattle cut out and ready to take them to their respective ranches. I felt that what was taking place was not proper, and besides, Hudson and Combs were riding around in the roundup with their heads together, talking, and they never spoke to me. It was obvious to me that they were ignoring and treating me with disrespect. I also knew that Hudson had skinned Nations out of a large sum of money by mortgaging more cattle than he had. Likewise, I knew that the one hundred they were holding for a feed bill was also a skin. The more I thought over the situation, the madder I got. Finally, I rode into the herd and spoke to Hudson and asked him if he was ready for me to work the roundup. Combs didn't give Hudson time to answer but spoke up and said, "Gober, you can't cut these Circle Bar cattle!"

That put my blood at boiling heat, and I said, "Combs, I never came here with any intentions of cutting the Circle Bar cattle, but your remark and the disrespect that you have shown me has caused me to change my mind. I'm starting Circle Bar's first! Turn one back on me, and it will be your last cow to turn." And I proceeded to cut out all there were, sixty-five head.

Combs ran to the four young boys that had been sent to take the cattle I cut to the herd up the river, and he forbade them to help me. The kids stood off in a bunch until I got through, and I started my sixty-five cows down the trail all by myself. When I had gotten a half-mile from the roundup site, Combs and three of his men came galloping up intending to scatter the cows from me so I couldn't drive them. I jerked my saddle gun, a .482 caliber, and threw a cartridge in the magazine and at the same time ordered them to stop. They stopped and held a consultation for a few minutes; then they struck a swift gallop for Woodward, which was seven miles away. After that party, intent on disrupting my mission, had dropped out of sight, the four kids ventured up to help me, and I stayed with them until they were within a mile or two of their herd. Then I loped on into Woodward.

When I got to Mr. Nations's office, I found him out in front, bareheaded and somewhat peeved or excited. It seems that Hudson and Combs had told him, in their own way, what had happened, and

When I had gotten a half-mile from the roundup site, Combs and three of his men came galloping up intending to scatter the cows from me so I couldn't drive them. I jerked my saddle gun, which was a .482 caliber, and threw a cartridge in the magazine and at the same time ordered them to stop.

Courtesy Private Collection

told him that they were going to sue him. Nations then remarked to me, "Gober, you will kill some of these thieves, and it will break me to get you out of it."

I replied, "Thieves must not insult or defy me unless they are wanting trouble." At this point I should say that this was the last work of closing out bad deals in the Woodward vicinity. In a few days, Mr. Nations had the cattle—about two thousand head—divided into two herds and had started them on the trail for pastures he had engaged for them.

Preparing to Right Another Wrong

Mr. Nations went back to his commission office in Kansas City, and I was enjoying real peace and pleasure with my wife and babies and looking after my little ranch west of Woodward, but my pleasure was of short duration. The duration of my peace of mind lasted just one week; then I received a long letter from Billy Flato, the vice-president of the Drumm-Flato Commission Company, informing me that Mr. Nations had asked him for my services to trace some cattle that had been driven out of the county from near Arapaho, Oklahoma. Nations held a mortgage on the cattle and had sold the notes to the Abell Brokerage Company of Kansas City. Both Mr. Flato and Mr. Nations were warm personal friends of long standing, and both thought highly of me. Therefore, I felt doubly obligated to grant the request.

The men that mortgaged the cattle and then drove them out of the county to parts unknown were Bailey Bingham and Tom Darlington, who were brothers-in-law. I didn't know either of them, but fortunately I had an old-time friend living on the Washita River near Bingham and Darlington, and his name was Jim Dobbs. We had been friends for many years in the Panhandle of Texas in the early eighties and all through my ordeal in Amarillo as sheriff of Potter County.

I packed my handbag and made the run down to Canadian, Texas, on the Santa Fe, then took the mail hack to Cheyenne and from Cheyenne to Arapaho. From there, I drove my team to Jim Dobbs's ranch, arriving there about five o'clock one afternoon. When I arrived at the ranch, I found Dobbs sitting on the front porch smoking his pipe. He was so glad to see me that he jumped up out of his chair and embraced me in a bear hug so tight that I could hardly breathe as he said, "Jim, I'm so darned happy to see you. You're like a long-lost brother!" When we finished exchanging kind words and love pats of friendship, we put my team up and fed them.

By six PM, his two boys and daughter had come home from school, and Mrs. Dobbs had supper ready. After supper, Dobbs and I indulged in recreating and reliving early days in the Panhandle, and we sat up until one AM. During our discussions, which occupied many hours, I questioned Dobbs in detail about his crop and home affairs and learned that his corn was laid by, and all his work was done, and he had nothing of importance to do until hay harvest, which was four weeks off.

Then I asked him how a job at five dollars per day, for him and his saddle horse, would suit him. He said, "If I can be of any service to you, it doesn't matter about the pay." "Well," I said, "the pay is coming from a source where you are not obligated, and they expect to pay for all services rendered. In this case, you will be helping catch two of your neighbors who have run off with mortgaged cattle." I told him their names and asked him to think the matter over and let me know by eight AM in the morning, and that I didn't want him to get into a

A Great Cattle Swindle: Tracking Men and Cattle
circa 1900

LEGEND

1 ✳ Gober Ranch

2 ✳ Cattle starting point

3 ✳ Dobbs Ranch

4 ✳ Darlington cattle found;
young man apprehended

5 ✳ Help from Sheriff J. L. Gober

6 ✳ Bingham cattle found

Gober's general route to find   - - ▶
misappropriated cattle

Estimated cattle route   ·········▶

ABBREVIATIONS

A.T. & S.F.   Atchison, Topeka &
Santa Fe Railroad

F.W. & D.   Fort Worth &
Denver Railroad

C.R.I. & P.   Chicago, Rock Island &
Pacific Railroad

© 1996 James R. Gober

deal that would cause him trouble. I cautioned him to think over the situation well before deciding.

Dobbs arched his eyebrows and frowned as I had seen him do many times in the distant past when anger darkened his countenance. He was emphatic when he said, "I can tell you right now, Bingham and Darlington are not friends of mine, and I am under no obligation to them, and conscientiously I feel obligated to assist you, Jim, in anything you may undertake, and I pledge my life that I will do it."

I felt that jolt of energy that you experience when you have the total, unreserved commitment of a friend to your task, so I said, "Then suppose we get up at six AM, and by breakfast, I will have plans. I must find those cattle."

We were indeed up at six AM next morning, and by six thirty we had had breakfast. I told Dobbs to saddle his horse and to put in the day among such neighbors as he knew to be friendly with Bingham and Darlington, and to try to find out where they were or when they left and the direction they went. Meanwhile, I would drive to Arapaho and get in touch with a cattleman I knew there and see if I could get any information from him. I instructed Dobbs to meet me in Arapaho that night, and we would compare notes and lay further plans.

I rode to Arapaho and found Mr. Howenstein, who handled more cattle than anyone in the locality and knew at all times what was going on in the cattle business, to include the comings and goings of the people involved. He informed me that Bingham and Darlington had gone south, but he didn't know their destination.

About six PM, Dobbs came in and informed me that all he could get out of any of the neighbors was that Bingham and Darlington had taken their cattle south, somewhere in west Texas, and he had also succeeded in getting the date and the point where they had crossed the Washita and where they camped the first night. It seems that they had been gone fifteen days.

Plans Made and Instructions Given

After we had supper and got out to ourselves, I gave Dobbs the following instructions: "Go home tonight, and get ready to start early tomorrow morning. You should move out in the direction of the point where the cattle crossed the river, and then you should be able to follow the trail. There were eight hundred head of these cattle, and there has been no rain since they left; therefore, you should be able to trail them, and their sign would be especially plain. You should be able to see where they bedded each night and get information from such people as, in your judgment, would be reliable."

I continued, "It's about 150 miles to the Fort Worth and Denver Railroad. You should make it in four days, and if the cattle keep a southerly direction, they will cross the railroad about Childress, Texas. I will take the mail hack to Weatherford, Oklahoma, in the morning. There I will take the train to El Reno, Oklahoma, and get on the Rock Island to Bowie, Texas, where the Rock Island crosses the Fort Worth and Denver. At that point, I will take the Fort Worth and Denver up to Childress, and you will find me at Childress after thirty-six hours from tomorrow morning."

Dobbs had gotten the information that two men that had broken out of jail at Arapaho and had gone with Bingham and Darlington. One of the men had been sentenced to the penitentiary, and the other was waiting trial on a charge that would have sent him to the same place. So, being aware of these circumstances, I advised Dobbs that if he should locate the outfit not to let his business be known and to get to a telegraph office and to wire me at Childress where to meet him. All was understood, and I shook hands with Dobbs, and he started for home.

Next morning I took the mail hack to Weatherford, Oklahoma, a distance of sixty-five miles. The crude railroad that ran from Weatherford to El Reno, Oklahoma, only made one trip a day. It came in late in the evening and laid over until eight AM the next morning, so I was doomed to stay all night in Weatherford, which was a rather lawless town. It was not unlike all new towns when they get their first railroad.

In order to kill time, I prowled from one place to the other until I thought that I could sleep. Then I went to bed in the crude hotel that had rough boards for part of the wall. For the other part, they had a tent, also for the ceiling.

Unfulfilled Expectations of an Encounter

Next morning, I hit the slow train for El Reno and got there about dark and had to wait until five o'clock the next morning to get a train for Bowie, Texas. The train arrived in Bowie at one PM that afternoon, and I took a bus, a horse-drawn conveyance, for town, as I had three hours to wait for the Fort Worth and Denver. I asked the bus man to let me out at a short-order restaurant, and, as it happened, I was the only passenger he had, so he went into the restaurant with me. He asked me to call him when I wanted to leave town, so I informed him that I would be leaving on the Fort Worth and Denver, westbound, and if he would wait until I ate my lunch I would go back to the depot, as I had just as soon wait there as to be in town.

Then he said, "You can ride back to my barn, which is halfway, and visit with me until train time, and then go to the train with me." I agreed, and by the time I was through with my lunch, he and I were chummy. When we got to his barn on the main street to the depot, we got comfortably seated, inhaling the odor of good Havana cigars that I had purchased. At this time my new friend broke the silence by informing me that he was expecting trouble any minute. He related to me the following story. "Dick Wagoner had taken a woman of easy virtue to the hotel with him, and he had proceeded to get drunk and go to sleep. Then the woman had slipped out of the room and had gotten me to take her to the train. She apparently went to Wichita Falls, and now Wagoner blames me, and he had made some threats, which he had voiced through other people, so that I would understand his intentions. This Dick Wagoner has killed four men that I know of, and now all I can do is to try to keep out of his way until he leaves town."

Once again, my tendency to help someone in trouble got in the way of my better judgment when I said, "I hope he doesn't come to kill you while I am waiting for the train, but if he does, I will guarantee your life to be safe." At that I ended my part of the conversation, for my blood began to heat from the time he'd mentioned Dick Wagoner's name. I knew every word the old man had spoken was the truth, for I knew Wagoner and knew that he had killed four men. The last one he had killed was a friend of mine he had murdered in cold blood by waylaying him. After that murder, I had met Dick Wagoner in a saloon in Amarillo, Texas, and he insulted me, and I beat his face into a pulp to where he had to be carried in a back room and washed and bandaged up.

The next day, he was walking the streets with a Winchester, and when I came to town, I was advised to go home, that Wagoner was hunting me. My reply to those well-wishers was, "I will find him and see what he wants." When I walked out into the street, my defensive posture became sensitive automatically as my eyes snapped quickly to the right and I scanned the row of buildings in that direction. Seeing nothing threatening or unusual, I rapidly shifted my eyes in the opposite direction. There, about one hundred feet away, I saw him coming down the street with his Winchester in his hand and his head bandaged up. I walked out in the street in plain view and stood facing Wagoner, and he walked right on by me. Just then, two Texas Rangers came following him. They were talking to him to try to persuade him to go out to the ranch owned by his brother-in-law.

I have never met Wagoner since that incident, but I always felt that if we did meet, I would be forced to have trouble with him. If I did have trouble with him, I had firmly set my mind to make it snappy and to finish the job. However, Wagoner didn't come to kill the bus man while I was there, so I escaped the anticipated opportunity of dealing with him.

It was now time for me to leave Bowie, so I caught the Fort Worth and Denver train and arrived in Childress that night, safe and sound.

The Search Continues

The next day I made inquiries of several different cowpokes that had come to town from different directions, but none had seen any cattle being driven on the roads or trails. Quite obviously, all I could do was stay there until I heard from Dobbs, and it was then four days since he and I had separated at Arapaho.

I went to the telegraph office and asked them, if any telegram came during the night, to deliver it to my room in the hotel. Then I retired early and was not disturbed during the night with a telegram.

The next morning I felt fresh and put in the time reading and writing a few letters. About four o'clock that afternoon, I received a telegram from Dobbs saying, "I HAVE CATTLE LOCATED x COME TO CLAREN-DON AT ONCE x, signed J. W. DOBBS x." Clarendon was one hundred miles west of Childress on the Fort Worth and Denver Railroad and sixty-eight miles east of Amarillo.

When I arrived at Clarendon at 10:40 that night, Dobbs met me at the train station and informed me that Theodore Piles, who was the cattle inspector for the Texas Cattle Raisers Association, had seen the cattle, and they were being held in a pasture twenty miles south, on the head of the Little Red River. The pasture was owned by a man named Shott. I immediately dug up the sheriff, Balley Oliver, whom I had known for years, and asked him to go with me the next morning to get the cattle and arrest the two convicts, if they were there. He readily agreed; then I found Piles, and he agreed to go.

Deputy Sheriff Bally Oliver, sitting third from left at the old Clarendon, Texas, "Saints Roost," ca. 1885. Courtesy Southwest Collection Photograph Collection 378-E1#21. Texas Tech University, Lubbock.

A Partial Success Is Enjoyed

Next morning, Dobbs, Piles, Oliver, and I saddled horses early and were on our way. We arrived at the Shott ranch about two PM. The ranch was located on the head of a rough canyon or bluff. The house and corral sat up on level ground, with mesquite timber all around. When we sited the house, we dismounted and tied our horses to mesquite trees and advanced on foot, keeping the brush between us and the house. Then I saw four men sitting on the very edge of the rim rock of the canyon, and just to the right of them was a huge pile of cedar posts, probably fifty feet long and eight feet high. I immediately took charge of the situation, and we slipped to the right until the pile of posts was between us and the men. Then I told Oliver and Pile to go around one end of the post pile, and Dobbs and I went around the other, all with drawn Colt .44 and .45 six-shooters; and each of us had our man covered by the time they saw us.

After thoroughly questioning the men, I found only one, a nineteen-year-old kid, who had any connection with the cattle deal. This kid had helped drive the cattle from Oklahoma and had been left with the cattle to look after them. I told him that I would have to take him back with the cattle. We then proceeded to round them up and had them on the trail towards Clarendon in two hours.

After hitting the trail, I turned my attention to the kid and treated him nice and began questioning him as to where Bingham and Darlington were. He told me that Bingham had cut his cattle out several days before and that he had gone on south when Darlington turned west. Also, he mentioned that Bingham was taking his bunch to the head of the salt fork of the Brazos River in Kent County. That meant that Dobbs and I must double back to Childress as soon as we could dispose of Darlington's cattle.

We got to Billy Christian's ranch that night and spent the night there. Next morning, I left the cattle with the other men and went into Clarendon and arranged with Mr. Cook, a banker who owned a good pasture near town, to take charge of the cattle and communicate with the Abel Brokerage as to what disposition to make of them.

That night I told the kid that I had found with the cattle that I would release him if he would promise to go home and be careful and not hire on with a cow thief again. He was a real happy kid and guaranteed me that he had had enough of working for crooks.

On with the Relentless Search

Dobbs had already taken the train back to Childress. The next morning I joined him, and we took the mail hack to Paducah, Texas, the county seat of Cottle County, and it took us until dark to get there. The distance, I believe, was eighty miles.

The sheriff of Cottle County was J. L. Gober, a cousin of mine. He also was a ranch owner, and I arranged with him for that night to furnish Dobbs and me each a good horse and saddle. Next morning, we were furnished with two splendid horses and saddles and were on our way early. We traveled all day through desolate country without seeing a living soul. Finally, we got to a post office and general store called Willington. It was about dark, and we were directed to a place where we were able to stay that night. Actually, we fared very well, with a breakfast the next morning that offered bacon and eggs and plenty of mesquite grass for our horses as well.

Joseph Lee Gober, first
sheriff of Cottle County,
Texas 1892-98, date
unknown. Courtesy Tom
G. and Peggy Taylor,
Maryville, Tennessee.

That night after we arrived and before going to bed, I went to the postmaster and asked him if there were any ranchers south of where we were. He directed me to a ranch five miles from Willington, owned by a Mr. George, and he informed me that George was a good man, and a square dealer. Next morning, Dobbs and I were off early on the trail, the same trail that we had left at dark the night before. By noon, the trail was fresh, we knew that the cattle couldn't be more than five or six miles ahead, and, according to directions the postmaster had given me, Mr. George's ranch would be about six miles ahead. We concluded that we would hit straight for George's ranch and get dinner and feed for our horses. Once we arrived, we would ask George to go with us to overtake the cattle and the men driving them.

A Quest for Anyone Willing to Help

We got to Mr. George's ranch about one thirty PM. It was Sunday, in the middle of August, and it was hot as blazes and dry. Mr. George came out of the ranch house, and I introduced myself and Dobbs. As

Courtesy Private Collection

Next morning, Dobbs and I were off early on the trail once more, the trail that we had left at dark the night before. By noon, the trail was fresh, we knew that the cattle couldn't be more than five or six miles ahead, and, according to directions the postmaster had given me, Mr. George's ranch would be about six miles ahead.

Dobbs and I both had Winchesters on our saddles, .45 six-shooters buckled around our waists, and our belts full of cartridges, I felt I must explain our presence and our business before asking any favors. So I told Mr. George we had followed a bunch of mortgaged cattle from Oklahoma and had left their trail fresh about six miles back and that we'd come to him for dinner and horse feed. He told his wife to fix our dinner; then he led the way to the shed stable and gave us shelled corn for our horses.

After dinner, I took Mr. George to one side and explained more fully what our plans and expectations were. I told him that it was Bailey Bingham and a couple of escaped convicts that were driving the cattle and that I expected to have trouble when I overtook them. Then I made it clear to Mr. George that I was a stranger in that country, and I understood Bingham had relatives on the river, and it would probably be at the river where I would overtake him. I told him that I would appreciate his services, if he would go with us to witness the transaction of receiving my cattle.

Berry Pursely, deputy sheriff of Kent County, Texas, ca. 1902. Courtesy Kent County Historical and Genealogical Society.

Mr. George studied deeply for several minutes. You could see him mentally going over various options, alternatives, and consequences as he thought seriously about what I had said and proposed. Then he frowned, and I could foresee that he didn't really want to say what he was about to tell me. "Gober," he said seriously, "I hate to refuse you, but I have cattle and horses all over this country. I know Bingham and also his relatives and have been on friendly terms with all of them, more out of necessity than for any other reason. If I were to take stock in this matter, they would ruin me. Can't you see what they would do to my stock? They are a hard-boiled bunch! Berry Pursely is deputy sheriff and has a ranch right on the river, about twelve miles away, and right in the vicinity of where your cattle are

As we neared the ranch, I noticed a column of smoke rising from the corral and several men and a bunch of cattle in one corral and a bunch of horses in the other.

going to. You go over to Pursely's and get him; then you'll be in the right area."

I readily agreed with Mr. George and thanked him for his kindness. Then Dobbs and I started for Berry Pursely's ranch on the salt fork of the Brazos River,[2] twelve miles from George's ranch.

Approaching a Possible Confrontation

We got to the river about four thirty PM and went down off of the table land over a high, rocky bluff onto the river valley. From our vantage point we could see Pursely's ranch for a distance of at least one mile before we reached it. As we neared the ranch, I noticed a column of smoke rising from the corral and several men and a bunch of cattle in one corral and a bunch of horses in the other. This scene of activities meant to me that they were branding cattle.

The road we were on ran between the house and the corral, and as I surveyed the scene at the ranch, I said to Dobbs, "We may find our men and cattle right here." Then I laid out the plan to him, "When we get opposite that corral, I will dismount and pretend to adjust my saddle, to give me a chance to draw my Winchester from its scabbard. You do likewise, for if it should be our men, the battle is on."

Norman N. Rodgers, sheriff of Kent County, Texas 1895-1902, date unknown. Courtesy Kent County Sheriff's Department, Jayton, Texas.

As we dismounted, the men stood motionless, just looking at us. One man came out to us, followed by a second man, while two remained at the corral. As the first man approached I introduced myself, and he replied that his name was Pursely but made no attempt to introduce the other man. The other man was a giant of a young man, about twenty-two years old. I said, "Mr. Pursely, you are deputy sheriff of Kent County, are you not?"

He replied, "I am."

I introduced myself, then told him, "I have come to you for assistance in helping me recover a bunch of cattle that Bailey Bingham and two escaped prisoners from Arapaho, Oklahoma, are driving." I explained to him that I was representing the people that held mortgages on the cattle.

When I was through with my explanations, the man that had followed Pursely out to where we were standing went hurriedly to the corral where the horses were, and Pursely beckoned me to follow as he walked ten paces away from Dobbs. Then he said to me, "By God, Gober, I can't go. I just killed a man a few days ago and have got to stand in with the gang until I get out of it. You go on to Clairemont, the county seat, and get Norman Rodgers, the sheriff. It's only nine miles, and you can get your cattle in the morning, but you won't find the men that are driving them. That boy that followed me out to you and heard you tell me what you were after is Bee Hardin, and a brother-in-law to Bailey Bingham. He is catching fresh horses right now to take to Bingham and notify him that you are after him."

I replied, "Well, Pursely, I have been in this western country since I was eighteen years old and have never seen any locality just like this, and the same spirit seems to exist over a considerable area." Then I continued by asking him, "Would you be obliging enough to loan me fresh horses and take care of our tired ones until I call for them?"

He replied, "I will," and went to the corral and lassoed three good horses. Dobbs and I changed the pack saddle to the fresh pack horse and our saddles to the fresh horses. Then we mounted them and struck a gallop for Clairemont as the oranges and pinks of the western sunset were being replaced rapidly by the purple shadows of the evening.

Further Annoying Complications

We arrived at Clairemont after dark, and I found the distance to be at least fourteen miles. Perhaps Pursely knew a shorter way, but it was nine o'clock when Dobbs and I got there.

The town consisted of a courthouse, jail, post office, general stores, and crude hotel combined with a wagon yard. We hunted up the sheriff, and I proceeded to tell him my business. I also explained to him what had taken place during my interview with Pursely, to include the actions of Bee Hardin in riding away to Bingham's location with fresh horses from Pursely's ranch.

Sheriff Rodgers was silent for a few minutes. Then he said, "Gober, you take your horses to the wagon yard, and you can get a bed there and sleep sound until morning, and we will go get your cattle, and that is all you care about. I want to ask you a favor to me: don't mention young Hardin taking horses to these men. His father is a good friend of mine, and a brother Mason. He is an only cousin to John Wesley Hardin,[3] and he and Billy Stantifer are at loggerheads, and I have been keeping down a killing between them for some time. If Stantifer heard of this kid assisting those fellows, for sure it would cause trouble to start anew." Billy Stantifer was cattle inspector for the Texas Cattle Raisers Association, of which I was a member, and I knew Billy but didn't know he was in that Godforsaken country until Rodgers told me. But I also didn't know Billy was straight and square. I felt considerable relief to know that I was going to find one man that was not obligated or intimidated by thieves and outlaws, so I asked Rodgers where I could find Billy. Rodgers then went with me, and we found Billy and arranged for him to go with us after the cattle the next morning.

The Missing Cattle in Deplorable Condition

Next morning, bright and early, Rodgers, Stantifer, Dobbs, and I took the trail back, crossed the river, and proceeded on through mesquite flats until we came to a crude rock stone building which housed a general store. We all dismounted, and Rodgers and Stantifer went into the building. I followed, since I wanted some chewing tobacco. When I entered the building, I found Rodgers and Stantifer talking confidentially with the proprietor, so I amused myself by looking at some rattlesnake hides and human skulls that were displayed on a table.

After a few minutes their conversation was finished, and the proprietor of the store came forward to wait on me. After sizing him up, I decided that I didn't want any tobacco, or at least I didn't want any tobacco from him or that he had handled. He was a slim, dark-skinned man with long hair and a beard that lacked soap and water and a comb. His whiskers were matted with tobacco juice, and many things could have lived undisturbed in his hair.

We all mounted, and Rodgers and Stantifer led out in a gallop. About five miles from the rock store, in a mesquite timber valley, we found the cattle scattered around for a mile, grazing. From the tracks we could see that three of the cattle herders had ridden in and out on ponies. The campfire was still smoldering where they had cooked their supper the night before. Also, fresh wagon tracks indicated that someone had come with a wagon and hauled their camp beds and cooking utensils away which they had been packing on a pony.

We rounded up the cattle and started them back to Clairemont. Some of the cattle were lame, and they all were in bad shape. They had been driven so hard that on the way back to Clairemont, I arranged with Billy Stantifer to pasture and look after the cattle and dispose of them as instructed by the Abel Brokerage Company.

The Finale and Interlude with an Old Friend

That night, Rodgers said to me, "Gober, you have your cattle and have finished your job. I suppose you are going to Kansas City."

I responded, "Yes."

Tom Powers, El Paso, date unknown. Courtesy The Heart of West Texas Museum, Inc., Colorado City, Texas.

Then he went on to say, "Well, I want you to take my advice. You take the mail hack in the morning that goes to Colorado City,[4] and take the train there for Kansas City. Let Mr. Dobbs take those horses back to Pursely and get yours, and go from Pursely's to Mr. George's ranch. There he can stay overnight. George will direct him to Paducah so that he can avoid this mesquite brush road or trail. At least, I don't want you to go back the way you came. I know the situation and the people." I liked Rodger's advice, and I readily agreed to follow it, and I gave Dobbs detailed instructions that night.

The next morning, I took the mail hack to Colorado City, a distance of seventy miles, and arrived there at eight PM. This mail hack was drawn by Mexican mules, and we changed every fifteen miles. The mules would have to be held by the heads at every station until we were ready to go, and when they were turned loose, they would run the first few miles before the driver could pull them down to a swift trot. Usually, the last five miles he could use the whip freely to keep them in a trot.

When I got out of the mail hack, the first person I saw was Tom Powers,[5] an old cowboy friend I had not seen in several years and one who I had lost complete contact with. As I shook hands with Tom, I noticed a big silver star shining on his weskit with the words "City Marshal." Without realizing it at first, my mind wandered in time back fifteen years and to the place, the Texas Panhandle, where I wore proudly the silver shield that read "Sheriff Potter Co. Texas." I was looking back in time and not realizing for a moment where I was until Tom said with concern in his voice, "Jim, are you all right?" I apologized and excused myself as having a lot on my mind and being pretty tired from the chase of the stolen cattle. Tom continued, "Since you have until eleven PM tonight for your train, let me show you the town." I readily agreed, and he proceeded to entertain me by taking me all over the town and showing me what they had.

Among other things, Tom Powers had a buggy team of spotted ponies, perfectly matched. They were well trained and beautiful to behold. Also, the city had just recently installed an electric light plant. Since it was the first one that I had ever seen, it was quite interesting and a real novelty to me. The three hours that I had to kill in Colorado City passed swiftly and pleasantly. Tom Powers accompanied me to the train and bade me goodbye.

The Major Turning Point

Lured by Attractive Business Propositions

I left Colorado City and went to Fort Worth on the Texas & Pacific Railroad, and from there I rode the Santa Fe to Kansas City. Arriving in Kansas City the second morning, I went straight to the Drumm-Flato Commission Company offices, where I met Billy Flato. He notified Mr. Nations by phone that I was there, and soon Nations arrived.

I presented a complete report on my work in their interests, including the disposition I had made of the Bingham and Darlington cattle. They were satisfied, and Mr. Flato asked me to come to the office the next morning, saying, "I want to talk over some future plans that I have been considering." Nations requested that I meet him at the Baltimore Hotel at six PM, have dinner with him, his wife, and daughter, and take a ride over the city after dinner. I cheerfully consented and spent a pleasant evening with them.

Next morning, I went to the Commission Company offices, and Mr. Flato took me into his private office and told me that he wanted me to go to Amarillo and open a general loan and soliciting office; also to go to Clayton, New Mexico, about 125 miles west of Amarillo, and buy and lease range enough to carry anywhere from seven to ten thousand head of cattle. This ranch would be maintained as a pool outfit on which to keep cattle that the company had to repossess. The idea was based on the expectations that customers would be unprepared to care for the cattle being taken back by the company, and at some location the company would have to take over and care for their cattle at a loss. His plan called for me to put my herd, which consisted of five hundred head of high-grade cattle, on this range and manage it there. That is, I would direct the management from my office in Amarillo at the same salary I was getting, which was $150 per month and expenses, with the privilege of buying more cattle when I chose.

Now, this looked like a real opportunity for me, and I knew Billy Flato was trying to help me, and he believed that he had found just the opportunity. I returned home to my little ranch near Woodward and began to arrange for the new and promising adventure.

The Work and Excitement of a New Ranch

On arriving home, I explained the future plans to my wife, then went to Amarillo to open my loan and soliciting office. I left my oldest brother, Wade Bowie, and Negro Sam to look after the ranch and help my wife pack the household furniture.

Arriving at Amarillo, I rented an office in the old McGregor Hotel. This hotel had been moved from the old town site of Amarillo to the new town. It had been built in the next lot as an annex to the new Amarillo Hotel.

I bought a four-room cottage from Mr. Jeff Cursey, adjoining his home, making a pleasant location for my wife, as Mrs. Cursey was a noble, kindhearted woman, and she and my wife's mother were good friends.

As soon as I had an understanding with Billy Flato as to future plans, I wrote to John Jones, my trusted friend and the same John Jones that worked for me on the Cimarron River ranch in Woods County, Oklahoma. His home was Clayton, New Mexico, and he knew the surrounding country well, so I detailed him to find a good location for the pool ranch, with suitable improvements for a headquarters ranch that would serve our purposes for the winter. I also informed him that we would have to care for twelve hundred head of cattle as soon as we could set up an acceptable location.

By the time I had gotten my office and home established in Amarillo, Jones had written to me to come right away to Clayton. When I arrived, Jones met me at the train and told me that we could lease a ranch with a good building and corrals and sheds for saddle horses. All that he had mentioned, together with a quantity of alfalfa hay, could be leased from the Miller brothers, located fourteen miles north of Clayton, and the country had free range for several miles north and east of his location. That seemed to be the best location available, so we hired a buggy and team and drove to the Miller ranch. I closed the deal with them, leasing the ranch and buying their feed, and then sent Jones to Woodward to ship my cattle. About seven hundred head in the herd belonged to three other cattlemen. Jones loaded the cattle, twelve hundred head in all, at Gage, Oklahoma,[1] late in November in a cold fall mist and rain. When they were unloaded at the Texas-New Mexico line, it was snowing heavily, and the cattle were driven twenty miles to the Miller Ranch. I had put Jones in charge of this cattle outfit and the ranch, and in the meantime I had a carload of oil cake[2] freighted in to the ranch.

Disaster Strikes

Wade Bowie had been with my cattle in Oklahoma and was still with the outfit. Mr. Car had left one of his men, so three men were left to look after and care for the cattle.

For three months, it seems as fast as one snowstorm would subside, another would come. The cattle would walk and bawl, and walk over the feed, and it seemed impossible to get them satisfied. As a consequence of all of this difficulty, we suffered a heavy loss by spring. However, the worst loss to me was that of my staunch friend Billy Flato. He had withdrawn his interest of one hundred thousand dollars from the Drumm-Flato Commission Company to attempt to prop up the Flato Commission Company of Omaha, run by his brothers. They failed, and Billy lost his money.

When Billy Flato withdrew his stock from the Drumm-Flato Company, the company reorganized and took the name of the Drumm Commission Company. That meant a readjustment of the affairs throughout the company.[3] This situation occurred the following spring after we had moved my cattle to the Miller Ranch. I was notified that the Drumm Commission Company had concluded to dissolve the pool ranch, and Messrs. Car, Clark, and Doren would take their cattle back to Oklahoma.

This situation had left me out on a limb that was bound to break under the weight, and it did break. The Drumm Commission Company also closed the loan office in Amarillo and curtailed my salary. Now things indeed were gloomy for me. I had sacrificed a nice little ranch in Oklahoma to indulge in this venture, which at the time had the appearances of being a gold mine but instead turned out to be fool's gold, and I was broke and in debt to the company. However, I really felt that the company was inconsiderate of my interests, and I

I had put a small bunch of cows that were having calves and not fit to ship in a pasture near Dalhart, Texas, and I sold them to Hawley Plemons, a brother-in-law of mine, to be received June 5, 1905. When that delivery schedule could be met, I would be through with the cattle and the commission company.

firmly believed that they should have balanced accounts with me. They did not, and as a consequence, I have never worried about my indebtedness to the Drumm Commission Company.

The Ultimate Sorrow

I shipped all of the cattle to them, and my part of the pool ranch was closed. Now, I was unsettled as to the future and, of course, worried. I had put a small bunch of cows that were having calves and not fit to ship in a pasture near Dalhart, Texas, and I sold them to Hawley Plemons, a brother-in-law of mine, to be received June 5, 1905. When that delivery schedule could be met, I would be through with the cattle and the commission company.

I rode over to Dalhart the evening of the fourth of June and went to Ike Manskers's Saloon, where I found my old friend, Jack Ryan, was tending bar for Ike. Jack handed me a letter that had been sent "in care of Manskers's Saloon." It was from Hawley Plemons, informing me that he would be one day late, so Ike Manskers invited me to his home for the night. The next day seemed to be a very long one, and I spent most of the day visiting with friends.

About four o'clock, while I was talking to Jack Ryan in front of Manskers' s Saloon, a messenger handed me a telegram. I signed for it and tore it open. The contents of that telegram gave me a lasting shock, for me a fatal blow from which I never have been able to recover, nor will I ever.

Just imagine the disbelief, the agony you would feel, had you been the one reading the following message concerning your loved one:

> AMARILLO TEXAS
>
> JUNE 5 1905
>
> 345 PM
>
> JAMES R GOBER x IN CARE OF IKE MANSKERS x DALHART x TEXAS x
>
> COME HOME AT ONCE x WADE BOWIE KILLED YOUR WIFE AND HIMSELF x
>
> SIGNED x JOHN JONES x [4]

The world turned black in front of my very eyes, and my heart and soul were suddenly crushed, and I was thrown headlong into the depths of a bottomless pit of unspeakable despair. I was crushed totally, to where I found myself gasping for breath as though I had been stomped by an unseen force. In this condition and speechless, I came to my senses, only to realize that I was pale and ready to fall in my tracks. Jack Ryan noticed my condition and gave me the chair that he had been sitting in. Ike Manskers came out just as I gave the telegram to Jack Ryan. Ryan read it and handed it to Manskers, and, without hesitating, Manskers left for the railroad depot, where he found a freight train that was due to depart for Amarillo in a few minutes, and he arranged for me to ride it. Manskers, Ryan, and several other friends half carried me, half steadied me and got me to the railroad depot and onto the train.

It was sixty-eight miles to Amarillo, but of the Fort Worth and Denver Railroad employees, most all knew me and were friends of long standing, and they were respectful of my tragic situation and made extra-fast time, arriving at Amarillo just as the shadows of darkness were settling over the horizon. The train slowed down when it whistled in station and came to a stop when it was opposite my home. John Jones and several other friends had come out to the street crossing, and as I alighted from the train, Jones took me by the arm and supported me from there to my home, a distance of one block. The little home in which I had been so happy just the day before was filled with friends and relatives in tears of grief. When I entered, I saw my devoted wife lying flat on a cooling board, with a bullet hole over her left eye.

No words can explain my mental agony and heart stricken grief. My wife's cousin, Minnie Wyand, who had been in our home a great deal and was a loved companion of ours, knew my nature, perhaps better than anyone except my wife. She had hastened to spread a quilt and pillow on the floor for me in a small room, and she took me by the arm and led me to the pallet. There I lay motionless for hours, with just one thought, and that of my five small children, the youngest only fourteen months old, and there being only two years between each of them. They were all babies, and now with no mother.

A Down-Spiraling Path to Self-Destruction

Fate had dealt me a double blow by the loss of my wife and the sorrow and pity I must bear for my little children. It seemed impossible to live under such pressure and keep my brain in balance, and it was impossible; for now, looking back, I can realize experiences that happened in those days, weeks, and months after I lost my wife where, I am convinced, I was mentally unbalanced.

My mother-in-law, Mrs. Plemons, had been with my children either in my home or in hers most of the time since we had moved back to Amarillo, and she was the image of a real mother to them. When the tragedy occurred, she took them to her home, where her four children were grown except the youngest, and he was fourteen.

I stood the heartrending grief of my wife's tragic death about two years, during which time I lived and paid for the keep of my five babies as best I could. Realizing that I was unfit for responsibility, quite naturally I would seek other idle company and found myself hanging around saloons and gambling joints. I soon began to drink after being a teetotalist for fourteen years. In addition, I joined in the poker games, and it seems I would do anything to allay the consistent heartaches and loneliness.

Soon I found myself an excessive drinker and fit for nothing else. I realized fully my worthlessness and was often thrown in jail by officers that I had always considered to be my friends. That knowledge added to my grief and saddened condition.

I thought constantly of my faithful wife, my friend from childhood, the one I loved so much. In my loneliness, I longed for her to be back by my side to be able to comfort me and our babies. I thought so much about it that these words became indelible on my mind:

I want you back to light the gloom,
That creeps somehow into each room
Since you've been gone, that renders mute
My heart that once sang like a lute.
I want you back across the table there,
So I may come and stand behind the chair,
That would hold two so well, and softly touch
With tender hand the silken hair I loved so much.
I want you back so I can see your eyes
Light up in wonder at some well-planned surprise,
So I may live again each joyous, golden hour
We lived so fully when love was in flower.
I want you back so when the day is done
And all the tiny stars creep one by one
Into the sky, then I shall seek again your chair
And I shall sigh content to know you're there.
I want you back so we may dream a space,
Your head against my heart, my lips upon your face.
No word to break the silence while you sleep,
While love and I o'er you our vigil keep.
And as I sit alone tonight, upon my breast
A drowsy head, so dear, seems to softly rest,
And I smile and lift glad hands to touch
Soft silken hair I once loved so much.
Only to drop a weak hand back to my knee,
Only to muse alone of nights I spent with thee
Only to start thoughts whirling on an old bitter track
Only to whisper brokenly, "Oh, I want you back!"

                                              Jim Gober

   I would often go to distant town but would meet acquaintances
and wind up intoxicated and dragged off to jail, there to suffer the
consequences of nervousness, embarrassment, and remorse. I was in
such shape that a drink of water would not stay on my stomach. No
friend or kin seemed to care or would come to my rescue.

A Racing Attempt at Escape

The Consuming Excitement

I sought every possible outlet to escape the thoughts of my wife's tragic death. My mind, quite naturally, turned to horse racing. The excitement of this sport was consuming, just what my tortured mind craved—a chance to escape, to travel, not remaining long in any place but being constantly on the move.

At the time that I lost my wife, I owned several race horses, because it was always my hobby and in my heart to love a good horse. As I began to think about my horses and dream about the tracks, the betting, the indescribable excitement of having a winning horse, my mind wandered back to my childhood in Denton County and a thrilling moment that came quickly and unexpectedly.

An Early Encounter with Sam Bass

It was after our family tragedy, when we lost our home, that I remember my first sight of Sam Bass at the first race that he matched with the Denton mare.[1] In Sam Bass's first horse race, he was using a race pony he had bought when she was two years old. She had become lame through following an immigrant wagon into Texas.

As I remember the circumstances of this encounter with Sam Bass, it occurred sometime in the summer of 1875, when he was nineteen or twenty years old and had been working in a livery stable in the town of Denton. Uncle John and I had gotten in our lumber wagon at Denton and started for home, a distance of nine miles. My uncle turned the team off the main trail and drove to the south into a level valley. There I saw approximately two hundred men and saddle horses—wagons, buggies, and all the different conveyances that had brought them to this spot. I saw paths straight as an arrow running east and west, probably with a fifteen-feet space between the paths, 444 yards in length.

Sam Bass was leading a beautiful, red sorrel mare on one of the paths. Tom Spotwood was leading a beautiful roan mare on the other path. On the Bass mare, better known as the Denton mare, was a small Negro boy about twelve years old; and on the Collin County mare, Spotwood's, was a white boy about the same age.

The crowd was divided. Each mare's friends and backers were near the path on which their favorite was being led back and forth by their respective owners and trainers.

I heard loud curses, boasts, and challenges, and saw men meet each other halfway between the paths and wager money, jewelry, knives, and pistols. As time went on, the men got louder and more boisterous, and wicked threats were shouted until finally a pistol shot rang out, and the two mares were running their fastest speed, neck and neck.

When they finished, I heard the judges decide that the Denton mare had won by a fraction of a nose. The roan mare's friends disputed the decision, and it was at this juncture that I had seen my first horse race and, in my young career, I was also observing the first men engaged in fighting. They were fighting with fists and quirts, some waiving six-shooters.

My uncle took me by the arm and hurriedly led me to the wagon. As I remember, he loped the team back to the trail leading homeward. Once the team leveled down to a moderate trot, Uncle John turned to me and said, "Son, let this be a lesson to you to stay clear of horse races. I brought you to see this race that you would know what kind of men indulge in racing and gambling." Although I was only nine years of age, this was my first experience at being in rough company, and I was frightened and at the same time excited. Still, I felt the spirit of sympathy in my heart for the losing side. Perhaps my sympathy was aroused more deeply for the white lad that rode the roan mare, crying, than for the little black skunk that rode the Denton mare, grinning and showing his white teeth. He was doing this in a way to convince me that he was elated over his victory of outperforming the white boy.

That spirit of sympathy created in my young heart took deep roots and grew to a substantial level. All of my life I have been for the underdog.

Sam Bass matched many races with his mare during the two years following this first race and won them all. Sam, although somewhat wild and reckless, had many friends and a few enemies, and he was honest in his everyday walk of life.

At this point I will return to the reality of the present. I knew that I had good, thoroughbred horses that could win with the right training and opportunities. That training and the right opportunities could and must be found.

It was then that I began to shower all my attention on my horses in an attempt to hasten my escape from the reality of the bitter hand that I had been dealt and the empty life that had resulted. I had been unable to find any other means of escape that seemed to work.

Into the Colorado Circuit

In March 1906, I shipped my race horses to Trinidad, Colorado, where the Colorado race circuit began. The circuit included one week of races at Trinidad, then to Pueblo for a week, thence to Colorado Springs for three days, and on to Denver for two weeks. I had my two little boys with me, for they were very fond of the horses and even begged to ride them in the races. Naturally, I refused such a request, as I was afraid that they might be injured, and besides, it was an embarrassment to even think of them being jockeys.

My reason for racing horses at this time, besides the most important one of helping me to forget my sorrow, was the sport of seeing my horses win. More than the money could ever do, the excitement of winning provided a thrill. This was better than any treatment I could have received to break the monotony of constant heartache and loneliness.

I had a dear friend with me who I depended on to train the horses and keep them fit to run. His name was Fred Bosman, born and raised in Kentucky and a natural sport. He would lay his last dollar on his judgment, and for the most part his judgment was bad, but he had a welcome place in my life.

A Shootout at the Trinidad Stables

Fred came to me one day wanting to match a race with Lofe Reede. I advised him not to do so, as I knew Reede to be tricky and quarrelsome, and I feared that Fred and Reede would have trouble. I was staying at a rooming house in town, and Fred stayed at the tracks and fairgrounds with the horses.

After I left the stables, went to town and could no longer interfere, Fred and Reede matched the race. Each one was to carry a certain weight, which was the weight of our jockey, and the race was to be run that evening.

At three PM, which was in the interim between the time that the race was matched and the time it was to be run, Reede offered our rider ten dollars to throw the race. The rider came to Fred and told him what had happened. Fred instructed the rider to accept the offer Reede had made him and to keep still about it. So Reede and the rider made the deal. All this was going on unbeknownst to me.

At the appointed hour, the two horses were on the track, our rider on our horse and Reede's on his. While the riders were galloping the horses around the track to warm them up for the race, Fred and Reede made several side bets.

After putting up all the cash that they possessed, and ready to start the horses off, Fred took our rider that had been bribed off of our horse and put another boy of the same weight on the horse. Quite a cussing match ensued, but the horses were started off, and our horse finished three lengths ahead of Reede's.

The next morning I was standing by the bank waiting for it to open that I might cash a check. A hack drove up and stopped, and the driver approached me. Just then, Lofe Reede passed us on horseback, headed for the post office to get his mail. The driver then said to me, "I just heard Reede abuse Bosman in a scandalous manner. He told Bosman that he, Reede, was going to make him leave the fairgrounds." It seemed that this happened while Bosman was in his shirtsleeves leading one of my race horses for exercise, so I asked the driver to take me to the fairgrounds as quickly as it was possible for him to drive me there.

When we arrived at the stables, which was only fifty yards from the gate, I knew that Reede would come in and pass directly opposite our stables, as Reede's stables were in the same wing as ours and thirty yards down the line of stables. I found Bosman standing in a stall with a shotgun in his hands. He told of the abuse that he had been forced to take from Reede, with Reede's .45 Colts leveled on him. I said, "All right, Fred, I will walk out far enough that I can see Reede as he comes through the gate. When he comes in at the gate, I will whistle at his approach. I will be situated so he will have to come between us. Don't make any wild shots; this is not exactly my fight, but we did come to Trinidad expecting to be treated decently, and we can't afford to be run away by any man as long as we are decent. So if you get scared and miss, I may get scared and shoot, and I have never missed."

After I walked out as far as I thought necessary to force Reede between me and the stables and had stood there ten minutes, Reede came through the gate in a sweeping trot. I whistled to Bosman and saw him bring his shotgun into position. Just as Reede was opposite Bosman's position, Bosman stepped out of the stall and said to Reede, "Fall off your horse and start fighting."

Bosman fired just as Reede fell off his horse, on the opposite side from Bosman. Reede pulled his gun as he hit the ground. Bosman had missed him with the shotgun and had discharged both barrels, but to my surprise Bosman drew a Colt .45. Bosman was taking deliberate aim at Reede every time he fired, and Reede was shooting at Bosman from behind his horse, and the horse was trying to get loose from Reede. Then Reede accidentally shot his horse in the foot, and the horse reared straight up and whirled away from Reede so he was left in the open uncovered. Each man leveled on the other and fired. I saw the dust fly from Reede's clothing, near the waistband of his trousers, and Reede went down.

I had stopped three of Reede's stable men halfway between their stables and the battle area by hollering at them to stop unless they chose to join in the action. When Reede fell, I told his men to come on and drag him in, and they picked him up and carried him away.

Blessed with a Lenient Lawman

Accompanied by Bosman, I went to the sheriff's office, and when we entered, I introduced myself as the ex-sheriff of Potter County, Texas. Then I introduced Bosman as my friend and the trainer of my horses and related the circumstances leading up to the shooting. I expressed regret that it was our fate to get mixed up with the most overbearing troublemaker in the West and that I would pay a guard until a bond was fixed. And furthermore, I told him I would be greatly appreciative of the favor if Bosman could be allowed to stay with my horses.

Just then Mr. McPherson, a deputy sheriff, came into the room and shook hands with me. I had gotten acquainted with him several years prior, and he had been a peace officer in the vicinity of Trinidad for many years and was a real man. The sheriff asked McPherson if he could take care of Bosman and me until he needed us. McPherson promptly replied that he would, with pleasure. McPherson, Bosman, and I walked out of the sheriff's office, and McPherson then said, "If you two don't buy me a drink every day, I will throw you in." In the meantime, we had gotten the word that Reede had been taken to the hospital, and his wound was serious but not necessarily fatal. The bullet had struck his watch in his vest pocket and ranged downward through his groin. We never saw McPherson anymore until the week's racing was over and we were ready to ship out to Pueblo.

Bosman and I went to the sheriff's office, and I told him that I wanted to leave for Pueblo and was willing to make bond for Bosman. The sheriff looked at me and said, "If you come bothering me anymore, I will throw you both in jail." So that incident appeared to be closed, and we never bothered him again.

The Dream Horse of a Lifetime

While at Trinidad, I bought a four-year-old horse whose sire and dam I had known, and I had seen this horse at the age of two years. John Ledbetter of Quanah, Texas, had bred and raised this colt, and his dam was finely bred and a thoroughbred mare but undersized, being only fourteen and one-half hands high. The sire was also small compared to most thoroughbred horses.

This colt had apparently bred back to an original large family. He was sixteen hands and one inch, and pure black. The man that bought him from Ledbetter and shipped him to Trinidad had spoiled him until he couldn't get him on the track. I was satisfied that it was because he neglected the horse's feet, and they had gotten sore. Perhaps he also had punished the horse while speeding. Anyway, I took a chance and paid the owner $150 for the horse. I began to take the best of care of him and made a friend of him and found that he had almost human sense.

After a week, he would not lie down to sleep at night until his keeper came in and made his bed down in his stall. Then the horse would back off and sit down on his hind quarters and gradually straighten out, with his head near the keeper's legs. Soon he would be snoring like a human.

By the time we arrived at Overland Park in Denver for two weeks of racing, this horse was in perfect condition and working nicely on the track. He was showing such speed that I felt assured that I had a winner, but I waited to enter him until I caught a fast field, so I would get long odds in the books. Finally, I caught a half-mile dash with four horses entered that were holding records for that distance. I entered my horse under the name that I had given him, Hindooman.

What a suspense I felt as he ran his first race for me, while all the time I just knew that he would win. Hindooman did win his race by a length, and I cleaned up thirteen hundred dollars.

A bookmaker by the name of Middleton made me a proposition: to ship this horse to Lamar, Colorado, where a short racing circuit was to start from Lamar, then on to Las Animas; thence to Pueblo; thence to Las Vegas, New Mexico. From Las Vegas, we would ship to Los Angeles, California, and start him in a three-fourths-mile race. Middleton would place money in every pool room in the U. S. to back this horse. I accepted his proposition with the understanding that I was to receive 25 percent of the money he made booking. We made Lamar on the way, after leaving Denver.

Unmistakable Signs of Trouble

After we had run some fifty miles and the train had stopped for water at a tank and section house in a canyon, the head brakey came back and met the rear brakey. After a short conversation, the head brakey came to the car door and asked me how many men I had. I said, "I have three men, a trick dog, and a Mexican goat." The dog belonged to my two little boys, and they had trained him to do many stunts. I wouldn't have taken fifty dollars for him. The goat I had bought to keep in the stall with a nervous mare. She was a very fast mare but hard to condition because she did not rest and moved around in the stall like a wild animal in a cage. After putting this goat in the stall with her, she was perfectly at ease. So I valued my goat highly. I naturally was concerned when this brakey said, "You will have to pay fare on your men, or unload."

I grabbed a hatchet and jumped out on the ground. The brakey ran, and I ran after him. Unfortunately, the dog and the goat jumped out and ran after me; the train whistled out, and I caught a boxcar on the move, but I lost my dog and goat.

Loss of Another Dream

We arrived at Lamar and raced for three days, then shipped to Las Animas. There I started my noble horse Hindooman in a five-and-one-half furlong race, and he won by several lengths.

While my rider was taking him to the stables, another horse struck my horse's hind tendon from behind, about eight inches above the ankle, with the sharp toe of a front plate, cutting my horse's tendon and almost causing his foot to be useless. This accident spoiled all my prospects of making a small fortune. It also broke my heart insofar as being interested in racing, for this was the best and fastest horse I had ever seen or expected to see. That unfortunate incident killed my interest forever in owning horses.

After getting my invincible racehorse Hindooman ruined at Las Animas, Colorado, it destroyed another area of happiness in my life. Quite naturally, that caused me to meditate over all other disappointments of the past, and I was in a melancholy mood most of the time.

I owned Boomer the Second, a high-class race horse that I was training, and a half-sister to Hindooman. She had been spoiled as a three-year-old and was track shy and crazy. The second fall after Hindooman was hurt, I had him well but didn't have the confidence in his speed that I had had before he was hurt, but I shipped these three to Dallas, Texas, to the fair, as racing was to be one of the important features.

The Destruction of Anticipated Pleasure

Cleve McNeal was, at that time, a traveling salesman for a wholesale whiskey firm in Fort Worth and had owned Boomer the Second and was fond of the races and of race horses. He happened to be on his way to Fort Worth and rode in a boxcar with me and my horses as far as Fort Worth. Cleve and I were reliving our school days at Bolivar, and Cleve said to me, "Guess who I saw on the train, between Fort Worth and Childress, as I was coming to Amarillo? Your first sweetheart, Augustine Alexander. She was coming to Childress to visit her daughter, and she asked me about you and said that she had rather see you than anyone in the world. Augustine is as beautiful and sweet as when she was a girl, but her hair is as white as snow." I told Cleve that since it would be a pleasure for Augustine to see me, then I would try to afford her that pleasure on my way home after the Dallas and San Antonio fairs were over.

After arriving in Dallas one week before the fair was to start and getting stalls for the horses, it began to rain, and the tracks soon got muddy, but we had to exercise the horses every day just the same. I put my exercise boy on Boomer and instructed him to let him go half speed one mile. Boomer was feeling ready to run and had took the bits and ran off with the boy and pulled with a badly bowed tendon.

The next morning, I sent the filly to the track, and she ran over the fence and hurt a hind leg. I was then left with only Hindooman, and he was no good in the mud. So I left Boomer and the mare, both crippled, and shipped Hindooman to Bowie, Texas, and won a three-fourths race there. Next, I shipped him to San Antonio, but he was kept on a local freight for three days and nights, and when I arrived, Hindooman had taken cold and was unfit to race. I left him in the livery barn and came back to Amarillo, disgusted with race horses. However, I could not stop thinking of that intelligent, fine horse, Hindooman, and how much sought-after pleasure I was deprived of by his untimely injury.

> Many years ago when life got dull and dark
> I would ship race horses to Overland Park
> Where I met men from many a state
> That on some horse's speed depended their fate.
> It was a battle of wits of spirited men
> Trying to pick a horse that would win.
> Bookmakers would make their slate,
> On their judgment depended their fate.
> The fastest race one-half mile I ever saw run
> Was Hindooman, and Joe D., Ute Chief's Son.
> Jennie Hughes and Honest John
> Were crowding these two right along,
> And when they finished under the wire
> A blanket would hide them with some to spare.
> Hindooman first by a nose,
> Joe D. second place,
> Jennie Hughes and Honest John tied for third,
> Over the results there wasn't a word.
> The bookmakers seemed amazed,
> They paid off tickets in a daze.
> They were bound to acknowledge defeat.
> For Joe D. the invincible was beat
> On Hindooman's success in that one-half-mile dash
> I drew from the bookmakers thirteen hundred in cash,
> Other friends of mine cleaned up fine.
> Hindooman was owned and trained by me
> And a faster horse I never expect to see.
>
> Jim Gober

Before I left San Antonio, I had picked up a paper and read an account about Augustine Alexander, burned while visiting her daughter near Childress, Texas. It seemed that she had lighted a gasoline cooking stove, and the stove exploded and burned her to death. One more anticipated pleasure was blasted into eternity.

The Quest For Peace and a
Meaning to Life

An Effort to Regain a Normal Life

After leaving the racing circuit for good and getting back to Amarillo, I opened a clubroom over Jim Burroughs's general store on the Bowery, composed principally of saloons, gambling houses, restaurants, and rooming houses.[1] I slept in the clubroom and ate in one of the best and nicest restaurants in the block. At this restaurant, Mrs. Pearl Smith was a waitress and only twenty-two years old, but she had been unfortunate enough to marry at the age of sixteen years to a husband who had proven himself unworthy of a respectable woman. She divorced him and had been unmarried for two years. Pearl Smith was a real innocent, beautiful woman, and she and I soon became warm friends.

An Attempted Assassination

Pearl's father and mother lived at Snyder, Oklahoma, and she concluded to visit them while I attended the Texas Cattle Raisers Association meeting at Fort Worth in March. The night we were to leave, I took Pearl to the Fort Worth and Denver depot, and I had some business I wanted Gus Mathis to attend to during my absence. Gus was tending bar for Z. Z. Savage, and the Savage saloon was probably fifty paces from the depot and directly in front of it. It was a miserable night, misting rain, foggy, and very dark. I told Gus my business, and he readily agreed to accommodate me, and I left the saloon and started back to the depot.

Automobile parade, looking north on Polk from Third Street, Amarillo, ca. 1909.
Courtesy Amarillo Public Library.

Fort Worth and Denver City Railroad Station, Amarillo, ca. 1910. Courtesy
Amarillo, Texas: The First Hundred Years 1887-1987, a Picture Postcard History
(Amarillo: Ray Franks Publishing Ranch).

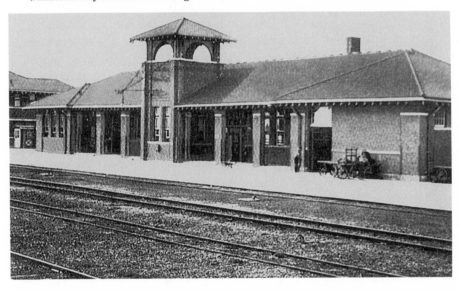

When I was halfway there, I was knocked flat by a blow on the neck. Gus Mathis and Barney Plemons[2] saw a man run up behind me and strike and run, and they gave chase while Al Chastine put me in his buggy and ran his horse to the offices of Dr. Pearson and Dr. Lumpkin. There they repaired nine arteries that were cut in my neck.

Barney and Gus caught the would-be assassin and landed him in jail. I went to the jail as soon as it was safe for me to walk and had Jim Keating bring the villain out where I could look him over. I would not appear as a complaining witness, so he was turned loose and warned to get out of town. As soon as I was notified that he was gone, I left town and stayed gone until I was an eyewitness, later, to that fellow's demise.

The Loss of Another Object of Affection

On her trip to visit her parents, Pearl Smith, as she alighted from the train at Snyder, Oklahoma, was struck by the force of a cyclone that hurled her against the depot structure, killing her instantly. Not long after this, I concluded to go some place where I could be alone and have absolute peace and quiet. I simply wanted to be left alone by the world and all its activities. The place I selected was my mountain lodge in Cimarron County, Oklahoma.

Off to the Oklahoma High Country

I rigged up a spring wagon and team from the six broncos that I owned. Just one of them had been broken to harness; the others had been ridden about three times. So I hitched my gentle pony and a bronc to the wagon and put my eldest boy, twelve years old, on a bronc to drive the other three behind the wagon. One of my acquaintances, named Tom Hughes, and my next eldest son, Johnnie, rode in the wagon with our camping outfit, consisting of bedding, cooking utensils, provisions, and grain for the ponies. We left Amarillo for Kenton, Oklahoma, an old cow town on the Cimarron River near the border of New Mexico and Colorado.

I had homesteaded a claim seven miles north of Kenton seven or eight years before, but my right had been forfeited because of non-residence.[3] My intentions were to make a reentry on this land, as there was running water there. The Carrizo ran through this claim, and it was surrounded by mesas and rough lands that were covered with mesquite and black grama grass, an ideal location for a small cattle ranch.[4]

Jim Gober's sons Temple (left) and Johnnie, ca. 1902.

We left Amarillo and drove twenty-five miles north, crossing the Canadian River at the best fording site in that locality. Our broncos were pretty well fagged out, so we decided to stop and camp. Our camp was located about four hundred yards from one of the old LX Ranch houses then occupied by Garnett Lee[5] and his family, whom I thought to be my friend. After we had hobbled our ponies and built a small campfire and were frying bacon and making coffee, Garnett Lee rode up on horseback and said, very gruffly, "You will have to move outside my pasture. If I let you camp here, others will camp here, and I am liable to get burned out." On this same ground I had enjoyed freedom and liberty and had extended hospitality and kindness to all humanity that came my way. I did this for a period of three years just thirteen years prior to this incident. Now, it seemed, there was nothing for me to do except hitch those tired broncos to the wagon and unhobble the other horses; saddle one of them for Temple, my boy; and move on three miles in the dark, or have trouble with Lee.

The next day we made a hard day's travel to Dalhart, Texas. There I had a cousin and his son running a livery and transfer barn, so we put up with them and stayed until the next day. We left Dalhart about noon and traveled about fifteen miles toward Buffalo Springs.[6] At the chosen site for our stop, we pitched camp across the trail, some four hundred yards from a farmhouse in a German settlement. Next morning, Tom Hughes and the two little boys got up early and spread out a tarp. They cut and scattered shelled corn for the broncos, and Hughes was preparing our breakfast when I heard the little boys fussing at something.

Looking out from under the wagon covers, I saw a large black mule fighting the ponies away from their feed. There was a bunch of horses some fifty yards away that this mule evidently had quit. I got my clothes on and crawled out of the wagon and herded the mule away until the ponies were through eating their grain.

After finishing our breakfast, we harnessed our team and saddled Temple's bronc and were on our way, hoping to make Buffalo Springs for the night. Soon Johnnie said to me, "Temple is having trouble with that mule." I saw Temple running the mule back in the direction we had come, and the bronc he was riding was not bridle broken, and before he could get her stopped and turned around, the mule would be back with the loose broncos, following the wagon. On seeing the situation, I hollered to Temple, "Just leave the mule alone until we come to a gate, and then we will be able to cut him out and shut the gate."

We drove some seven or eight miles before coming to the Buffalo Springs pasture fence. There we shut the mule off and drove on, probably ten miles; then the boxing overheated in one of our wheels, and the wheel stuck and refused to turn. There was nothing for us to do but camp. While Hughes was getting dinner, I tried to get our frozen wheel loose from the axle, but I only succeeded in breaking the boxing.

After we ate, I put Temple on the only gentle pony we had and tied the broken boxing to his saddle. I started him to Buffalo Springs Ranch, approximately ten miles away, instructing him to ask the ranch foreman to order a new boxing from Texline[7] by mail. Temple's instructions were for him to stay at the ranch until the boxing came and then to come back to our camp.

The next day at noon, Temple came in with the boxing, and the sheriff of Dalhart, Rube Hutton, was with him. I had known him twenty-five years back when he was a cowboy and also when he was

Rube Hutton, sheriff of Dallam County, Texas 1904-6, date unknown. Courtesy XIT Museum, Dallam-Hartley County Historical Association.

sheriff at Miama, Texas, but never had associated with him as an intimate friend. In fact, as I remembered him, he had somewhat of a selfish disposition and the reputation of being overbearing.

On dismounting, Hutton asked me if I had seen or heard of a bunch of mules. I told him that the only mule I had seen had followed our wagon eight or ten miles the day before, until we had come to a gate where we had shut him off, and I directed him to the location of the gate. Hutton remarked that he would go by and get the mule and that it belonged to a Dutchman who thought the mule was stolen.

An Unscrupulous Lawman

After our dinner, Hutton asked me where we intended getting to that night. I told him that we would make Buffalo Springs, and he bade me goodbye and rode in the direction where we last saw the mule. With Hutton's departure, we harnessed our team and saddled Temple's bronc and started for Buffalo Springs. We arrived there about sundown and camped. It was threatening rain, and I told Tom

Hughes to take the little boys to the ranch house and to get a bed for him and the boys, and I would sleep in the wagon to guard the outfit.

Next morning Sheriff Hutton waked me up at daylight and said to me, "You will have to go back to Dalhart with me and square that Dutchman. He swore out a warrant for you for stealing his mule." It was only a few months until election, and Hutton was running for reelection. He had gone and found the mule and had taken it to its owner and apparently persuaded him to go with him to Dalhart and swear out a warrant for my arrest, making the Dutchman believe that I was a desperado and thief. Expecting to make a great reputation with the entire Dutch colony, he had the owner of the mule well coached, and the fellow swore some manufactured lies that might have caused me some trouble if I had been a stranger.

I appeared before Judge Joseph Inman, the county judge, and he had known me for years. After Hutton's trained witness had testified, or I should say recited the lesson that Hutton had taught him, I took him for cross-examination. I asked him only two or three questions when Hutton left the room. Then I took the stand and was sworn. I related all the circumstances concerning the mule, just as they had happened. Judge Inman promptly ruled, "The defendant is dismissed." When I walked out of the courtroom, I found Hutton sitting on the courthouse steps. I only stopped and looked at him and wondered how such a man could live in a civilized community, much less get to be sheriff, even of a small-populated county.

I had some real friends in Dalhart, especially J. L. Gober and son and Jesse Jenkins, who were as near to me as brothers. They stood high in the community and had considerable experience in elections. As a final settlement, I asked them, in the way of a favor, to see that Hutton was defeated for sheriff in the coming election. Hutton was defeated, and if he has ever held public office since, I am unaware of the fact.

Unscheduled Change in Plans

Tom Hughes, the little boys, and I took the Fort Worth and Denver train that night from Dalhart to Texline. The next morning, I hired a rig to take us to Buffalo Springs.

The following morning we were on our way to Kenton. It took us two days to arrive at my old claim, where I expected to find the little box house that I had put there eight years before. But when we

Jim Gober, date unknown.

arrived, there was no sign of a house ever being there. Nevertheless, we pitched camp and fixed things up the best we could.

The next day, I began a search for my house and found it about three miles from where I had left it. The man that had it on his premises told me who he had bought the house from, and it was a man I knew and thought of as a friend. He lived at Woodward, Oklahoma, and so I wrote him a letter and demanded that he put the house back or build me another one at once. On receipt of my letter, he immediately took the Santa Fe train to Amarillo and then changed to the Fort Worth and Denver bound for Clayton, New Mexico. From Clayton, he took the mail stage out to Kenton, and I hired a team to bring him to my camp.

He apologized for his actions and arranged for another house to be built, so we shook hands and parted peacefully and respectfully, but I was much surprised and disappointed in his character. I could only conclude that he had taken the course of disrespect and lack of consideration that many continue to follow to this day.

I went to work to fence my claim, and Tom Hughes kept camp and cooked. There I put in six weeks of the hardest work I have ever done to bring my land back to the condition that I had left it eight years before.

Business matters required that I return to Amarillo, and I brought the smallest boy and Tom Hughes with me, leaving Temple at a neighbor's, just one-half mile from our shack. Temple was to look after the ponies and take care of our things until I returned.

Within a week, I concluded to remain in Amarillo. I wrote Temple to come and bring the ponies, which he did. After deciding to spend the latter part of the summer and perhaps fall and winter in Amarillo, I began looking for a job of any kind to make a living.

Too Mean to Die

An old-time cowboy friend, Joe Phillips, was running a hotel, one of the oldest in town, called the Southern. He also was running three cabs of the kind that were used before automobiles. Phillips gave me a team and cab to drive on percentage, and after I had been driving some two weeks, about the sixth of September, a cold rain had been falling for two days and nights.

I had met a train and had come back to my stand on Polk Street, in front of a day-and-night restaurant. At that moment I was standing on the sidewalk waiting for a customer that had gone in the restaurant to eat. Suddenly, I turned deathly sick but managed to get on the cab seat and drive to the barn and put my team up. I went to the hotel and told Mr. Phillips I was sick and was going to my room and go to bed.

In a few minutes, Phillips came to my room and found me with a hard chill, and he piled all the extra covers on me that he could find. Next morning, I had a high fever, and Mr. Phillips sent for Dr. Patton, who pronounced my case as typhoid fever.

My eldest sister, Annie, was running a rooming house several blocks from the Southern Hotel, and my mother, eighty-three years old, was living with her. When Mother found out I was sick, she and Sister had me moved to Sister's home and rooming house.

Dr. Patton had the reputation of never losing a case of typhoid fever, but after two or three days he began bringing his partner with him when he came to see me. His partner was Dr. Gist, whom we had known from the time he was a small boy; in fact, his father and mine were neighbors and friends in the first settlement of Denton County, Texas.

After I had been sick two and one-half months, both doctors were called in about three PM. The world was dark to me, and I could not tell one person from the other except when they spoke, nor could I move a muscle. When the two doctors examined me and felt where my heart should be, I heard Patton tell Gist to fix a strychnine hypo. I knew that it was the doctors working with me by their voices, and my knowledge of what was going on was normal, but I was blind, speechless, and helpless, insofar as being able to move. I heard Gist say to Patton, "This is the last we will have to do for Jim"; then they raised my left arm and injected the strychnine. All I realized was the raising of my arm.

They left the room and me for dead and told my sister that she should wire my other sister, Sallie, who lived at Canadian, Texas, and a brother, John, at Woodward, Oklahoma. My mother heard the doctor and fell to the floor in a faint. All of these things were occurring unrecognized by me. I was dead, so far as any sense of the body or mind was concerned.

My sister wired my brother and other sister, and they got to Amarillo at seven forty-five the next morning and walked into my room. Brother took hold of my hand and spoke, and I recognized his voice, the voice of his wife, and that of my sister. Then I realized that they were all really there, but it seemed that they were in the dark. Gradually my sight came to me, and I felt like I had awakened from a long sleep.

Soon I could talk, but my speech was weak and feeble. I passed over the danger and was on the road to recovery, providing no complications set in. Slowly and gradually I improved, but my mother was confined to her bed in the same room. She was suffering from the shock of hearing the doctor say I was dying and had no chance to live.

In a week, I was able to be propped up in a rocking chair and would sit up a little longer each day. The second week, I got my brother to bring me a billiard cue, cut off the right length to use for a walking stick, and I began to move around the room. Within a few days, I was able to get out into the yard.

A Difficult but Worthwhile Sacrifice

The following week I received a letter from Oliver Tucker, urging me to come to Boise City,[8] the county seat of Cimarron County,

Oklahoma, the county where I had my homestead. I was a witness for the prosecution in the case where a doctor that performed a criminal operation on Tucker's wife and caused her death had been indicted on the charges. I thought that if I could get there, it would help my mother to see me able to get up and go. Also, I felt that I had been a great burden to my sister, she being a widow who was slaving her life away to make a living.

I mustered all the courage, strength, ambition, and pride that I had and ordered a cab to take me to the Fort Worth and Denver train. The cab man and my brother helped me into the cab and helped me out at the depot and on the train.

I had several difficult things to deal with on this journey: first, a suitcase that would weigh forty or fifty pounds; second, changing at Dalhart and taking the Rock Island to Texhoma;[9] third, riding the mail hack from Texhoma for sixty-five miles in real cold weather.

When I arrived at Dalhart, I arranged with the train porter to help me off of the train and into the depot. He was also to get me a cab to take me to the Rock Island depot.

By the time the Rock Island train arrived, I had arranged for help to get on the train. It was a fast train called the Golden State Limited, and it was only an hour run on the train to Texhoma. For some reason unknown to me, the train just barely checked at Texhoma; then it started again. I pulled the bell cord, but the train had proceeded one-half mile before stopping, because it took that amount of time for the conductor to realize what he had done.

He and the porter helped me off of the train onto the bleak Oklahoma prairie. The train had left me one-half mile from the town in the early dawn, with a cold winter wind that soon had my hands and ears aching. I got down on my knees and ran my billiard cue through my suitcase handle, pulling the cue over my shoulder with one hand and putting the other hand on frozen ground to help my weak legs get me on my feet. Four times I had to stop and rest and then go through the same process before reaching the hotel.

The mail hack left the hotel for Boise City promptly at seven AM. I was helped into the hack and a comfort wrapped around my legs. In that situation, I started on my last lap of a nerve-wracking adventure.

The hack hadn't gone far until snow began to fall and the wind blew furiously, keeping the snow blown out of the road pretty well. We had to change teams every fifteen to eighteen miles, and the hack finally arrived, with its frozen human cargo, about seven PM.

I was well acquainted with Mother Louis, who ran the hotel, and she gave me a nice warm meal and put me to bed. I was completely exhausted, but I felt that I had accomplished a righteous deed by relieving my sister of her long, tedious burden of caring for me. Also, I was about to fulfill my obligation to my friend, Oliver Tucker, to appear as a witness against the man that had unscrupulously murdered his beautiful wife and left him heartbroken and two little boys motherless.

My accomplishments cheered my feeble spirit to the extent that I rested very well and got some real sound sleep. The rest and sleep put me in very good condition to take the witness stand the next morning.

I had driven Mrs. Tucker to Kenton to see this doctor and was cooking for the family when the doctor made his second call on her. That is how I became a material witness. When I took the witness stand, I simply testified to the circumstances that happened on, and in a few days prior to, Mrs. Tucker's death. At the conclusion of the trial, the defendant was sentenced to serve two years in Leavenworth prison.

The Loss of a Noble Lady

After the trial was over and we all were dismissed, I joined Mr. Tucker's party, and we started in a spring wagon for his home, forty-five miles distant. It was four o'clock when we left Boise City, so we drove most of the night. I had arranged with Tucker to stay at his house until I had regained my strength.

It appeared that I could not escape the specter of sadness even now in my weakened condition. I had been there only three days when I got a letter from my sister to come back to Amarillo at once, because my mother was going to die.

The only conveyance I could get was to take Tucker's team and a lumber wagon and get a Mr. Austin to drive me to the road where the mail stage passes, which was a distance of twenty-two miles. The stage would pass the crossroads at one thirty PM, and it was understood that Austin was to get back home that evening to tend to the stock. Mr. Tucker was away, and a bad storm had come up with snow, sleet, and rain.

We got to the crossroads at two PM, but the stage had passed thirty minutes before we arrived. I got my walking stick and ran it through the handle of my suitcase and bade Mr. Austin goodbye, and he started back home.

I headed up the road for Clayton, New Mexico, wading in snow eight inches deep and with the snow still falling. I realized that I must gauge my speed according to my strength, but by all means I must keep moving, or perhaps I would get numb and freeze to death.

It was twenty-three miles to Clayton from the crossroads where Austin left me, and there were no settlements in sight from the road save a homestead now and then. I waded the snowy trail until eleven o'clock that night; then I came to a small, new, one-room shack, not more than ten by twelve, with a small picket shed. It seemed that I knocked and hollered at least five minutes before I could get a response. Finally, a man opened the door, and I explained who I was and how I came to be out in the storm.

He asked me in and built a fire out of cow chips in a small sheet-iron stove but expressed his regrets that he could not keep me through the remainder of the night, saying, "I have only been married a few days and just have the one room and one bed and no extra bedding." Finally, his wife called his attention to a wagon sheet they had in the picket shed. So I told him that I would appreciate the sheet—I could wrap up in it and sit up in the shed until daylight, and I would then be rested enough to travel on.

Next morning, I shook the snow off and started down the road. I had walked, or rather waded, until nine o'clock when a man driving a team to a spring wagon came up the snow-laden trail and overtook me. He asked me to ride with him, and I thanked him with all my heart. Two hours later we arrived at Clayton.

In Clayton, I was forced to wait until nine PM for a train to Amarillo. The consequence of all these unfavorable circumstances was that my mother was already buried by the time I got to Amarillo. At least I knew in my heart that I had made a desperate effort to get to her. And so, under such cruel conditions I lost another loved one.

I have reflected back, many, many times to that walk in the snow and the suffering I endured from the cold. Each time I think of the incident it gives me joy, because I was suffering and enduring an inhuman task, prompted by the love and respect I bore for the noblest woman of God's creation, my mother.

Kindly take this message from a friend,
Our mother is our dearest sweetheart since time began.
Mother will give us love and care,
No other will all our troubles share,
So when she has toiled and slaved until we are grown

We should claim some burdens to be our own,
And keep them from her heart and mind, and give her peace
   and repose,
For no sweetheart like her, a son or daughter ever knows.

Jim Gober

A Return to the Homestead Ranch

I remained in Amarillo through the balance of the winter. The next spring, I went back to my claim alone, as I wanted the boys to go to school in Amarillo. I had worked very hard and gotten forty acres into cultivation, planted maize and sowed nine acres in alfalfa. I had hired a Mr. Cooper and his mule team and had taken my team of horses, and we went up the Carrizo about four hundred yards, hitched onto slips or scrapers,[10] and started building a sand dam. Cooper helped me only a few days; then I put in a week alone and threw up a sand dam twenty-five yards long and ten feet high in the midstream, tapering off on the ends to the level of either bank.

Then I started on an irrigation ditch to my alfalfa. By the time I had my ditch completed, the earth literally had burst open with grasshoppers, and in three days my alfalfa was cleaned off the ground as neat as a well-kept front yard.

In a few months, I harrowed the ground, and it was then fall, and my team was pretty well jaded. Just when I was finishing up, an old friend by the name of Jess Tanner came along. He had a cattle ranch out in Colorado and had been in the vicinity of Kenton for several days buying cattle. Tanner ate dinner with me, and when he got ready to leave, he sized up my worked-down team and said, "It's only seventy-five miles to my ranch. Now, if you will hitch those old ponies to that old buggy and come up and stay a week with me, I will give you a good saddle horse."

Tanner had been one of my early-day, Panhandle, cowboy friends, and he knew that I was serving, at that time, as deputy sheriff in that corner of old No Man's Land, and that I needed a good horse. So I set a time when I would come, and at the appointed time, I hitched my old team to the old borrowed buggy that Willard Cole had been good enough to loan to me.

The first day, I drove to Jim Stenson's sheep ranch and stayed all night. The next day I went through Springfield, Colorado, and camped that night in a canyon that was a very desolate place. One of my horses got sick, and I could go no farther.

The following day, I arrived at Tanner's ranch on Clay Creek about two PM. Tanner and his entire family made me feel like I was in a brother's or sister's home. I stayed with them three days and begged off staying any longer because I had to return home. My sick horse was still in bad shape.

Mr. Tanner sent one of his sons to round up and corral thirty head of cow ponies. After they were in the corral, Tanner pointed out one old pet horse and said, "Leave that one out, and pick any other you want." I roped out a nice buckskin pacing pony with black paints, left my sick horse, and hitched the buckskin with my well horse and bade the entire family goodbye. We had gotten into my buggy to start on the journey home when Mr. Tanner halted me, saying, "Wait until I go in the house and return. I have something for you."

The Receipt of an Unpredicted Result

Tanner soon reappeared with a flour sack, stuffed until it could barely be tied. He raised the flap from behind the seat of the wagon and shoved the sack under the seat and said to me, "Now, promise me that you will not open this sack until you get home."

I drove to Springfield that day and stayed all night, and the next day I drove home, getting there about four PM. Before feeding my team, I turned them loose to browse while I prepared my dinner. After I had gotten my dinner and fed the team, I went to get my things out of the buggy, and of course I came across the sack, about which I had completely forgotten. It seemed so light to be so full.

I didn't take time to untie it, but instead I cut the string and found it was tobacco, the best odor I ever smelled and of a beautiful color. Without question I had never seen any tobacco like this before. Immediately, I got my big, strong briar off the shelf and mashed up enough to jam the big pipe full. I packed it well, thinking all the while how I was going to enjoy the richest smoke that I had ever had.

I lit my pipe, got a book, and selected my favorite chair, then sat down and began to puff and curl the smoke from my much appreciated home-raised tobacco. In about three minutes, the house began to turn over, and I managed to get to the bed, but it would turn on its side. Within a few seconds I got on the floor and crawled to the door and lay flat on my stomach, holding on to the door sill, heaving, praying, and cussing my friend Tanner. I continued each of those activities, in that order, over the next several minutes.

I had always known Tanner to be full of jokes and pranks, but this seemed too serious for any friend to impose on another. This was one action that was very difficult for me to understand, but I finally got back to my bed and went to sleep. The next morning, I felt no bad effect.

After two or three days, I ventured to put a small portion of the golden leaf with my Prince Albert pipe tobacco, and from time to time increased the natural until finally I was smoking it straight. Then I conscientiously forgave my friend and spent many lonely hours enjoying the rich aroma of my present from Tanner. Without a doubt, it was the most beautiful hand-cured tobacco that I ever hoped to find.[11]

My alfalfa, after its earlier devastation, came up to a most beautiful stand. All the neighbors passing by would remark what a splendid stand I had, and I felt assured that the nine acres would be worth at least nine hundred dollars per year.

The winter set in early in November, and the ground froze. It seemed that before one freeze would thaw, another would come. About the third freeze, the ground cracked open as though a charge of dynamite had exploded, and my alfalfa vanished once again.

I worried on until spring and planted some Indian corn[12] and quite an acreage of maize. In a bend of the creek, I prepared an acre of rich, black, sandy soil for a garden, and I planted most of it in Irish potatoes. While I was planting the potatoes, John Labrier came by on horseback. John had lived in that vicinity for twenty years and handled cattle and sheep. He spoke to me with a grin of wisdom and said, "You are just throwing your labor away—you can't raise potatoes here." I wondered why John said, "You will find out."

My potatoes came up to a fine stand and grew real fast, as the land was subirrigated. I would get out early in the morning and cultivate the thrifty vines and wonder why John had tried to discourage me from planting them.

On Saturday evening, about the tenth of July, John Jones and his lovely wife, whom I had known from a girl of seventeen years old, came by and asked me to have dinner with them at their ranch Sunday. Their ranch was three miles up the creek from my place. To go to their ranch the next day, I crossed the creek at the potato patch and looked at my flattering prospect with much pride and satisfaction. I ate dinner and visited with my good friends until three PM, and then I started for my lonely cabin, crossing the creek at the same place as when I left home. I was looking toward the direction where my potato patch was when I left, and, shocked and astounded, I found that the vines were literally devoured with army potato bugs. They were still digging at the stubs of the vines as I rode by, and then I realized why John Labrier grinned at me when I was planting the potatoes and told me that I was throwing my labor away.

My Indian corn, about five acres, was also on the creek valley on very rich land and had grown very well, although we had no rain of consequence. When it was just in roasting ears, I cut it by hand and shocked it in large shocks.

About the time I had shocked my corn, I made a deal with my neighbor, Tucker, to lease his place that joined mine on the south, lying on either side of the Carrizo Creek. He had about one hundred acres in cultivation, besides a school section[13] leased from the state for grazing. His teams, farm implements, chickens, and milk cows went with this lease.

Tucker was a hard-working, honest man and had recently lost his wife. She had left him with two small children, both boys, one four and the other six years. Tucker was still a heartbroken and discouraged man, and I readily understood his situation and could sympathize with him wholeheartedly.

My son, Temple, had been in east Texas working for my father-in-law's brother as a guard on the county farm of Wood County. While there, he had married and left the position, gone to Temple, Texas, and secured a job with the Santa Fe Water Department, but had agreed to come out and live with me and file on 320 acres of land that joined me on the north. The Colorado and Oklahoma state line was the dividing line between this land and mine.

I hauled my shocked corn to the Tucker place and put it in a large rick and prepared to make the Tucker place my home, as it was better improved than mine. Then I received a letter from Temple saying that his wife wasn't able to make the trip and wouldn't be for six weeks, but that he could come and file on the land, and his wife would come as soon as it was safe for her to undertake the trip. He also stated that he was short on money and asked me to send him fifteen dollars to help pay his railroad fare.

I went to John Jones and borrowed the fifteen dollars and went to work for him at one dollar per day to pay it back. About all he had for me to do was to stay at the ranch with Mrs. Jones and her sister. John had to go receive some cattle he had bought, quite a distance away. He knew that I would be as a father to Mrs. Jones and her sister in his absence.

Another Tragedy to Face

The second morning that I had been at John's ranch, I went out to a small pasture that was used for saddle horses to catch a horse to ride the fence line of the large range to see that all gates were closed. By the time I had caught the horse, I looked back towards the ranch house, approximately one-fourth mile, and saw Mrs. Jones running toward me. That scene unnerved me and made me speechless, knowing that she was in a delicate condition and that she was subjecting herself to danger. I realized that something of a serious nature must have happened, so I started running toward her as fast as it was possible for me to move.

When I met Mrs. Jones, she was almost breathless but managed to make me understand that a telegram had been forwarded to me, over the phone, from Clayton, New Mexico. When we arrived at the house, Mrs. Jones said, "Mr. Gober, perhaps I had better talk over the phone and tell you the contents of the message." I sat down and waited until Mrs. Jones got through taking the message; then she turned, facing me, and was as pale as a ghost and said sadly, "Mr. Gober, your son that you were expecting has been murdered at Temple, Texas."

I said to Mrs. Jones, "I must leave at once for Amarillo and arrange for the body to be shipped to Amarillo for burial."

Then that blessed little friend said, "Mr. Gober, I will write you a check for what expense money that you think you will need."

And I replied, "Twenty-five dollars would be sufficient, as I have relatives that will help me when I get to Amarillo." Mrs. Jones gave me a check, and I hired a livery team at Kenton to take me to Clayton, New Mexico, where I took the Fort Worth and Denver for Amarillo that same night at nine thirty PM. When I got to Amarillo the next morning, I engaged the Eakle undertaking to negotiate the shipment of my boy from Temple, Texas, to Amarillo, and also to superintend the burial.

Later on, I went to Temple, Texas, and investigated to my satisfaction that my son was foully and brutally murdered by his wife's brother, who was a Santa Fe brakeman. I stayed until the grand jury convened, and not one witness could be found or had ever been sought. I was familiar with the conditions that had existed in Temple, Texas, for years, and I knew that it was only a joke for the home guards there to kill a stranger. I don't know of any other town in Texas where more men have been killed and the killer has gone free than in Temple, Texas.

I came back to Kenton, Oklahoma, and disposed of what few belongings I had, including my land and improvements. I deeded my home to R. A. Owens, who was county clerk, and told him that if he ever sold it, to divide what he got out of it. I have never seen Owens since then, but I understand that he still lives at the county seat of Cimarron County.[14]

While in Amarillo after Mother had died, I met an old friend—in fact, his father and mine were friends in the first settlement of Hunt County, Texas, before the Civil War. I will call this man J. C. He had been sheriff of an east Texas county and had married his cousin when he was a very young man. She had died a short time before I had met him here in Amarillo.

Mr. J. C. had taken to drink to drown his sorrow and was in a nervous condition. While talking to him, my two sweet little daughters came to me, and I told my friend how I had lost their mother, and he made over them and bought them some small presents.

My oldest daughter was past fifteen, and the youngest was thirteen years. Woodie was the oldest, and both of them were living with their grandmother and going to school. Woodie was in the eighth grade and Jimmye in the seventh, and I was placing my fondest hopes on the future when they would both finish high school and I could have a home of our own, no matter how humble. It would be a great pleasure to have my children once more in a happy family circle.

J. C. informed me that he should return home, that his farm was going to be sold under a hatched-up judgment by of his wife's kin folks. Since he and his wife had no children, there was something peculiar about the deed on his property, and he told me that if I would take him home and straighten up his business, he would pay me liberally. I accepted his offer and took him home and sold his interests for two thousand dollars. Besides, I sold cotton, oats, and corn to the amount of one thousand dollars, and then I took J. C. to Oklahoma City and put him in the McKenley whiskey cure.

I put up at a hotel where there was a clubroom located in the hotel, run under locked doors. The Oklahoma legislature was in session, and naturally business was thriving in private places that were under protection.

Still Another Loss that Pierced the Heart

I was making some money gambling every day and still not making myself conspicuous. After being at this clubroom for a week, I walked out early one morning and went to the Steward Hotel for breakfast. After I had finished my meal and stepped out on the sidewalk, a plainclothes detective tapped me on the shoulder and asked my name. I told him, and he said, "We have been looking for you for three days. There's a telegram at the police station for you." I was getting suspicious of telegrams and dreaded to know their contents.

I went straight to the station and opened the telegram, and it informed me that Woodie was dead. Since the telegram was sent three days previous, naturally, my daughter already was buried when I arrived at Amarillo. It seemed I was destined to suffer yet another blow to my heart and spirit and I realized that one more bright hope was shattered forever.

My low spirits would only permit me to leave Amarillo, so I went to Woodward, Oklahoma, and stayed there for a month. The Wichita Falls and Great Western Railroad had been built through Woodward and was completed eighty miles to Forgan, Oklahoma.[15]

I went to Forgan and opened a restaurant. In Forgan I found the most unscrupulous den of thieves and robbers that I have ever had the misfortune of coming in contact with, and the mayor was the brains of the bunch. I stayed there three months and sold my outfit, mostly on a credit.

From Forgan, I went back to Woodward and leased the old Cattle King Hotel. It had been running for some time in a disgraceful manner. There had been bootlegging, crap shooting, and lewd women permitted there, and of course they had been paying off the officers. As soon as I took possession, I ordered everyone to vacate, except two men who held positions in business firms in town. The third evening, the night marshal, without my knowledge, sent a woman to get a room. She inquired for work, and when I informed her that I hadn't any opening, she asked if she could get a room. I told her to register and gave her a nice room upstairs.

About ten PM, I went to bed, leaving a man on duty in the office with positive instructions not to allow anyone to go upstairs unless registered. My room was upstairs, near the landing. Around eleven PM I was startled by a knock on my door. Ever since my cowboy and lawman days, I have always slept "with one eye open," so I was up quickly, and when I went to the door and opened it, I found that it was the man I had left on night duty. He came in and said, "Mr. Gober, the night marshal has gone back to the room that the woman is occupying, and I told him that is against the rules."

I pulled on my trousers and, accompanied by the night manager, rushed back to the room in question. We reached the door just as the light was snapped out. I rapped on the door loudly and said, "Sir, I must have you open this door immediately." There was no reply. I spoke again, "If I have to kick this door in, you will have to be taken away in an ambulance." He opened the door, and I took his gun and guided him to the stairway with fist and foot. I went back and made the woman dress and then guided her downstairs and out of the door.

In a few days, this same marshal and a deputy sheriff came rushing in the office and started to enter the hall leading to the rooms on the ground floor. I stopped them and required that they come back into the office, saying to them, "Gentlemen, this is my home and my place of business. It isn't a payoff joint anymore. Hereafter, if you have business here, make your business known to me, and I will be courteous enough to allow you reasonable privileges."

Two weeks later, the sheriff tried a dirty scheme on me, and it failed. I saw that I was in another nest of degenerates hiding under the cloak of officers, but in reality petty larceny thieves. Convinced that I should leave, I sold out after being there a year and went to Shattuck, Oklahoma,[16] in 1914, just as the war broke out. I opened another restaurant and found another lowbred bunch of officers in authority, but I skirmished along and stayed there seven years. The last two years I served as city marshal, and all respectable, honorable citizens of Shattuck are my friends.

In July 1923, I left Shattuck for San Francisco, California, to work as a detective until I acquired the knowledge of running a real detective agency. I chose San Francisco because my only living daughter and her husband lived there, and I would get to be with her while picking up the knowledge that I sought. I went to work for the Mars Agency and worked for them for ten months, then went over to the William A. Pinkerton Agency,[17] where I spent another ten months. Believing that I had the knowledge that I desired, I made plans to leave San Francisco to return to Amarillo.

Grasping the Vision
of a Detective Agency

Police Connections

I left San Francisco the evening of May 23, 1925, arriving home in Amarillo the evening of the 26th. My objective was to obtain the first paying job that I could get, as I was anxious to start a detective agency in Amarillo as soon as possible.

Early after my return, I met H. L. Gaither, a patrolman in the Amarillo Police Department. Gaither's wife was the daughter of Jim Dobbs, an old-time friend of mine, although I had never had any acquaintance with Gaither. Somehow I felt as though I already knew him because of the high regard I had for his wife and mother-in-law. Those relationships had caused me to form a good opinion of Gaither. Jim Dobbs had died several years before, and his wife was living with her daughter and Gaither.

The chief of police was Captain Blackwell, and it wasn't but a short time after I met Gaither until Captain Blackwell got into trouble, was indicted, and lost his job over putting some woman in jail. I will state that I think that Captain Blackwell was unjustly treated in this matter. A new chief of police was to be appointed soon by the mayor.

Gaither eventually came to me and said, "If you can't get the job, I would like for you to help me get it." I told Gaither that I had no intentions of trying to get the job and that I would do all that I could to help him get the appointment. He thanked me and said, "If I

Jim Gober in his security officer uniform, ca. 1927.

become chief of police, I want you to come work for me." I thanked Gaither for his confidence in me.

A Misplaced Effort To Help

Before Gaither's quest for the police chief's position could even be pursued, Blackwell had discharged Gaither—before Blackwell got into trouble. Gaither was taking watchman jobs and had told me that he was not making a living and was unable to supply the necessities for his family. I went to the home of the mayor, Lee Bivins,[1] and I felt comfortable in doing that, for I had known him for twenty-five years. I talked to Mr. Bivins for one hour and made every favorable impression possible for Gaither. At the time I believed that I was doing the right thing. I felt that I was trying to help the wife of my old friend Dobbs and his daughter by getting Gaither the job as chief of police. Whether or not my pleadings to Mayor Bivins had any effect on Gaither's cause, I am not able to say, but Gaither was appointed chief of police.

After he had taken over the reins as chief, I went to see him, and he told me that he thought that he could put me on the police force, but first he wanted to talk to the mayor. After that, I would see him every few days, and he would speak up and say, "I haven't gotten a chance to see the mayor yet."

After two weeks of suspense, Harve Avery, the assistant city manager, recommended me to the city commissioners to take charge of sixty guards that were maintaining quarantine on the smallpox cases. The city manager, Mr. Bartlett, called me into his office and told me that I would be commissioned under Gaither, but in reality I would not be under anyone except the health office and specifically him, Bartlett. He told me to get a capable man to assist me in handling the guards at night and suggested John Snider.[2]

I had known John Snider from boyhood and had known him as chief of police of the Amarillo Police Department just a few years back, and I knew him to be a capable man. So I readily sanctioned Bartlett's recommendation. Then Bartlett suggested I speak to the chief, as a matter of courtesy. To Mr. Bartlett's way of thinking, Snider would have to be commissioned by Gaither.

I went to Gaither and asked him if it would be agreeable to commission Snider to help me. Gaither informed me that it wouldn't suit him, as all old-timers in Amarillo were dead, politically. From that very remark I realized why he had not placed me on his force, and, further, I realized that he didn't intend to. So I selected another man, and I never raised the issue about Snider because I needed work badly and hoped eventually to harmonize with the department.

Help to the City of Amarillo

As I remember, there were eighty or ninety cases of smallpox, and the health officer, whose name was Dr. Fuller, had out sixty guards at five dollars per day. Most of the cases were in the Mexican district, on the east side of town. These Mexicans had been employed by the Santa Fe Railroad.

After a few days, I conceived an idea to cut the enormous expense such a guard force was costing the city. I discovered a Mexican dance hall located at about the center of the Mexican settlement, and I planned to rent the dance hall and turn it into a pest house and put all the Mexicans in it. My plans were then to put a Mexican nurse and a Mexican cook there to help take care of the patients. That would enable Dr. Fuller to see all the patients at one location. Instead of sixty guards, I would use two, one in the daytime and one at night.

I laid out my scheme to Harve Avery, and he explained it to the manager, and they agreed on the plan. They arranged for me to discuss it with the mayor and the city commission, which I did. Mayor Bivins gave his approval and told me to arrange for the dance hall.

I immediately went and saw the Mexican that owned the hall and made a deal with him to use it indefinitely. In three or four days we had all the Mexican cases in our emergency hospital. The first day I released forty of the guards and continued to release additional guards until finally the city was paying only me and two guards each five dollars per day, instead of paying for sixty guards. Besides, we then had the smallpox epidemic under absolute control, and in a short while it was stamped out entirely.

A Windfall Job with a Discouraging Outcome

I felt that I had shown my ability to be of value to the city of Amarillo. I could see, however, that Gaither did not appreciate my being in the city services, and I surmised that I was about to be out of employment, as there was no need of a boss over two men. If my motives had been self-directed only for the purpose of ensuring my future employment, I would not have made a proposal for a change that would have caused the elimination of my job.

To my surprise, Mr. Bartlett called me in his office and informed me that the city commission had concluded to furnish the five banks of Amarillo with a day and night guard, and they had agreed to give me that detail. I was to select a good man for the night job, and that man would be under me; although I would be commissioned under Gaither, I didn't have to answer to roll call or pay any attention to police matters. My job was independent of the police force, and as long as I pleased the banks, I would please the city officials. I felt very grateful, and so I expressed gratitude to Mr. Bartlett; also to Mr. Avery, for I knew that Avery was really the man that had boosted my stock.

I could see that this new job that was another thorn in Gaither's side, as he had shown that he was envious of any other man's capability. Soon news reached me that Gaither had accused me of trying to get his job, and this word came to me repeatedly. In each instance, I told my informant that such information was totally unfounded and that I would not accept Gaither's position even if it were offered to me.

Several times matters came to my attention that pertained to lawbreaking or other matters of interest to the police department, and I would tell Gaither. I soon saw, by his demeanor, that he didn't appreciate information from me, so I paid no more attention to him.

The Chief with Questionable Judgment

About the tenth of July, after I had taken the bank job in February 1927, Gaither approached me where I was standing on the corner of Fourth and Polk Streets. He informed me that a detective by the name of Powell from Fort Worth would come to me between two and three o'clock PM and introduce himself. Gaither also told me that this detective only wanted certain other parties to see him talking to me, to leave the impression on them that Powell was familiar with me. I said, "Gaither, what is the object in this stuff?" He replied, "There are some bank robbers in town, and we are setting a trap for them." Then Gaither walked on.

About fifteen minutes until three PM, Powell came up and introduced himself, and I had known him as a dirty cur that had been fleecing women out of money for several months. He asked me if the chief had spoken to me about him. I informed him that the chief had. Then Powell said he and the chief wanted to see me at once at the Oliver-Eakle Building,[3] on the fourth floor, at Judge Anderson's

Oliver-Eakle building, Amarillo, ca. 1927. Courtesy *Amarillo, Texas: The First Hundred Years 1887-1987,* a Picture Postcard History (Amarillo: Ray Franks Publishing Ranch).

office. I told Powell that I could not leave until the banks closed at three PM. Powell then said, "Make it ten minutes past three; we must see you right away."

After the banks closed, I studied this mysterious problem, and about fifteen minutes after three PM I went to the fourth floor of the Oliver-Eakle Building. I was standing, looking for Judge Anderson's sign, when Gaither came up on the next elevator and led the way to Anderson's office. We found Anderson and Powell seated on one side of a medium-size table. Gaither took a seat at the end of the table, and I sat on the opposite side from Powell and Anderson. Powell spoke up and said, "Mr. Gober, you understand that I am the go-between from the chief to the bank robbers. There are six in the gang. They are stopping at the Herring Hotel,[4] and I have had a room there for two weeks, getting acquainted and getting their confidence.

266

Herring Hotel, Amarillo, ca. 1928.
Courtesy *Amarillo, Texas: The
First Hundred Years 1887-1987,* a
Picture Postcard History (Amarillo:
Ray Franks Publishing Ranch).

"I have succeeded in getting familiar with three of them, and they
have agreed to crack the safe in the First National Bank next
Saturday night. In order to convince them that I have the chief fixed,
you will have your night man let one of them into the bank Friday
night to see that the plugs connecting the burglar alarm are pulled.
Then Saturday night they will have to tie up and gag your night man,
but they guarantee not to hurt him. In the meantime, the chief and
I and a couple of other good men will hide and kill the whole bunch."

I was shocked, surprised, and outraged. There is no doubt that I
showed my indignation as I looked each of those three devious men
over carefully. I can say truthfully that never in my forty years of
experience in dealing with crooks have I ever gazed on three more
cowardly, treacherous-looking beings.

Even though Gaither was the chief of police, I bore down on him
in anger with knife-like questions. "Do you really know that the men
you are framing and planning to murder are bank robbers, and if

267

First National Bank, Amarillo, ca. 1927. Courtesy *Amarillo, Texas: The First Hundred Years 1887-1987,* a Picture Postcard History (Amarillo: Ray Franks Publishing Ranch).

so, were there warrants issued for their arrest and rewards offered for them?"

Powell spoke up, "There is plenty against them," and then turned his conversation to Gaither in a way that gave the impression that the plans were all fixed, and they were not about to entertain any more questions from me.

In a few minutes, I got up from the table and walked out into the hall. Gaither came out, and we took the elevator and came down to the Polk Street landing. We walked two blocks without a word being spoken. Then Gaither stopped and asked me what I thought of the plan. I told him, "I knew Powell to be the dirtiest crook that was ever in Amarillo, and the likes of him wouldn't be allowed to stay in Amarillo if I were chief of police." I continued, "In the second place, I would not be part of a scheme that induced any man to commit a crime and then murdered him for committing it. Furthermore, you had better start using your head as a peace officer and, in fact, a leader of peace officers, and not be led by such scum as Powell."

I knew, at the conclusion of this conversation, that Gaither would use all the prestige in his power to get me fired from the bank job. He did succeed in getting the manager to give him the authority to ask for my commission, and the manager, the commissioners, and the mayor withdrew their liberal support from the banks as an alibi for giving Gaither the privilege to take my commission.

I went home and stayed there most of the time for six weeks, until Harve Avery drove out to my home in a car and told me that Mr. B. T. Ware,[5] president of the Amarillo National Bank, had sent for me. When I walked into Mr. Ware's office, he instructed me to go to Wiley Pollard, the sheriff, and get a commission and then return to my bank job once more. I thanked Mr. Ware and Mr. Fuqua,[6] president of the First National Bank, and also Mr. Ray Wheatley,[7] president of the Amarillo Bank and Trust Company, for I knew that they were trying to right an injustice that had been done to me by Gaither and other officials, the entire leadership of the city of Amarillo.

After two months, Gaither, through a certain stockholder in the Bank of Commerce and also the American State Bank, induced those two banks to withdraw the financial support they provided that was part of my salary, which amounted to one dollar per day each. That left only Ware, Fuqua, and Wheatley supporting my work and amounted to a cut in salary of from $150 down to $90 per month.

With this final blow from Gaither, I then and there decided to start the James R. Gober Detective Agency. I gave that work my spare time and averaged one hundred dollars per month profit on detective work. Once the agency was well established, the business began to expand significantly. I felt grateful indeed to the three bank presidents that stood by me, for they made it possible for me to start my agency by giving me a salary sufficient to live on.

Genesis of the Gober Detective Agency

I began operating the James R. Gober Detective Agency in April 1928. About the tenth of May, a man and his two sons came to me with a request that I investigate an incendiary case involving a cotton mill that had burned two hundred miles south of Amarillo, in Fisher County. I detailed an operative who I believed to be capable and kept him on the job for thirty days. He ascertained the fact that the gin, while closed awaiting the ginning season, had been used by a gang of bootleggers and poker players. Further, it was determined that the fire was caused by their carelessness with cigarettes, or cigars, or perhaps the explosion of a small still. These gamblers and bootleggers had gotten a key to the gin and had as many duplicates made as suited their convenience, but there was no plausible motive for an incendiary charge against anyone.

The Case of a Cunning Blackmailer

I had not finished with the incendiary case when I was awakened at midnight by a prominent citizen of Amarillo and his uncle. They were both excited and uneasy; in fact, the nephew was badly scared. He handed me a typewritten letter written on stationery from a hotel in Utah, and the envelope also carried the name of this same hotel, and the signature on the letter was that of Ray Pollack. Inside of the envelope, the letter contained the following:

> As an amateur detective, I am an ace. I run an ad in the Amarillo paper. Your wife answered it, and I went on the job. Your wife wants to see you and the blond behind bars.
>
> Last Saturday at two PM, you picked up the blond on Tenth Street. You were in a Dodge car with a commercial bed, and you went west following the 66 highway. I pulled in after you just keeping well in sight of you. You stopped at Bovina and took on gas. Then you stopped at Texico where you had taken supper. You drove to the Travelers Inn at Portales, just after dark. I drove in the shadow of a filling station where I could see into the office of the hotel. You took a careful survey of the surroundings. No one but you and the blond and the hotel clerk were in the hotel office when you registered as Mr. and Mrs. Thomas. You and the blond and the hotel clerk went upstairs, then I got mine, I got the sheet out of the hotel register.
>
> Now I figure that you can pay me more than your wife can. You mail a cashier's check payable to Ray Pollack for one thousand dollars ($1000). Just address the letter to Ray Pollack, general delivery, Amarillo, Texas, and no shadowing the post office. I will get it not later than Saturday and get me a car and hit the road for Utah, where the Mann Act is not so strict.

That ended the letter from the person claiming to be Ray Pollack.

I read this letter over the second time. Then I said to my client, "Is it true that you carried this woman across the state line and registered as man and wife?" He answered that he had. Then I said, "Is the description of your travel correct?" He also answered yes to that question. Then I asked him, "How long have you known this woman?"

He replied, "Three months."

Next I asked, "How did you happen to form her acquaintance?"

His answer was, "She has some mining property in New Mexico, near Santa Fe. I have done some drafting work for her. She intends to organize a company, and I anticipate taking some stock."

I continued my questioning by asking him, "Do you believe that this woman is square?"

He responded, "Absolutely. I hate this on her account, as bad as my own." Then he asked me, "Do you think that you can find Pollack?" Without letting me answer, he continued by remarking, "I want to find him and pay off and get shut of him, and I have got to leave tomorrow, and I will be gone for two weeks."

My response to all he said was, "That is fine. I am glad that you are getting out of the way. I will have everything fixed when you get back to Amarillo. Now be kind enough to give me your lady friend's name and address and an accurate description of her." My client promptly did as I had requested. Then I asked him, "Have you and your wife been congenial for the past several months?" His answer was no. My next question was, "Does your wife know this woman friend of yours?" He answered that she did. Then finally I asked him, "Where is your wife at present?" He told me that she was visiting her mother in south Texas. "That is all," I told him. "I will proceed on the case tomorrow; in the meantime, you need not suffer further uneasiness. I will guarantee that I will find Ray Pollack and settle matters satisfactorily with him."

After bidding my client and his uncle goodnight, or rather good morning, as it was one AM, I dressed, sat in my rocker, read this letter over many times, and studied every phase. By daylight, I had formed my conclusions.

The first conclusion was that the description of my client's movements were too accurate to be obtained by someone traveling separately. My second conclusion was that the composition of this letter was that of one composed by a woman. Third conclusion—that there was no mining property around Santa Fe, New Mexico, that hadn't been worn out one hundred years ago. Therefore, this woman was trying to bunco suckers out of money under false pretenses, and that was one form of blackmail.

I arose from my rocker fully convinced that my client's lady love was the composer of the letter and, in fact, she alone had planned the entire scheme to scare him out of one thousand dollars. In the meantime, this sham was scaring my client out of his socks on the way to getting his money.

I went to my office at seven thirty, called an operative, and instructed him to go to the hotel where the lady love was stopping and ask to be admitted to her room to see her on business. I told him that he could pretend to have a rooming house for rent and had been referred to her. His real business was to see whether or not there was a typewriter in the room.

I called in a second operative and took him to the general delivery window and arranged with the postal clerk that handed out the mail that if anyone called for Ray Pollack's mail, for him to slam the letter down unusually hard. This was to be done in order for my operative to know that the postal clerk was calling his attention to that letter. I instructed my client to mail the letter according to the directions, except that he would leave out the check for one thousand dollars.

In due time my operative returned from lady love's hotel and reported the existence of a Corona typewriter in her room.

The following day, I called in a lady operative that had experience as a stock saleswoman for a building and loan company. I instructed her to call on my suspect and tell her that she, the operative, had been in Santa Fe, New Mexico, for the purpose of securing options on mining property. She had noticed the suspect's name in the records as owning some property, and her object in getting options was that she had an uncle in New York City who was a very prominent businessman and experienced in selling stock. She was going to pay him a visit, and she had faith in her uncle's capability to dispose of such stocks as she might secure option on. My instructions to the operative were for her to attempt to secure some kind of typewritten instrument as a sample before she left the suspect's room.

My operative brought me a typewritten, ninety-day option on eighty acres of worn-out placer mines. I compared the type with that of the letter that demanded one thousand dollars from my client. There could be no mistake as to the two instruments being written on the same machine. The stem carrying the letter W set the W a noticeably unusual distance from the balance of the letters in the sentence. Also, the stem carrying the letter T threw the top of the T slanting to the left. Several other letters were out of line.

My operative reported, after being on watch at the post office for two days, that the letter addressed to Ray Pollack had never reached the general delivery department. This report annoyed me, for quite naturally I thought this operative had been off the job and that this letter had slipped by.

After considerable study of the situation and a thorough review of all possible circumstances, I went to the inspector at the post office and described the envelope and gave him the name Ray Pollack and told the inspector the hour, to the minute, two days prior, that the letter had been mailed. The inspector got busy and found the letter in the directory searcher's department. I then put the letter in my pocket but left the operative and the general delivery clerk with the same instructions I had previously given. The reason that the letter had miscarried was because my client had failed to write "general delivery" on it.

Within one hour after I had taken the letter out of the post office, my lady suspect came to the general delivery window and asked for Ray Pollack's mail. My operative promptly reported, giving me her description, which was identical to the one my client had given to me.

The next day was Sunday, and I went to the hotel where my suspect was stopping and asked the room attendant at the desk to phone this lady and tell her that a gentleman was waiting to see her in the lobby. She phoned back and asked the room attendant who the gentleman was. I instructed the attendant to inform her that it was Mr. James Gober, of the Gober Detective Agency, and that I must see her at once.

In about ten minutes, she came down the stairway very slowly. When she left the last step and was on the lobby floor, I moved toward her and shook hands and introduced myself, saying, "Madam, I have some typewritten instruments in my office that concern you, and I want you to come to my office at 110 Central Building. I desire to ask you some questions. When will it suit your convenience to come?"

After a considerable pause, she said, "I guess I can come at one PM."

I threw back my coat lapel, exposing my badge[8] and gun, and said, "Let there be no guess, if you are not there promptly at one PM, I will be after you." Then I turned and went hurriedly out of the hotel and back to my office. I placed an operative in a room adjoining my office and then shut the door. Then I placed a chair by the closed door to seat the lady in when she arrived.

Promptly at one PM she came in the front door and raised her hands and said, "I suppose that you want to shake me down for some money, and I haven't any."

I took her by the arm and seated her. I said, "Madam, you have misjudged me. I make my money by running down shakedown people and sending them to prison." I became very investigative in my discussions with her as I said, "Now, on a certain day you left Amarillo with a prominent citizen. This person is a married man and a man that was so favorably impressed with you that he trusted your honor and took you to Portales, New Mexico. You and he registered at a hotel as man and wife under an assumed name. After you returned to Amarillo, you concluded that he was an easy touch and that you would scare him out of one thousand dollars. So with that plan in mind, you wrote him this letter on that old, worn-out Corona machine that you have in your room." At this point, I held the letter in front of her so that she could see it very plainly.

Then she said, "I wrote that letter for that man Pollack, because he threatened to turn me in."

I said to her, "Why did you call at the general delivery window for this letter?" I drew from my pocket the decoy letter that was supposed to have in it the cashier's draft. At this point, she sank down in her chair and shed some cold, forced tears.

I called in my man from the other room, and I then dictated a confession for him to type. Then I handed it to her, and she read it and said, "Yes, I will sign it." She did sign the confession and then began to cry once more.

I said, "Madam, I have done all that I am paid to do. So far as this agency is concerned, this matter is closed, but knowing my client as I do, I believe that when I give my report to him with your confession, he will be so outraged over this affair that he will take these documents and hand them over to the federal district attorney, who is also a personal friend both of his and of mine. If he does, I will guarantee that you will get a term in the federal penitentiary for using the United States mail for blackmail purposes. You will be locked up so long that cosmetics wont hide your age."

She arose and went out of the door in a stooped position. I immediately called the Negro porter to mop the floor.

The Final Roundup

Reflection

Looking back across the sixty-five years that I have been allowed to live on this earth, I see what amounts to a cavalcade of family, friends, associates, and adversaries of many kinds who have impacted my life through the events of which they have been a part. As you the reader have shared those experiences with me, you may have wondered what happened to those individuals. For each of them is woven into the tapestry of my emotions, reflected in the mosaic of my personality, and colored into the painting of my life. I will start with one who I have not mentioned previously but who typifies the qualities that I respect the most in a human being.

A Most Memorable Example and Meaning

Many years ago, I knew an old Dane who was a carpenter by trade. He was an honest, conscientious man to whom I gave considerable employment, and I had every confidence in his skill and honor. His name was Anderson, and my association with him was at Woodward, Oklahoma, in the early 1890s, when Woodward was a wild cattle town. There, the saloons and gambling houses were the most popular businesses, the most attractive and most patronized by the various classes of people in the surrounding territories.

If I had a house to build, I would send for Anderson and tell him what I wanted and give him an order for material. When he finished the job and brought me the bill for his labor, it was a pleasure to pay him.

Perhaps I would not have occasion to see the job for weeks; still I had confidence that I had just what I had ordered, for I knew this man liked me and appreciated me as a friend and customer and placed the value of our relationship and my trust in him far beyond selfish gain. I have known many men that I have had such confidence in, and when I call them to memory, it's a satisfaction to realize that once such men lived.

Mr. Anderson always when greeting me would say, "Good morning, Sir, are you happy?" I have pondered over his consistent question extensively and wondered why that question always followed his greeting, and I always came to the conclusion that it was his appreciation of my friendship that caused a desire in his heart to know that I was happy. Mr. Anderson typified the type of attitude, care, and concern for fellow men that my heart always tried to reflect in my life and that I so cherished in the lives of others.

Final Appearances on the Stage of Life

In the case of some of the important players in my life— my father and mother, George and Amanda; my beloved wife, Belle Helen; some of my children; my first sweetheart, Augustine Alexander; and others—the final events of their lives were so integral to mine that you have experienced those with me. But then there are others who also had made a major impact on my life. Whatever happened to them? When they appeared in this story, their effect was felt and recorded, but they probably appeared to have ridden off into the sunset, never again to be heard from or about.

Whatever happened to Judge W. B. Plemons, W. M. D. Lee, Tom Harris, Jesse Jenkins, Lem Woodruff, Jim East, Tobe Robinson, Temple Houston, Sam Bass, and many others who played important roles in the shaping of my life? I will relate what I believe to be true concerning certain of the final events in their lives.

Judge W. B. Plemons, one of the finest gentlemen I've ever known, a true hero of the Civil War, a most capable attorney, city mayor, first county judge in two counties of Texas, also served notably as a Texas State representative to the legislature in Austin and was a candidate from Texas for the U.S. Congress. These are only some of the many highlights of his life. His accomplishments could fill a book, but most important to me was his love and devotion to his family and to me, his son-in-law. He was one of the very best friends that I ever had.

Judge Plemons died in Amarillo, Texas, of apoplexy, December 4, 1901, in his fifty-eighth year of life.

W. M. D. Lee, a man I found difficult to respect because of his methods of dealing with people, sold his interest in the Lee-Scott Cattle Company to Mr. Scott soon after the LS Pat Garrett rangers were killed in Tascosa in 1886. Then, attempting to promote a town site near the Gulf of Mexico, he undertook the dredging of the Brazos River, which he hoped to make navigable from the Gulf to his proposed town. He spent all of his own capital and all that he could induce his friends to invest in the project but failed to accomplish his objective and died a broken man, in spirit, courage, and finances.[1]

The spring following the shootout in Tascosa, Tom Harris, with the Isaacs brothers,[2] moved their cattle to a much better range some two hundred miles east, near the city of Canadian, Texas. A few months later, Harris drove to Canadian for supplies, left his wagon and team in the wagon yard for the night, and the next morning was found dead in the bunkhouse.[3]

Jesse Jenkins sold his saloon and attained success as a cattleman with large land and cattle holdings near Corona, New Mexico, in which community he is a prominent and respected citizen.

With money supplied by friends, Lem Woodruff went to Hot Springs, Arkansas; underwent a successful operation; and later married a wealthy old lady from Boston, Massachusetts.

Jim East was defeated for sheriff by Tobe Robinson in the November election of 1886, went into the saloon business, and moved to Douglas, Arizona, where he died in 1930.

Tobe Robinson, after being reelected sheriff, found life rather dull and monotonous, got to drinking and gambling, and married a woman known as Santa Fe Moll. When he had served about one year of his second term, he resigned, and they emigrated to Bisby, Arizona. One morning, Moll concluded a quarrel with Tobe by picking up a Winchester and shooting him in the back, killing him instantly.

Temple Houston, my good friend and benefactor, lived the balance of his life in and around Woodward, Oklahoma, where he continued his brilliant career as a defense lawyer. In 1898, in Taloga, Oklahoma, he was delivering one of his colorful defenses when it was cut short by an attack from a sickness from which he suffered. He seemed to recover from this illness, and soon he was able to return to the busy schedule in his law office in Woodward. However, within a short period, Temple went to Roger Mills County, Oklahoma, where he defended some criminal clients. He left there for Canadian, Texas, for another case but suffered a seizure in the wilderness of the prairie. He apparently lay near death for some time until a cowboy discovered him, but Temple showed an amazing ability to rebound and participated in a trial the next day.

When he returned from Texas, the illness hit him once again, and he was taken to the hospital in Topeka, Kansas, where it was found that an infection had spread throughout his body. On August 15, 1905, he suffered through the final phase of his infirmity, a brain hemorrhage, and died within minutes in his home in Woodward. Temple was only forty-five at the time of his death, and it was a sad revelation indeed to know that my friend, such a dynamic person in life, was now gone. I shall never forget him.

In the early spring of 1877, Sam Bass, other boys from Denton, and Tom Spotwood and Joel Collins of Collin County went to the south Texas coast. There they hired on as cowboys to drive a herd of wild longhorn cattle to Nebraska. It took them until late summer or early fall to get to their destination. When the cattle were delivered and the boys paid off, they were set free to "paddle their own canoe" and get home as they pleased. Now, Nebraska was a wilderness in its crudest state, and the few towns that existed were composed of supply stores, saloons, gambling houses, and dance halls.

The boys made splendid cash customers and were royally entertained until the last one was out of funds. Then their reception grew cool, cooler, and cold. This "temperature," this coolness, was felt principally from their lady loves that had been so affectionate while their money had lasted, but now they had become unbearable.

The boys held a council of war and decided to rob the Union Pacific train, and they did rob the train and got more 1877 twenty-dollar gold pieces than they could carry. Strange to say, they came back to Denton County, and I am quite sure that one of those 1877 twenty-dollar gold pieces was the first twenty-dollar gold piece that I ever saw, but soon they were common property. These boys spent them as free as though there was an unending supply, but their home visit was of short duration.[4]

A man named Jim Murphy was well-known by me and for years by the Bass gang and trusted by them as a best friend. Their trust in him was such that they gave him a liberal quantity of their gold. However, Murphy slipped off to Round Rock and arranged with the bank to get the Texas Rangers there, with him acting as a spy and leading the Bass gang up to the slaughter. All was arranged, and the Bass gang was killed, save Frank Jackson, with whom I had been in company many Sundays while I lived with his sister, Mrs. Ben Keys, whose husband was a distant relative of my mother.

Jim Murphy came back to Denton, where he was a regular customer at Ben Pascal's saloon. When he fell ill one day and was taken to the Shipley Hotel, where he eventually died, several hours before his death both eyes burst in his head. As a boy, I had not the least sympathy for Murphy and what had befallen him, for as well as I knew him, I could not respect a man that would induce and influence a man to commit a crime knowing full well that he would be killed. It would have been just as easy for Murphy to induce those bighearted, rough boys to disband and go to some other country and start life anew, as Frank Jackson did, and Frank was considered the most daring man of the gang. Since the Round Rock experience, Jackson has been a hard-working, honest man. My eldest brother met Jackson many years ago in a Colorado mining town where Jackson had worked in the mine during the Ouray and Cripple Creek excitement. He became a law-abiding citizen in 1878, but he suffered his share for the recklessness and thoughtlessness he demonstrated when he was a mere uneducated lad.

The Vision of a Desired Rest in Paradise

As I bring this long and sometimes tortuous story to an end, I will share this vision of paradise from the mind of an old man who fought the battle of life to win but now realizes that all one can hope for is a draw:

> I have been a slave sixty-five long years
> Laboring for other folks' troubles and cares.
> Now, I am tired and feel worn out
> And I am wondering what this world struggle is all about.
> I nor no other man has figured it out,
> But today I have made a plan
> To take a rest from being an office man.
> Next September, the first month of fall,
> I am going where the pines grow large and tall.
> I will find some good water in a hidden stream
> That no other man has ever seen.
> I will build me a cabin under trees shady and tall,
> In hearing distance of a waterfall.

I will listen to its music, sweet and rare.
I will have wild turkey, fish, and deer as my bill of fare,
And when I lay down to sleep and rest,
My dreams will be of the joy in the Golden West.
It is then that my mind, heart, and soul will see peace and rest.
Mockingbirds will wake me at dawn
With the sweet musical songs they are singing on.
I will stroll out and inhale the mountain breeze
And watch gray squirrels playing in the trees.
I will observe the rising sun, perhaps two hours
As the dark shadows of the night it slowly devours.
Then I will watch the huge rocks on mountain peaks
As the morning sun colors them in shades and streaks;
Then I will take my Springfield and go on a quiet prowl
And listen for the whistle of a buck or a bear's growl;
Perhaps if I find a fresh track,
I will be carrying a saddle of venison or bear on my back;
And if my friends happen to come my way,
They will share in the good old spirit of the Pioneer Days.

Jim Gober

Notes

Introduction

1. James R. Gober, "A Philosophy of Morals and Ethics," James R. Gober Collection, Albuquerque, New Mexico.

2. "'Jim' Gober, Potter's First Sheriff, Dies; Final Rites Monday." Amarillo Sunday *News-Globe,* April 23, 1933.

The Formative Years

1. Robert Washington (Bob) Wright married Arcanie Roseana Elizabeth Gober, the daughter of prominent Denton County resident John Wesley Gober. See family Bible, Gober Family Collection.

2. A major tributary of the Sabine River, Long Branch Creek unites with the Short Branch in southeastern Greenville in Hunt County. See Fred A. Tarpley, *Place Names of Northeast Texas* (Commerce: East Texas State University Press, 1969), 116.

3. Named for Indian trader Jesse Chisholm (ca. 1805-1868), the Chisholm Trail served as a principal thoroughfare for Texas cattle traveling to Kansas railheads between 1867 and 1876. Comprising many feeder routes originating in the cattle-breeding regions of southern Texas, the trail forded the Red River at several points, Red River Station being the most popular crossing. After leaving the river, herds bore northward through the Oklahoma Territory to Abilene and, later, Wichita, Kansas. By 1877, quarantines against Texas cattle had closed the trail in Kansas; by this time, the Western Cattle Trail and Dodge City had become the main route and terminal of the droving trade. Wayne Gard's *The Chisholm Trail* (Norman: University of Oklahoma Press, 1954) offers the best overview of this historic route.

The trail was sometimes erroneously called the Chisum Trail, in reference to prominent cattleman John Simpson Chisum (1824-1884). Over the years Chisum's cattle traveled many trails, including the Goodnight-Loving Trail in West Texas and New Mexico and the Jones and Plummer Trail through the Texas Panhandle. See *The Handbook of Texas,* 3 vols. (Austin: Texas State Historical Association, 1952, 1976), 1:342-43; James W. Mullins, "Says Chisholm and Chisum Trails are Being Confused," Amarillo Sunday *News and Globe*, June 27, 1926; Georgia B. Redfield, "The Historic Chisum Trail," *The Cattleman* 32 (Nov. 1945): 26-27, 56-57.

4. Lock Stubblefield Forester (1844-1913) was born in Tennessee but moved as a small child with his family to Denton County, Texas, in 1850. The Forester family established a home on the Mill Branch tributary of Clear Creek in 1852. The old Chisholm Trail passed through the Forester ranch, crossing Clear Creek at what is known as "Trail Crossing." Like his father, Forester became a substantial stockman, running the "Two I" brand with the "Jinglebob" mark on both ears. During the Civil War, Lock Forester served with state troops defending the frontier from Indian raids along the Red River in northern Texas. See Mrs. Paul Simpson, "Two I Jinglebob Brand," *The*

Denton County Sunday Morning Enterprise, March 10, 1974; and Karen Muncy, "County Roots: Forester Ranch Dates to 1853," *Denton Record-Chronicle*, October 16, 1974.

5. In the days of the open range, states established estray laws to regulate the disposition of free-roaming cattle and horses. Most such laws required the finder of stray stock to post descriptive notices in county newspapers to enable owners to locate it. If not claimed within a set period, strays were usually sold at auction and the money deposited with the county treasurer. See Ray August, "Cowboys v. Rancheros: The Origins of Western American Livestock Law," *Southwestern Historical Quarterly* 96 (Apr. 1993): 457, 485, 497.

6. Founded in 1859 on Clear Creek, a few miles northwest of Denton, Texas, the farm and ranch community known as Clear Creek Settlement took the name Bolivar in 1861. See Edward F. Bates, *History and Reminiscences of Denton County* (Denton: McNitzkey Printing Company, 1918), 84-85; *Handbook of Texas*, 1:183. The three forks that comprise Hickory Creek arise in the northwestern part of Denton County and flow southeast for thirty miles to the Elm Fork of the Trinity River, in the southeastern part of the county. See ibid., 1:804-5.

Cattle and the Open Range

1. Three branches of the Pease River (north, middle, and south or tongue) rise in Motley County. After the branches unite in northern Cottle County, the Pease, named for Governor Elisha M. Pease, flows east for 110 miles, joining the Red River near the town of Vernon. See *Handbook of Texas*, 2:352.

2. William Crow Wright (1837-1906) was born at Clarkesville, Texas. At the age of twenty-one, Wright moved to Denton County, where he founded a horse ranch and amassed substantial land. Wounded in the Civil War, Wright organized a militia unit during a local Indian campaign in 1866. Like his brother Bob, Crow Wright also married a daughter of John Wesley Gober, Julia Ann Amanda Gober. See Bates, *Denton County*, 86, 308; Family Bible, Gober Family Collection.

3. Called Oregon City until 1878, the town of Seymour, named for a local cowboy, became the seat of Baylor County. Astride the Western Cattle Trail to Dodge City, the town boomed briefly with the arrival of the Wichita Valley Railroad in 1890. See *Handbook of Texas*, 2:594.

4. Three branches of the Wichita River head in Dickens and King Counties. The north fork joins the middle fork in Foard County, the south branch in Baylor County; it then flows northeast to join the Red River in northern Clay County. The river was named for the Wichita Indians, who inhabited that region. See ibid., 2:905.

5. Sometimes known as New Henrietta, Cambridge was a thriving community in 1878 but withered after losing the race for county seat to

Henrietta in 1882. See William Clayton Kimbrough, "A History of Clay County" (M. A. thesis, Hardin-Simmons University, 1942), 116; *Handbook of Texas*, 3:137.

6. Henrietta was established in 1860 but was abandoned and reoccupied twice before permanent inhabitants arrived in 1873. The Fort Worth and Denver and the Missouri, Kansas, and Texas Railroad lines made the seat of Clay County the hub of regional trade. See ibid., 1:798-99.

7. The Little Wichita River rises in Archer County, Texas, flows northeast, and empties into the Red River from Clay County. See ibid., 2:65.

8. Groesbeck Creek rises in two streams, north and south, in eastern Childress County, and flows east across Hardeman County to join the Red River. See ibid., 1:740.

9. Joseph F. Glidden (1813-1906) and Henry B. Sanborn (1845-1912) located the Frying Pan Ranch on 250,000 acres in Potter and Randall Counties in 1881. It was the first fenced ranch in the Panhandle. Glidden and Sanborn dissolved their partnership in 1894, Sanborn retaining some twenty-five thousand acres. In 1898 Glidden deeded the ranch to his son-in-law, William H. Bush. For brief sketches of this famous outfit, see Laura V. Hamner, *Short Grass and Longhorns* (Norman: University of Oklahoma Press, 1943), 207-15; Pauline Durrett Robertson and R. L. Robertson, *Cowman's Country* (Amarillo: Paramount Publishing, 1981), 97-99.

10. Temple Houston (1860-1905), the youngest son of Sam Houston, studied law at Baylor University and was admitted to the Texas bar in 1878 at age nineteen. After serving briefly as Brazoria County attorney, Houston relocated to the Panhandle, where he became the first district attorney of the Panhandle judicial district. In 1884 he was elected to the first of two terms in the Texas senate. With the opening of the Cherokee Outlet in Oklahoma, Houston moved his family and his law practice to Woodward.

A flamboyant dresser and brilliant orator, Houston stood six feet tall, wore his hair long, spoke several European and Indian languages fluently, and was well versed in the classics. Houston died of a brain hemorrhage on August 15, 1905. He is the subject of Glenn Shirley's fine biography, *Temple Houston: Lawyer with a Gun* (Norman: University of Oklahoma Press, 1980) and also figures prominently in Shirley's *West of Hell's Fringe* (Norman: University of Oklahoma Press, 1990).

11. Founded in 1875 on Sweetwater Creek in Wheeler County, Mobeetie served as a trading post for buffalo hunters and soldiers from nearby Fort Elliot. In 1879 Mobeetie became the county seat, and it retained its economic prominence until the late 1880s. Without rail service and severely damaged by a cyclone, the town dwindled into obscurity in 1890s. The county seat moved to Wheeler in 1907. With the coming of the Panhandle and Santa Fe Railroad in 1929, a community known as New Mobeetie sprang up on the tracks two miles north of the old town. See Frederick W. Rathjen, *The Texas Panhandle Frontier* (Austin: University of Texas Press, 1973), 230; G. C.

Boswell, "Some Early Activities Around Mobeetie," *West Texas Historical Association Year Book* 12 (Jul. 1936): 45-55; *Handbook of Texas,* 2:220.

12. Born in St. Lawrence County, New York, H. B. Sanborn migrated to DeKalb, Illinois, in 1864. In 1874 he began to market barbed wire, invented by J. F. Glidden, in Texas. After selling most of his interest in the Frying Pan Ranch, Sanborn promoted the town site of Amarillo and became one of that community's most prominent citizens. See James Cox, ed., *Historical and Biographical Record of the Cattle Industry and Cattlemen of Texas and Adjacent Territory* (St. Louis: Woodward and Tiernan Printing Company, 1895), 500-503; James D. Hamlin, *The Flamboyant Judge* (Canyon, TX: Palo Duro Press, 1972), 4.

13. A sparsely traveled trail connected Dodge City, Kansas, and Springer, New Mexico, by way of Fort Bascom, an army post established in 1863 on the north bank of the Canadian River, near the Texas-New Mexico boundary. The route eventually included the towns of Tascosa and Mobeetie in the Texas Panhandle. The two-hundred-mile daily mail run between Mobeetie and Fort Bascom required fifty-nine hours on horseback. See John L. McCarty, *Maverick Town, The Story of Old Tascosa* (Norman: University of Oklahoma Press, 1946), 12-14, 67-68, 70-71; C. Robert Haywood, *Trails South: The Wagon-Road Economy in the Dodge City-Panhandle Region* (Norman: University of Oklahoma Press, 1986), 60-61.

Sierrita de la Cruz Creek, better known to Panhandle cowpunchers as the "Sweet Lacruse" or "Sweetly Croose," rose in Oldham County and emptied into the Canadian River about ten miles below Tascosa. The LS Ranch maintained a line camp near this confluence. See Dulcie Sullivan, *The LS Brand* (Austin: University of Texas Press, 1968), 42, 72, 132.

14. Las Tecovas Creek emanates from a spring northwest of present-day Amarillo in Potter County and flows north for fifteen miles into the Canadian River. Before becoming headquarters for the Frying Pan Ranch, the spring was the site of commerce between Hispanic traders from New Mexico, known as *comancheros,* and Comanche and Kiowa Indians, who exchanged stolen cattle for trade goods. See J. Evetts Haley, *The XIT Ranch of Texas* (Chicago: Lakeside Press, 1929), 26; *Handbook of Texas,* 2: 718.

15. Located at the confluence of the Canadian River and Atascosa Creek in Oldham County, Tascosa was settled in the 1870s by Hispanic sheep raisers from New Mexico under the leadership of Casimero Romero. Anglo ranchers and tradesmen soon joined and outnumbered Romero's colonists.

Tascosa was named the county seat of Oldham County in 1880 and became the center of regional trade. While the range cattle industry flourished, Tascosa became a rowdy cowtown. But when the Fort Worth and Denver Railroad bypassed Tascosa in 1887, many businesses relocated to a new site on the railroad across the Canadian. Neither location prospered, and in 1915 the county seat was removed to Vega. The life and death of this colorful community is amply chronicled in McCarty, *Maverick Town.*

16. Front Street comprised the principal business district in Dodge City during its heyday as a cattle town. The famous Long Branch Saloon contributed liberally to the town's wild and unsavory reputation. See Robert R. Dykstra, *The Cattle Towns* (New York: Alfred A. Knopf, 1968); Odie B. Faulk, *Dodge City: The Most Western Town of All* (New York: Oxford University Press, 1977). Cowboys sometimes referred to liquor as "wild mare's milk." See Ramon Adams, *Western Words,* rev. ed. (Norman: University of Oklahoma Press, 1968), 347.

17. Born at sea about 1839 and raised in Maine, Jack Bridges drifted west and by 1869 was a U. S. deputy marshal in Kansas. An efficient lawman, Bridges was seriously wounded in a Wichita gun battle in 1871 but recovered to serve as marshal of Dodge City, Kansas, from 1882 to 1884. See Bill O'Neal, *Encyclopedia of Western Gunfighters* (Norman: University of Oklahoma Press, 1979), 46-47; Dan L. Thrapp, *Encyclopedia of Frontier Biography,* 3 vols. (Glendale, CA: Arthur H. Clark, 1988), 1:168.

18. In 1880, the firm of Gunter, Munson, and Summerfield established the T Anchor Ranch on Palo Duro Creek, in present-day Randall County. By 1883, W. B. Munson (1846-1930) had acquired his partners' interest in the enterprise. Two years later he sold the brand, along with 225 sections of land and twenty-four thousand head of stock, to the British-owned Cedar Valley Land and Cattle Company. In 1895 the company began downsizing its operations and in 1902 ceased ranching altogether. Its remaining lands were broken up and sold to farmers. See C. Boone McClure, "A History of Randall County and the T Anchor Ranch" (M.A. thesis, University of Texas, 1930).

The Cowboys of Old Tascosa

1. Leavenworth entrepreneurs William McDole Lee (1841-1925) and Lucien Scott (1834-1893) organized the Lee-Scott Cattle Company and LS Ranch in the Texas Panhandle in 1881. Expanding upon individual holdings acquired earlier, the partners bought several surrounding outfits and by 1882 owned about eighty thousand acres outright and grazed additional grass on the public domain. The partnership lasted until 1890, when Lee sold out to Scott. This historic outfit is the subject of several good accounts. The best are Sullivan, *LS Brand,* and Hamner, *Short Grass and Longhorns,* 216-27.

2. The color of whiskey led to names like "red liquor," "redeye," "red ink," and "red disturbance." See Adams, *Western Words,* 178.

3. During the 1880s, several cattle trails crossed the Texas Panhandle. The most important of these routes, the Jones and Plummer, Adobe Walls, and Tuttle Trails, followed established wagon roads leading from the Panhandle to the railroad shipping pens at Dodge City. When Tascosa became a trading point, freighters forged a branch of the Jones and Plummer Trail known as the Dodge City-Tascosa Trail. Leaving Oldham County in a northeasterly direction, the new branch intersected the main trail about a mile south of present-day Beaver, Oklahoma.

In 1885, Kansas quarantine laws forced the Panhandle cattle trails further west to Colorado and the northern plains. Texas herds traveling the westernmost branch of the Potter and Bacon Trail, also called the Potter and Blocker Trail, skirted the western edge of the Panhandle on their way north. By the mid-1890s, fencing and farmers closed these northbound routes as well and brought an end to a colorful era in western history. For an overview of Panhandle cattle trails see Haywood, *Trails South,* and Jimmy M. Skaggs, *The Cattle Trailing Industry: Between Supply and Demand, 1866-1890* (Norman: University of Oklahoma Press, 1973), 106-7.

4. W. M. D. Lee was born in Pennsylvania but raised in Wisconsin. After serving as a Union quartermaster during the Civil War, Lee traded with the Indians on the southern plains. When the buffalo hide trade played out he moved to the Texas Panhandle, where he embarked on a successful ranching partnership with Lucien Scott. Lee is credited with introducing the Aberdeen Angus breed to the western range. When the profitability of cattle ranching declined and his partnership with Scott soured in 1890, Lee and his capital looked elsewhere for fertile fields of investment. Donald F. Schofield's *Indians, Cattle, Ships and Oil: The Story of W. M. D. Lee* (Austin: University of Texas Press, 1985) is the most complete biography of this energetic capitalist.

5. The strikers met in March of 1883 and drafted an ultimatum on wages, demanding fifty dollars per month for regular hands and cooks and seventy-five dollars for range bosses. Led by LS wagon boss Tom Harris, rebellious cowboys representing the LS, LE, LIT, LX and T Anchor ranches threatened to strike on April 1 if employers did not meet their demands. Although only twenty-four cowboys signed the strike ultimatum, some estimates placed the total number of participants at more than three hundred.

The recent influx of large corporate ranches, which imposed rules governing cowboy conduct and forbidding employees from owning land or cattle, also contributed to the labor unrest. Failing, however, to win long-term concessions from owners, the strikers ended their walkout after just over two months. Many returned to cowboy jobs in the region, although some ranchers blackballed participants. Evidence suggests that at least a few strikers drifted into New Mexico and began rustling the cattle of their former employers. Robert Zeigler provides an overview of the strike in "The Cowboy Strike of 1883: Its Causes and Meaning," *West Texas Historical Association Year Book* 47 (1971): 32-46. For a Marxist interpretation of the same event see Jack Weston, *The Real American Cowboy* (New York: Schocken Books, 1985), 99-105.

Little is known of the origins of the charismatic Tom Harris. The federal census of 1880 recorded his presence in the Panhandle as a Texas-born herder, age twenty-two, whose parents both hailed from Alabama. After leaving the Panhandle in the wake of the cowboy strike, Harris operated a ranch in New Mexico for several years. In November 1886 he married Clara Paulis in Fayette County. See Ernest Archambeau, "The First Federal

Census in the Panhandle—1880," *Panhandle-Plains Historical Review* 23 (1950): 123; *The Tascosa Pioneer,* September 1, December 15, 1886.

6. Although clearly a leader among the livestock interests in the western Panhandle, W. M. D. Lee never headed any formal cattlemen's organization. Nor did he even belong to the well-known Panhandle Stock Association, organized in 1879. For a history of this organization see B. Byron Price, "Community of Individualists: The Panhandle Stock Association, 1879-1889," in *At Home on the Range,* ed. John R. Wunder (Westport, CT: Greenwood Press, 1985), 73-93.

7. Patrick F. Garrett (1850-1908) was born in Alabama and grew to manhood in Louisiana. Garrett worked briefly as a cattle drover before becoming a buffalo hunter in west Texas. After killing a hide skinner in 1878, he moved on to New Mexico. Elected sheriff of Lincoln County in 1880, Garrett killed the notorious outlaw Billy the Kid at Fort Sumner the following year. In 1884-85, Garrett headed a squad of special rangers in the Texas Panhandle. Returning to New Mexico, he promoted an ill-fated irrigation project in the Pecos Valley, acted as a private detective, established a horse ranch, and served a two-year-term as collector of customs at El Paso. He was murdered near Las Cruces, New Mexico, probably by Wayne Brazel, a local cowboy. Leon Metz's *Pat Garrett* (Norman: University of Oklahoma Press, 1974) offers the most reliable account of this renowned lawman.

8. When hard feelings persisted and rustling increased in the wake of the cowboy strike of 1883, W. M. D. Lee induced Governor John Ireland of Texas to commission a group of special rangers to help suppress rustlers. He then persuaded Pat Garrett to lead the force, which was also expected to enforce a new state law prohibiting the wearing of side arms.

Garrett brought his brother-in-law, Barney Mason, and cowboy George Jones with him and recruited seven LS loyalists, including Ed King, Lon Chambers (with Garrett in his pursuit of Billy the Kid), Charley Reason, Bill Anderson, John Land, Albert E. Perry (a stock detective), and G. H. "Kid" Dobbs (a former buffalo hunter). The rangers received sixty dollars monthly, twice the prevailing cowboy wage. Garrett received five thousand dollars annual salary plus some cattle.

The actions of Garrett's sometimes overbearing charges antagonized many cowboys and smaller ranchers, many of whom were not allowed to work the general roundup and who were often accused of being a part of the rustling element. Although the rangers were disbanded in the spring of 1885, animosity over their activities lingered in the region for many years. The story of this ill-fated organization is detailed in McCarty, *Maverick Town,* 129-39; Schofield, *W. M. D. Lee,* 67-74; Metz, *Pat Garrett,* 142-48.

9. Stealing and branding large, unmarked calves, known as mavericks, was the most common form of rustling in the Panhandle during the 1880s. For a complete account of the ways and means of cattle theft in the region see Haley, *XIT Ranch,* 107-28.

10. The cattle pool known as the Tom Harris Syndicate or the Bar WA attracted an estimated eighteen to fifty investors, most of them cowboys and small ranchers who contributed capital to the enterprise in exchange for a share of the profits. See McCarty, *Maverick Town,* 123-24.

11. Located three miles west of the Texas border and thirty-seven miles east of Tucumcari in present-day Quay County, New Mexico, the town Endee took the name of the nearby ND Ranch, established by John E. and George Day in 1882. See Jerry L. Williams and Paul E. McAllister, *New Mexico In Maps* (Albuquerque: University of New Mexico Press, 1979), 53, 55; T. M. Pearce, ed., *New Mexico Place Names: A Geographical Dictionary* (Albuquerque: University of New Mexico Press, 1965), 54.

12. Harris was only twenty-four in 1882. His bearing and maturity, however, obviously impressed Gober as those of a much older man.

13. Dakota Territory was created in 1861 from parts of Minnesota and Nebraska. Montana and Wyoming Territories were carved from Dakota Territory later in the decade. In 1889 the remaining area was divided into the present states of North and South Dakota. See Dale L. Morgan, *Rand McNally's Pioneer Atlas of the American West* (Chicago: Rand McNally, 1969), 30.

14. The brother-in-law of Tom Harris, Jesse Jenkins was a prominent Panhandle rancher, co-owner of a popular Tascosa saloon, and a champion of the so-called "little men." Jenkins and his brother Lon helped Harris organize a cattle pool in New Mexico in the wake of the cowboy strike. He later moved to the town site of Hartley, north of Tascosa, where he led the homesteaders in their fight against the mammoth XIT Ranch over the location of the county seat. Jenkins was a longtime director of the Panhandle Stock Association, owned several ranches, and became the president of a Dalhart, Texas, bank. In the 1940s he still operated a ranch at Corona, New Mexico. McCarty, *Maverick Town,* 110-12, 123-24, 131, 134, 155, 173-74, 194, 234-35, 237.

15. H. A. Russell erected the Exchange Hotel on Main Street in Tascosa in 1881. See ibid., 54-55.

16. The card game known as monte originated in Spain and was widely played in the American Southwest. Like most games of chance, there were many variations, but the odds always favored the dealer. For a description of monte see Robert K. DeArment, *Knights of the Green Cloth* (Norman: University of Oklahoma Press, 1982), 395-96, n 9; Winfred Blevins, *Dictionary of the Old West* (New York: Facts on File, 1993), 223.

17. Born in Illinois, James H. East (1853-1930) came to Texas at fifteen and became a cowboy. He drove herds to Kansas and Nebraska before hiring on with the LX Ranch in the Texas Panhandle. In 1877 he helped Pat Garrett capture Billy the Kid at Stinking Springs, New Mexico. Four years later, the cowboy vote elected East sheriff of Oldham County. Considered a cool and efficient officer, East killed gambler Tom Clark in a saloon shooting in Tascosa in 1889. East once owned the Equity Bar and the Cattle Exchange Saloon, famous Tascosa watering holes.

After leaving the Panhandle he moved to Arizona, where he engaged in law enforcement and the saloon business. He died in Douglas, Arizona. For a biographical sketch of East see J. Evetts Haley, "Jim East, Trail Hand and Cowboy," *Panhandle-Plains Historical Review* 4 (1931): 39-61.

18. Lower Tascosa, or Hogtown, lay about a quarter mile from the "respectable" part of town and was home to numerous saloons, gambling dens, and houses of prostitution and was the scene of regular mischief. See Sullivan, *LS Brand,* 56; Pauline Durrett Robertson and R. L. Robertson, *Panhandle Pilgrimage,* 2d ed. (Amarillo: Paramount Publishing Company, 1978), 108.

19. Emma Horner was probably the Tascosa prostitute known as "Rocking Chair Emma." McCarty, *Maverick Town,* 142-43, 175.

20. Flowing from near Raton Pass in Colfax County, New Mexico, the Canadian River bisects the Texas Panhandle through Oldham, Potter, Moore, Hutchinson, Roberts, and Hemphill Counties before entering Oklahoma. The Canadian eventually drains into the Arkansas River. See *Handbook of Texas,* 1:288.

21. Gough's first name was John rather than William. See *Tascosa Pioneer,* June 25, 1887.

22. Fredericksburg is located in central Gillespie County in the Texas Hill Country. See *Handbook of Texas,* 1:643.

23. Theodore Briggs, an ex-soldier from Fort Union, New Mexico, and a friend of Tascosa founder Casimero Romero, established a ranch six miles west of town, near Rica Creek, in 1876. He maintained rental property in Tascosa and ran unsuccessfully for Oldham County judge in the early 1880s. See McCarty, *Maverick Town,* 17, 36, 40, 133, 151, 208; *Tascosa Pioneer,* December 22, 1886.

24. Most sources credit Fred Chilton with killing Sheets, who had stopped in Tascosa the previous year with his wife and five children on their way to Oregon. See McCarty, *Maverick Town,* 144, 147-48, 150, 152.

25. The most complete description of what became known as "the big gunfight" of March 21, 1886, may be found in ibid., 140-55. This narrative includes Gober's account of the wounded Lem Woodruff's escape from Tascosa to Theodore Briggs's ranch. Although Gober persists in identifying some participants in the fight as LS Rangers, that body had already been disbanded for nearly a year.

26. Bostonians W. H. Bates and David T. Beals founded the LX Ranch in Colorado in 1876. The following year, the partners moved their herds to the Canadian River in the central Texas Panhandle. By the early 1880s the LX possessed nearly two hundred thousand acres occupying parts of five counties. Ownership of the LX passed to the American Pastoral Company Ltd. of London in 1884, and by the 1890s the new owner had expanded its holdings to about four hundred thousand acres. Beginning in 1910 the company liquidated its holdings to cattlemen Lee Bivins, R. B. Masterson, and Joe T. Sneed. Bivins got the brand, the new Bonita Creek headquarters,

and one hundred thousand acres. See Margaret Sheers, "The LX Ranch of Texas," *Panhandle-Plains Historical Review* 6 (1933): 45-57; Robertson and Robertson, *Cowman's Country,* 115-17.

27. According to the historian of Tascosa, "Several did put in a few shots who have never been mentioned as participants." See McCarty, *Maverick Town,* 149.

Another Ranching Experience

1. Charles A. Siringo (1855-1928) was born in Matagorda County, Texas. After fifteen years as a cowboy and trail driver, Siringo became an undercover operative for Pinkerton's National Detective Agency. He retired in 1907 and moved to Santa Fe.

Siringo took up writing while still a cowpuncher and authored several books, including the first cowboy autobiography, *A Texas Cowboy, or, Fifteen Years on the Hurricane Deck of a Spanish Pony* (1885). His attempt to write about his detective career, however, resulted in a painful lawsuit and years of hostility between the ex-detective and his former employer. Siringo died in Hollywood. Ben Pigenot provides the most authoritative account of Siringo's fascinating life in *Charles Siringo* (College Station: Texas A & M University Press, 1989).

2. Hispanic sheepherders from New Mexico moved into the plains of western Texas as early as the 1860s and by the early 1870s had established plazas along the Canadian River Valley and camps further south in Yellow House and Blanco Canyons. Flocks owned by several British-based partnerships and corporations followed these early entrants in the late 1870s. By 1880 some 400 *pastores* grazed more than one hundred thousand head of sheep in the Panhandle. Within a decade, however, challenges from cattlemen for the free grass of the public domain had reduced this number to only about ten thousand head.

Of the five sheep ranchers occupying the Yellow House Canyon region by 1880, the most prominent was Mississippi-born Zachary Taylor Williams, who placed a flock on three sections as early as 1877. In 1884 the Western Land and Livestock Company of Iowa bought him out and established the IOA Ranch. A reliable account of sheep ranching in northwestern Texas can be found in Paul Carlson, "Panhandle Pastores: Early Sheepherding in the Texas Panhandle," *Panhandle-Plains Historical Review* 53 (1980): 1-16. For information on Zachary Taylor Williams see Lawrence Graves, ed., *History of Lubbock* (Lubbock: West Texas Museum Association, 1962), 38-39, 50, 64.

The Yellow House Draw, comprising the upper reaches of Yellow House Canyon, was created by Yellow House Creek, an intermittent stream rising in northwestern Hockley County, Texas, and flowing east-southeast for fifty-two miles to join the Double Mountain fork of the Brazos at present-day Lubbock. The canyon drew its name from the yellow soil of its walls. See Graves, *History of Lubbock,* 29; *Handbook of Texas,* 2:943.

3. Gober probably refers to George Singer's store, a famous area landmark and the first business in the region. Most sources agree that Singer's mercantile was open by 1881. See Graves, *History of Lubbock,* 55-56, 65-66.

4. Gober encountered a remnant of the once-prolific bison herds that roamed the southern plains. By 1880 hide hunters had harvested most of the shaggy beasts, although a hunting party in the Panhandle reported seeing about three thousand head in small bunches as late as 1886. See Haley, *XIT Ranch,* 48; McCarty, *Maverick Town,* 208-9; Miles Gilbert, ed., *Getting a Stand* (Tempe: Hal Green Printing, 1986), 69-70.

5. Green, Tant, and Sanders Estes moved their herd onto the range around Yellow House Canyon about 1882. XIT Ranch fencing operations forced their departure about 1885. Haley, *XIT Ranch,* 49.

6. In 1886 Jim Newman relocated his herds from XIT range in the Yellow House Canyon area to a salt lake about twenty miles northeast of Portales, New Mexico. See ibid., 49.

7. Doak Good, a former buffalo hunter, settled at Portales Spring, six miles southwest of the present town of Portales, in 1878, where he began a small ranch. He left New Mexico in the late 1880s, living at Colorado City, Texas, for a time before moving to San Diego, where he found work on a railroad grading crew. See Jack Potter, "Tragedies of the Portales Road," typescript, John McCarty papers, Amarillo Public Library, Amarillo; Haley, *XIT Ranch,* 48; Pearce, *New Mexico Place Names,* 124-25.

8. Billy the Kid and his confederates often used Los Portales as a way station and refuge. See McCarty, *Maverick Town,* 81; Robert M. Utley, *Billy the Kid: A Short and Violent Life* (Lincoln: University of Nebraska Press, 1989), 129, 133, 145-46, 150, 166, 250.

9. Gober probably refers here to the head of Blackwater Draw, located about seven miles northeast of present-day Portales. The draw ranges southeast into Texas, where it joins the Yellow House Draw to form Yellow House Canyon in Lubbock County. See Pearce, *New Mexico Place Names,* 18; Graves, *History of Lubbock,* 25.

10. Tierra Blanca Creek flows east and northeast from its origin in Curry County, New Mexico, through Deaf Smith and Randall Counties in Texas, joining Palo Duro Creek east of the town of Canyon. The junction of the two creeks forms the Prairie Dog Town fork of the Red River. See *Handbook of Texas,* 2:780.

11. At the time, Grissom was serving as the Frying Pan range boss.

12. Several Texas ranches maintained finishing ranges for their cattle on the Yellowstone River in Montana. Cowboys were often called upon to swim their herds across this formidable watercourse. See Donna M. Lucey, *Photographing Montana 1894-1928: The Life and Work of Evelyn Cameron* (New York: Knopf, 1990), 134-35.

13. Duane F. Guy, ed., *The Story of the Palo Duro Canyon* (Canyon: Panhandle-Plains Historical Society, 1979) and Dan Flores, *Caprock Canyonlands* (Austin: University of Texas Press, 1990) offer stimulating over-

views of the history and geography of the Palo Duro Canyon and surrounding region.

14. For an account of this devastating winter see David L. Wheeler, "The Blizzard of 1886 and Its Effect on the Range Cattle Industry on the Southern Plains," *Southwestern Historical Quarterly* 94 (Jan.1991): 415-32.

15. The JA Ranch was founded in 1877 under a five-year partnership agreement between Irish investment banker John G. Adair and cattleman Charles Goodnight (1836-1929). Goodnight, who had located a herd of cattle from Colorado in the Palo Duro Canyon the previous year, provided the stock and ranching expertise, and Adair the operating capital. By the mid-1880s the JA owned 100,000 head of cattle and 650,000 acres outright and leased or grazed a like amount of range.

John Adair's death in 1885 and distressed conditions in the cattle business brought an end to the partnership in 1887. The assets were partitioned, with Adair's widow, Cornelia Wadsworth Adair, retaining ownership of the JA brand.Upon Cornelia Adair's death in 1921, ownership of the nearly four hundred thousand acres of JA range passed to her heirs, who still operate the ranch. The early history of this famous Texas outfit is well documented in Harley T. Burton, *A History of the JA Ranch* (Austin: Von Boeckmann-Jones Press, 1928). See also J. Evetts Haley, *Charles Goodnight, Cowman & Plainsman* (Boston: Houghton Mifflin Co., 1936).

16. Mulberry Basin lies near the head of Mulberry Creek in northwestern Armstrong County. See *Handbook of Texas*, 2:247.

17. The Panhandle blizzard that began on January 7, 1886, raged for two days and three nights, with winds clocked at fifty-eight miles an hour and temperatures of -10 degrees F. Area cattlemen lost thousands of head, and some ranchers were forced out of business. John Hollicott, manager of the LX, recalled that his cowboys skinned 250 cattle per mile for thirty miles along one section of drift fence. See Wheeler, "The Blizzard of 1886," 415-32; McCarty, *Maverick Town*, 165.

A Target of Opportunity

1. John Hollicott managed the LX Ranch continuously from 1881-1898, except for a brief hiatus in the early 1880s. Earlier he had managed George Littlefield's LIT Ranch. Hamlin, *Flamboyant Judge*, 29-30.

2. Liberty, the first civilian settlement in Quay County, New Mexico, was located near Fort Bascom. Whiskey peddlers arrived first, followed by a store and a post office. See Virginia Morton, "Early Settlement of Quay County, New Mexico," *Panhandle-Plains Historical Review* 19 (1946): 74.

3. Wilson Waddingham recorded the Bell brand in San Miguel County, New Mexico Territory, on March 15, 1875. About the time Gober roamed the Bell range its boundaries encompassed some 855,000 acres, and its cattle herd numbered 52,000 head. See David Remley, *Bell Ranch: Cattle Ranching in the Southwest, 1824-1947* (Albuquerque: University of New Mexico Press,

1993); Don Ornduff, "A Historical Overview of the Bell Ranch," in George F. Ellis, ed., *The Bell Ranch as I Knew It* (Kansas City: Lowell Press, 1973), 2-45.

4. Gober's view of the man known as the Catfish Kid reflected the prevailing local sentiment. John B. Gough, who participated on the side of Lem Woodruff in the "big fight" of 1886, was tried and acquitted of murder for his part in the incident. In June of 1887, however, Gough was convicted of killing unarmed Pete Fulton in cold blood and sentenced to sixteen years in prison. See McCarty, *Maverick Town*, 104-5, 144, 146, 149, 151, 155, 176; *Tascosa Pioneer*, June 25, October 8, 1887.

5. Matt Atwood eventually drifted into Oldham County and home-steaded on the Rita Blanca. He was defeated in the 1886 county sheriff's election by Tobe Robinson. Although the editor of the *Tascosa Pioneer* thought him a "general good fellow," XIT ranch officials considered him a rustler. He was eventually charged with the crime but escaped his captors and disappeared. See *Tascosa Pioneer*, June 19, September 1, November 10, 1886, August 27, 1887; Haley, *XIT Ranch*, 110-12.

A Deputy Out on a Limb

1. The popular Tobe Robinson, a Tascosa businessman and rancher, served as the county sheriff of Oldham County and later became the first sheriff of Hartley County. In 1891 he was wounded in a shootout in Channing, Texas, with the Graham brothers, who were intent on murdering XIT manager A. G. Boyce. See Haley, *XIT Ranch*, 180-81; *Tascosa Pioneer*, November 10, 1886, December 22, 1888; McCarty, *Maverick Town*, 235.

2. Federal troops occupied a cantonment on Sweetwater Creek in present-day Wheeler County in 1875 to protect travelers and local settlers. The new post was christened Fort Elliott in 1876 and abandoned by the army in 1890. See James M. Oswald, "History of Fort Elliot," *Panhandle-Plains Historical Review* 32 (1959): 1-59.

3. Fort Sill lies at the junction of Medicine Bluff and Cache Creeks in present-day Comanche County, Oklahoma. Continuously occupied by the army since 1869, Fort Sill played a key role in the subjugation of the Indian tribes of the southern plains. Wilbur S. Nye's *Carbine and Lance: The Story of Old Fort Sill* (Norman: University of Oklahoma Press, 1937) is still the best history of the early years of this important military installation.

4. The army occupied Camp Supply in present-day Woodward County, Oklahoma, in 1868, as a base of operations for Indian campaigns. The post became Fort Supply in 1879 and continued in active use by the military until 1895. See Robert C. Carriker, *Fort Supply Indian Territory: Frontier Outpost on the Plains* (Norman: University of Oklahoma Press, 1970).

5. Chartered in Texas in 1873, the Fort Worth and Denver Railway Company began to survey a route from Texas to Colorado but was soon delayed by a national depression. In 1881 construction resumed to Wichita Falls, where work was again halted until 1886. During the hiatus in Texas,

a rail line was extended from Denver to Pueblo. The Texas and Colorado lines were finally connected on March 14, 1888. See *Handbook of Texas,* 1: 634-635.

6. Located on land owned by Jesse Jenkins, Rag Town (or Amorilla Village, as it was also known) was typical of the mobile communities that served railroad track layers throughout the West. See Crudgington, "Old Town Amarillo," 84; Hamlin, *Flamboyant Judge,* 4.

7. The nefarious pleasures conducted in Fort Worth's Hell's Half-Acre are amply exposed in Richard F. Selcer's *Hell's Half Acre* (Fort Worth: Texas Christian University Press, 1991).

8. Frontier communities commonly required saloons and other places of entertainment to take out operating licenses as a means of regulation and taxation.

A County to be Formed

1. Born in Macon County, North Carolina, William Buford Plemons (1844-1901) served in a state regiment in the Civil War and was wounded three times. After the war he moved to Wood County, Texas, then to Henrietta in Clay County, where he was elected mayor and, later, the first county judge. Moving to the Panhandle after two terms, Plemons became the first Potter County judge beginning in 1887 and served similarly in the forty-seventh district before being elected to the legislature in 1894. During his tenure in Austin, Plemons authored the important Four Section Settler Act, which facilitated settlement of the semi-arid plains of western Texas. After an unsuccessful bid for Congress, he practiced law in the Panhandle until his death. See Hamlin, *Flamboyant Judge,* 12-13; Thomas F. Turner, "Prairie Dog Lawyers," *Panhandle-Plains Historical Review* 2 (1927), 321-22; *Handbook of Texas,* 2:386; William Clayton Kimbrough, "A History of Clay County" (M. A. thesis, Hardin-Simmons University, 1942), 154; Della Tyler Key, *In the Cattle Country: History of Potter County,* 1887-1976, 2d ed. (Quanah, TX: Nortex Offset Publications, 1972), 281.

2. Claiborne W. Merchant (1836-1926) was born in Nacogdoches County, Texas. In 1858 he became a storekeeper in Denton County. After serving in the Confederate army, Merchant took up the cattle business in 1869 and in 1874 moved to Callahan County, where he established the 74 Ranch in partnership with Jasper McCoy. He later acquired interests in the Half Circle and Ten Ranches and in the San Simon Cattle Company of Arizona. Merchant lost heavily in the cattle market crash of 1885. He located and promoted the town of Abilene in Taylor County in 1881, acquired a homestead in the Panhandle, and eventually became the Fort Worth and Denver Railroad livestock agent for Amarillo. See Jim Bob Tinsley, *The Hash Knife Brand* (Gainesville: University Press of Florida, 1993), 13; *Handbook of Texas,* 2:176.

3. James T. Berry arrived in the Panhandle in April 1887 to scout a likely town location on the Fort Worth and Denver Railroad. The following

month he filed on Potter County section 188, containing a playa lake that could be used to water the cattle sure to be shipped from the region on the new line. The following year he promoted the town site of Oneida as the county seat. See Crudgington, "Old Town Amarillo," 83.

4. Taylor County land and cattle dealer James T. Holland served on the first Potter County commissioners court, organized Amarillo's first social and business club in 1889, operated a ranch northwest of town, and, in partnership with John H. Wills, owned an early Amarillo realty company. The Holland addition of Amarillo is named for him. See *Amarillo News,* August 14, 1938; Hamlin, *Flamboyant Judge,* 18-19; Crudgington, "Old Town Amarillo," 88-89, 95, 106.

5. Charlie Gillespie did not run for sheriff; instead, he ran for county commissioner, precinct 3. See Crudgington, "Old Town Amarillo," 86.

6. R. M. "Mack" Moore did not run for the Potter County Commission in 1887. He ran successfully for commissioner in 1888. Appointed Amarillo's first postmaster, Moore also ran a coal business. According to one prominent Panhandle resident, Moore possessed a "vicious disposition," especially when drunk, and killed at least two men. After leaving Amarillo, Moore established a feed store in the community of Texico and later moved to Tahoka, on the south plains. See Crudgington, "Old Town Amarillo," 92, 98; Hamlin, *Flamboyant Judge,* 184-85.

7. H. T. "Tuck" Cornelius established the first livery stable in Amarillo. Cornelius closed out the H Dot Ranch in Snyder, Texas, and arrived in town with his wife, a covered wagon, and a remuda of horses. He was elected a county commissioner in 1887 and became a leading citizen in early Amarillo. See Crudgington, "Old Town Amarillo," 88, 94.

8. Contrary to Gober's recollection, John Bain had significant opposition from four other candidates in his successful quest for the position of Potter County treasurer. See ibid., 86.

9. Gober's reference here is probably to the Mexican Plaza located on the Canadian River about a mile downriver from Tascosa. This plaza was established on the south bank of the Canadian in the winter of 1878-79 by Ventura Borrego of New Mexico. See *Tascosa Pioneer,* August 14, 1886; Carlson, "Panhandle Pastores," 5.

10. Several Hispanic families from New Mexico also settled on Arroyo Pescado, "Fish Creek," on the north side of the Canadian, about a mile and a half below Tascosa. Neither the Pescado nor the Mexican Plaza settlements, however, appears to have figured in Potter County voting. See Haley, *XIT Ranch,* 35.

11. The Round Rock shootout between Texas Rangers and local lawmen and the Sam Bass gang occurred on July 19, 1878, not in 1880, as Gober remembered. Bass was mortally wounded as he attempted to hold up a bank in the Williamson County community. He died two days later. Wayne Gard has produced the most complete biography of Bass to date, *Sam Bass* (Boston: Houghton Mifflin, 1936).

12. Three town sites appeared on the ballot for the position of Potter County seat: Adessa (section 22), owned by Jesse Jenkins; Oneida (section 188), owned by James T. Berry; and Plains City (section 156), owned by H. B. Sanborn. See Crudgington, "Old Town Amarillo," 83-84.

13. According to early Amarillo attorney James D. Hamlin, Holland went to New York City for the purpose of "outwitting" a group of confidence men who had defrauded one of his friends. Holland's plan, which involved buying counterfeit bills, went sour, and in the melee that followed Holland killed one man and wounded another. He surrendered to police and was tried and acquitted of murder after a costly defense. Historian J. Evetts Haley thought Holland possessed "an impeccable record of character and propriety." See Hamlin, *Flamboyant Judge,* 18-19.

14. Gober defeated Bill Ruth by a margin of 34 to 16. Gillespie was not in the sheriff's race. See Crudgington, "Old Town Amarillo," 86.

15. With the help of John Hollicott, LX Ranch manager, and the votes of LX cowboys, who were promised town lots in exchange for their votes, Berry's town site won the election as the Potter County seat. The name Oneida was soon abandoned in favor of Amarillo. See ibid., 83-87, 93, 109.

16. Garrett Johnson was appointed the first hide and animal inspector of Potter County on November 30, 1887. He became a deputy sheriff under A. F. Criswell in 1889. An imposing six feet, four inches tall, Johnson was friendly as well as fearless. See Paul Timmons, "Peace Officers [of] Potter Co.," 1-2, typescript, folder 69, McCarty papers.

17. Jack Ryan had been a Tascosa saloon keeper and a top hand on the LX Ranch. See McCarty, *Maverick Town,* 50, 55, 172, 177, 232.

18. In September 1887, the Fort Worth and Denver agreed to locate its depot near Wild Horse Lake on James T. Berry's section 188. See Crudgington, "Old Town Amarillo," 87.

19. Former LX cowboy Frank Anglin paid the first occupation tax in Amarillo on January 1, 1888. See ibid., 92.

20. Between 1892 and 1897, Amarillo was the largest cattle shipping center in the United States. Each spring and fall, drovers trailed herds as far as four hundred miles to the Fort Worth and Denver shipping pens. Seven or eight Amarillo saloons and gambling houses entertained visiting cowboys at the end of the trail. See Hamlin, *Flamboyant Judge,* 6, 10; Clara T. Hammond, ed., *Amarillo* (Amarillo: George Autry, 1971), 66.

21. Wallace owned a one-eighth interest in Berry's Amarillo town site. See *Tascosa Pioneer,* June 23, 1888, 166; Key, *Cattle Country,* 43.

22. H. H. Brookes edited and published the first Amarillo newspaper, The *Amarillo Champion,* on May 17, 1888. In subsequent years he issued papers under other titles, including *The Amarillo Northwest, The Texas Northwest* and *The Daily Northwest,* before finally reverting to *The Amarillo Champion.*

Charles F. Rudolph, editor and publisher of several Panhandle newspapers including *The Tascosa Pioneer,* briefly published *The Amarillo Northwest,* a weekly, before selling out in 1891 to R. F. Cates. See Jerry Hollingsworth, "Trial and Travail of an Editor, or 'I'll Do Anything for a Block,'" *Panhandle-Plains Historical Review* 48 (1975): 27-41; Crudgington, "Old Town Amarillo," 91.

23. R. M. Moore was not a member of the first county commission. See Crudgington, "Old Town Amarillo," 88.

24. After the November 1888 election, Potter County commissioners appointed D. N. Quinn to succeed W. B. Plemons as county judge, Plemons having been appointed by the governor as judge of the recently organized 47th judicial district of Texas. See Hammond, *Amarillo,* 23; Crudgington, "Old Town Amarillo," 98, 105, 111.

25. The minutes of the Potter County commission meeting of August 17, 1888, place the final cost of the new courthouse at thirty-three thousand dollars. See Crudgington, "Old Town Amarillo," 98.

The Pursuit of a Desperate Man

1. Richard L. McAnulty located the first herd of cattle bearing the Turkey Track brand in present-day Hansford and Hutchinson Counties in 1878. McAnulty sold out in 1881 to Word and Snider, who relinquished their holdings two years later to the Scottish-financed Hansford Land & Cattle Co., under the leadership of Kansas City banker James M. Coburn. For two decades the ranch flourished under the capable management of C. B. (Cape) Willingham, grazing thirty thousand head of cattle on 430,000 acres of Texas grass and additional range near Roswell, New Mexico. The ranch and brand were later acquired by W. T. Coble and is still operated by his descendants. For sketches of the Turkey Track, see Robertson and Robertson, *Cowman's Country,* 152-53; Hamner, *Shortgrass and Longhorns,* 131-40.

2. Located in Moore County, Texas, Evans Canyon took the name of B. C. Evans, a surveyor who erected a house there about 1882. Blue Creek flows through the Evans Canyon and empties into the Canadian River. "Evans Canyon," typescript, Hutchinson County Museum, Borger, Texas.

3. The present-day Oklahoma Panhandle counties of Beaver, Texas, and Cimarron, consisting of some 5,670 square miles, were long the subject of disputed claims involving Spain, France, England, the United States, and the Republic of Texas. When the U.S. Congress failed to assign the area to any administrative unit following the Compromise of 1850, the area took the name No Man's Land. Although finally incorporated into the Territory of Oklahoma in 1890, the sparsely populated area remained a refuge for the lawless for many years. See Carl Coke Rister, *No Man's Land* (Norman: University of Oklahoma Press, 1948); Francis L. Fugate and Roberta B. Fugate, *Roadside History of Oklahoma* (Missoula: Mountain Press, 1991), 279-80; Joseph B. Thoburn and Isaac M. Holcomb, *A History of Oklahoma* (San Francisco: Doub and Company, 1908), 168-69.

4. Gober recounted his capture of Lee Fuller in "Potter County's First Sheriff Tells of Bad Men," *The Amarillo Sunday News-Globe,* December 1, 1929.

Corruption Plans a Murder

1. Although Holland was certainly of like mind, most sources credit Sanborn as the main force behind the drive to relocate the town site. The flooding of Berry's section in the spring of 1889 abetted Sanborn's plans as many residents moved their homes and businesses to higher ground in his new addition. See B. Byron Price and Frederick W. Rathjen, *The Golden Spread* (Windsor Publications, 1986), 69-70; Crudgington, "Old Town Amarillo," 105-8.

2. In 1887 James T. Berry and John Hollicott built a two-story frame hotel known as the Amarillo House on the new town site of Amarillo. Two years later H. B. Sanborn bought the building from the owners and moved it to the Sanborn addition, where it became an annex to the new three-story Amarillo Hotel. See Hamlin, *Flamboyant Judge,* 4, 113-15; Crudgington, "Old Town Amarillo," 93-94, 108.

3. M. M. Givens had not been appointed constable but elected by an overwhelming margin in November 1888. Gober killed Givens on the afternoon of January 10, 1889. The constable had gone to L. B. Collins's saloon to serve papers on several gamblers when, according to eyewitnesses, he got into an argument with bystanders who objected to his warrants. As words were exchanged, Givens pulled his pistol, pointing it at one of his critics and then in the direction of Jim Gober, John Hollicott, and B. Hawley Plemons, who had arrived twenty minutes earlier and were standing with others across the room. Givens ignored Gober's warning to hold up and trained his gun on the sheriff, who drew his own pistol and fired, mortally wounding the constable.

Two witnesses later testified that Gober had told them the shooting was accidental. James G. Davidson swore that he heard Gober say, "I threw my gun down on him to make him drop his pistol. The shot was accidental." Gober told another bystander that "the pistol went off without my knowing it." Nevertheless, some townspeople branded the young sheriff a killer. See Key, *Cattle Country,* 59-61; Crudgington, "Old Town Amarillo," 93-94, 108.

4. Gober was charged with the murder on January 14, 1889, and surrendered to deputy Eben F. True. Justice of the Peace W. M. Andrews fixed Gober's bond at five thousand dollars and set the trial for September 9, 1889, in the new Potter County courthouse. See file box 15, case 1, district clerk's office, Potter County, Amarillo; Key, *Cattle Country,* 59-61; Crudgington, "Old Town Amarillo," 103.

5. English born and Virginia educated, W. H. Woodman came to the Panhandle from Henrietta, Texas. By December 1885 Woodman was attorney for the Panhandle district, and on November 6, 1888, he was elected to a similar post for the thirty-first district. He practiced law at Mobeetie before relocating to Washburn in Armstrong County, where he established a legendary reputation as a criminal attorney. Woodman dressed impeccably and possessed shoulder-length black hair and an authoritative demeanor. Blessed with an exceptional memory, he never referred to notes in court, and his

penchant for dramatic oratory gave rise to rumors that he had been a Shakespearean actor. Some called him the "Lone Wolf of the Yellow House." See Key, *Cattle Country*, 300; Hammond, *Amarillo*, 23; Willie Newberry Lewis, *Between Sun and Sod*, (Clarendon, TX: Clarendon Press, 1938), 161; *Handbook of Texas*, 2: 931-32.

6. Lewis Carhart, a Methodist minister, established the town of Clarendon in Donley County in 1878. The religious proclivities of the town's founder and first colonists earned it the nickname "Saint's Roost." In the late 1880s residents relocated the community six miles south to a new site along the Fort Worth and Denver Railroad. See Lewis, *Between Sun and Sod*, 65-75.

7. H. H. Wallace, a distinguished Tascosa lawyer born in Virginia, was elected Oldham County judge in October 1886. He later served as forty-seventh district judge in Amarillo. See *Tascosa Pioneer*, October 13, November 10, 1886; Hamlin, *Flamboyant Judge*, 55-56; McCarty, *Maverick Town*, 177.

8. In 1881, Frank Willis of Montague County, Texas, was appointed the first judge of the thirty-fifth district, sometimes known as the "jumbo district" because it contained the entire Panhandle and part of Indian Territory. In 1887, Willis was the subject of celebrated impeachment proceedings over state grass leases to ranchers. See J. Evetts Haley, "The Grass Lease Fight and the Attempted Impeachment of the First Panhandle Judge," *Southwestern Historical Quarterly* 38 (Jul. 1934): 1-27; Haley, *Charles Goodnight*, 359, 365-66, 397-98.

9. Eben F. True, a native of Winthrop, Maine, was a bartender, gambler, and veterinarian who was responsible for many years for the LX Ranch remuda. He lived to age eighty-five. See Sheers, "LX Ranch," 45; Hamlin, *Flamboyant Judge*, 15, 22.

10. A warrant was issued on November 8, 1888, for the arrest of Moore in the stabbing of E. F. True. See Crudgington, "Old Town Amarillo," 102.

The Bitter and the Sweet

1. Although the marriage of Belle Helen Plemons and Jim Gober is widely recalled as the first in Potter County, official records are silent as to the exact date.

2. Sallie Gober married A. W. Tolbert. See Key, *Cattle Country*, 281.

3. Soft-spoken Sam McMurray (1847-1914) was born in Gallatin, Tennessee. A Confederate veteran, McMurray came to Texas after the Civil War and became a cattle drover. He joined the Texas Rangers in 1877 and served a tour of duty in the lawless Nueces Strip. McMurray was promoted to lieutenant in 1880 and the following year was named captain of Company B. He resigned from ranger service on January 31, 1891, and later became a salesman for a Louisville, Kentucky firm. He died in Kentucky but was buried in Saint Louis. See Robert W. Stephens, *Texas Ranger Sketches* (Dallas: privately printed, 1972), 99-102.

4. According to court records, Judge J. M. Thomason was originally chosen as a special judge to try the case. H. H. Wallace and Thomas F. Turner were employed as attorneys for the defense. Jurors included Gober's friends W. W. Wetsel and James Dobbs. The trial lasted three days, with a not-guilty verdict rendered on September 11, 1889. See file box 15, case 1, district clerk's office, Potter County, Amarillo; Key, *Cattle Country,* 59-61; Crudgington, "Old Town Amarillo," 103.

5. Jacob Lowmiller, who ran an Amarillo draying business, was appointed to finish Givens's unexpired term as constable. See Timmons, "Peace Officers," 1.

6. Earlier in the year, bad blood between Gober and Lowmiller had resulted in the sheriff charging the constable with assault. See Crudgington, "Old Town Amarillo," 103.

A New Election and Its Aftermath

1. Gober's chronology is flawed. Here he describes the1888 election and its aftermath, not that of 1890. Gober, with fifty-one votes, defeated Lowmiller, with ten votes, and M. V. Kinney, who captured seventeen ballots in the Potter County sheriff's race. See ibid., 98.

2. At a meeting of the Potter County commissioners court on September 9, 1889, the same day Gober's murder trial opened, H. T. Cornelius asked to be relieved as surety for several county officials. Other sureties were also declared insolvent, and new bonds were ordered for county clerk, treasurer, justice of the peace, hide and animal inspector, and sheriff. Gober's bond was raised to twelve thousand dollars as county tax collector and five thousand dollars as state tax collector. Commissioners later reduced Gober's security to five thousand dollars but rejected the sheriff's new sureties and those of county treasurer John Bain. On October 12, 1889, the court declared the treasurer and sheriff/tax collector positions vacant. See Key, *Cattle Country,* 61; Crudgington, "Old Town Amarillo," 90, 103-4.

3. On October 14, 1889, the commissioners chose from among three applicants for sheriff's office. Gober applied for his old job, as did A. F. Criswell and J. P. Flores. The court cast three votes for Criswell, two for Gober, and none for Flores. Commissioners Charles Gillespie and John Henry probably voted for Gober.

Criswell had served as a deputy sheriff in Amarillo in 1888. He too encountered bond trouble and was not able to make a satisfactory arrangement, causing the commissioners court to appoint J. M. Grude Britton to take his place in August 1890. See Crudgington, "Old Town Amarillo," 104-5, 110; Key, *Cattle Country,* 61; Timmons, "Peace Officers," 2.

4. J. H. Hamlin, a water well driller, received eight lots in James T. Berry's town site for locating a water well there. Hamlin installed a windmill and tank and sold water to residents by the barrel. H. B. Sanborn bought Hamlin's property and well in March 1889. Later that year Hamlin drilled a

well to provide water for Sanborn's Amarillo Hotel. See Crudgington, "Old Town Amarillo," 107-8.

5. The chronology of Gober's account of events following his refusal to relinquish the post of Potter County sheriff is somewhat garbled and at odds with other records. Forty-sixth Judicial District Judge G. A. Brown suspended Gober from office on November 1, 1889, and directed the county attorney to sue Gober for tax money not paid to the county treasurer. The following day, the Potter County commissioners court employed an attorney to sue to remove Gober from office. A few days later, the court suspended Gober's pay effective November first.

Brown's order was, however, vacated on March 14, 1890, by order of the district court, signed by special Judge W. D. Williams. The plaintiff appealed, and the judge's order was reversed in Donley County. See Crudgington, "Old Town Amarillo," 104-5; Key, *Cattle Country*, 61.

6. The colorful William J. "Bill" McDonald (1852-1918) succeeded Captain S. A. McMurray as commander of Company B of the Texas Rangers at Amarillo in January of 1891. McDonald was born in Mississippi and moved to Rusk County, Texas, in 1866. During the 1870s and 1880s the ex-penmanship instructor and grocer served variously as deputy sheriff, special ranger, and U. S. deputy marshal of the northern district of Texas and the southern district of Kansas. He later guarded Presidents Theodore Roosevelt and Woodrow Wilson on official visits to Texas. The veteran lawman succumbed to pneumonia in Wichita Falls. His exploits are best described in Albert Bigelow Paine, *Captain Bill McDonald, Texas Ranger* (New York: J. J. Little & Ives, 1909); and Walter Prescott Webb, *The Texas Rangers* (Austin: University of Texas Press, 1965), 458-60, 466-69.

7. Gober may refer here to A. L. Henson, a local rancher. See Key, *Cattle Country*, 146.

8. By 1890 Gober's parents and siblings had joined him in Amarillo. Here Gober refers to his brother, John. See ibid., 281.

9. Gober's recollection of his confrontation with McDonald and Criswell is flawed by the facts that Criswell left office in August 1890 and McDonald did not arrive to take over the ranger company in Amarillo until January 1891. R. M. Warden was sheriff at the time of McDonald's arrival. See Timmons, "Peace Officers," 2-3.

10. Gober refers here to his brother Tom, who never married.

11. In 1886 Brown was a law partner with Judge H. H. Wallace in a prominent Panhandle firm. Wallace lived in Tascosa, and Brown in Clarendon. See McCarty, *Maverick Town,* 198; *Tascosa Pioneer,* April 30, 1887; October 6, 1888.

12. Dr. Thomas F. Magee practiced medicine in Henrietta before moving to Amarillo around 1890. He became the organizer and leader of the Potter County Medical Society. Besides his medical practice, Magee acted as a local school trustee. He died in 1933. See Key, *Cattle Country,* 92, 109, 123, 125; *Amarillo News,* February 3, 1933.

13. The Gobers named their first child Willie. See Key, *Cattle Country,* 281.

14. C. B. Vivian, who had lost an arm in a battle with outlaws, was elected the first county clerk of Oldham County. In the late 1880s Vivian moved to Amarillo, where he served on the Potter County finance committee and operated the Elmhurst Hotel. He later migrated to south Texas. See Hamlin, *Flamboyant Judge,* 20; McCarty, *Maverick Town,* 62, 184; Crudgington, "Old Town Amarillo," 103, 111.

Beginning a Life Without a Badge

1. Canadian, Texas, on the Panhandle and Santa Fe Railroad, became the seat of Hemphill County in 1887. See *Handbook of Texas,* 1:287.

2. Born in Tennessee, John Simpson Chisum arrived in Texas in 1837 and settled at Paris. He entered the cattle business in Denton County in the mid-1850s and served as a Confederate Army beef contractor during the Civil War. During the war he moved his herds to the Colorado River in Concho County. In 1873, Chisum established a ranch at South Springs in the Pecos Valley of New Mexico. This range once carried as many as sixty thousand head bearing Chisum's distinctive long-rail brand and jinglebob earmark. Chisum died in Eureka Springs, Arkansas. See Cox, *Historical and Biographical Record,* 299-302; *Handbook of Texas,* 1:342-43.

3. For additional information on these early Potter County sheriffs, see Timmons, "Peace Officers," 1-5.

4. The Gobers named their first son Temple, after Temple Houston. See Key, *Cattle Country,* 281.

5. The opening of the Cheyenne-Arapaho reservation to white settlement actually occurred on April 19, 1892. See W. David Baird and Danney Goble, *The Story of Oklahoma* (Norman: University of Oklahoma Press, 1994), 299; Donald J. Berthrong, *The Cheyenne and Arapaho Ordeal: Reservation and Agency Life in the Indian Territory, 1875-1907* (Norman: University of Oklahoma Press, 1976).

6. A tributary of the Red River, the Washita River and its various branches drain most of south-central Oklahoma. Cheyenne, Oklahoma, became the seat of Roger Mills County in 1892. See George Shirk, *Oklahoma Place Names* (Norman: University of Oklahoma Press, 1965), 44, 217.

7. Sergeant Major Creek, a tributary of the Washita River in Roger Mills County, was named for Sergeant Major Walter P. Kennedy, killed at the Battle of the Washita in 1868. See ibid., 189.

8. Headquartered in present-day Beaver County, Oklahoma, the YL Ranch purchased range and cattle from the Texas Land and Cattle Company in Hemphill County, Texas, in 1888. In Oklahoma, the YL pastured large herds from the Cherokee Outlet to the eastern reaches of No Man's Land. See Robertson and Robertson, *Cowman's Country,* 103; Carl Coke Rister, *No Man's Land* (Norman: University of Oklahoma Press, 1948), 35.

9. Jim and Belle Gober named their second son John T. Gober.

10. Rush Creek rises from Rush Springs on the Chisholm Trail in southern Grady County, Oklahoma. See Shirk, *Oklahoma Place Names,* 189.

Across the Oklahoma Border

1. Home to about five hundred residents, two banks, and twenty-three saloons in the early 1890s, Woodward, Oklahoma, was a booming cattle shipping point with a wild reputation in the tradition of Abilene and Dodge City. Louise B. James covers Woodward's tumultuous early days in *Below Devil's Gap: The Story of Woodward County* (Perkins, OK: Evans Publications, 1984). See also Shirley, *West of Hell's Fringe,* 385.

2. Gober probably refers here to George T. Berry, Jr., a nephew of Amarillo town site promoter James T. Berry and early Amarillo postmaster. See Crudgington, "Old Town Amarillo," 92.

3. Gober was admitted to St. Francis Hospital in Kansas City.

4. The Cherokee Strip, more properly known as the Cherokee Outlet, originally consisted of more than 6.5 million acres running from the 96th to the 100th meridian, granted to the Cherokee Nation in 1828. This area was reduced in 1866 to about six million acres. Between 1883 and 1890 the Cherokee Strip was controlled by members of the *Cherokee Strip Live Stock Association,* who leased the land from the tribe for cattle grazing. In 1890 the federal government purchased the land from the Cherokees and opened it to settlement three years later. For a fine analysis of the origin and disposition of this region see William W. Savage, Jr., *The Cherokee Strip Live Stock Association* (Norman: University of Oklahoma Press, 1990).

5. According to the historian of Woodward, Oklahoma, the Dew Drop Saloon was often called "Dolly's Dew Drop Inn," in reference to Mary Elizer Kezer, a town madam known as Miss Dolly. See James, *Below Devil's Gap,* 89.

6. Former Amarillo saloon keeper L. B. Collins established one of the first saloons in Woodward. See ibid., 83.

7. A landmark in early Woodward, the Cattle King Hotel probably housed prostitutes as well as regular guests. See ibid., 121.

8. James Butler (Wild Bill) Hickok (1837-1876) was born in Illinois, served the Union during the Civil War, and made his reputation as a tough cowtown lawman in Kansas in the 1870s. Jack McCall assassinated the card-playing Hickok in Deadwood, South Dakota. Joe Rosa has produced the best biography of the famous gunman, *They Called Him Wild Bill,* 2d ed. (Norman: University of Oklahoma Press, 1974).

9. Wyatt Earp (1848-1929), the legendary western lawman, joined the Dodge City police force in 1876, serving intermittently as policeman and assistant town marshal until 1879, when he departed Kansas. He made his way with his brothers to Tombstone, Arizona, in 1880 and, as a deputy of his brother Virgil, participated in the fight at OK Corral on October 26, 1881. Earp left Arizona for Colorado and lived in Kansas, Idaho, and Oklahoma before settling in California. He participated in the Klondike and Alaska gold

rushes, then settled in Los Angeles, where he died. Earp's career has inspired many writers and much misinformation. One of the best works is Ed Bartholomew's *Wyatt Earp: The Man & the Myth* (Toyahvale, TX: Frontier, 1964). For a briefer treatment, see Thrapp, *Frontier Biography,* 1:448-49.

10. William Matthew Tilghman (1854-1924) was born in Fort Dodge, Iowa. He hunted buffalo before becoming a saloon keeper in Dodge City in 1875. During the 1880s he launched a stellar career as a lawman, from town marshal of Dodge City to U.S. deputy marshal in the Oklahoma Territory. He hounded the train-robbing Bill Doolin gang and captured Doolin at Eureka Springs, Arkansas. Tilghman served two terms as sheriff of Lincoln County, Oklahoma, and in 1911 he became chief of police of Oklahoma City. He was murdered in 1924 while serving as town marshal of Cromwell, Oklahoma. Tilghman's biographers agree that he seldom resorted to firearms and was not the killer Gober painted him to be. The best treatment of Tilghman's life and career is Glenn Shirley's *Guardian of the Law: The Life and Times of William Matthew Tilghman* (Austin: Eakin Press, 1988). Zoe A. Tilghman also wrote a memoir of her husband, *Marshal of the Last Frontier: Life and Services of William Matthew (Bill) Tilghman* (Glendale: CA: Arthur H. Clark, 1964).

11. Luke L. Short (1854-1893) was born in Mississippi but came to Texas as a child. As a youth he trailed cattle herds to Kansas. In 1876 he joined a party of whiskey peddlers selling liquor to the Indians in Nebraska. After a brief hiatus in Arizona, where he killed a man in Tombstone in 1881, Short returned to Kansas and bought part interest in the Long Branch Saloon. He engaged in a sharp and prolonged disagreement with town officials over prostitution and gambling and was forced to leave town. Short moved to Kansas City and then Fort Worth, where he killed famed western gunman Jim Courtright in 1887. He died of dropsy in Kansas. See O'Neal, *Western Gunfighters,* 284-85; Thrapp, *Frontier Biography,* 3: 1301.

12. C. E. (Tobe) Odem (sometimes spelled Odom), a prominent Bee County cattleman, bossed herds to Kansas and delivered steers on government contract to Indian reservations. In the late 1870s Odem established a range on McClellan Creek and the north fork of the Red River in the Panhandle and in 1884 brought ten thousand south Texas steers to this range. Drought and cold reduced the number to fifteen hundred by 1887 and forced him to sell out. See Robertson and Robertson, *Cowman's Country,* 77, 148; Jesse James Benton, *Cow by the Tail* (Boston: Houghton Mifflin, 1943), 41, 46, 74, 92; Haley, *XIT Ranch,* 45.

13. Located two miles from the Texas-Oklahoma border in Lipscomb County, the town site of Higgins developed when the Panhandle and Santa Fe Railroad passed through the area in the early 1880s. See *Handbook of Texas,* 1:807.

Secrets of the Oklahoma Territory

1. W. J. Sullivan, better known as "John L." Sullivan, had been a sergeant in Bill McDonald's company of Texas Rangers. Sullivan stood six feet, six inches tall, and was colorful and vain in dress and expression but also fearless. His religious proclivities led his fellow rangers to dub him the "Church Fiend." Sullivan authored *Twelve Years in the Saddle for Law and Order on the Frontiers of Texas* (Austin: von Boeckmann-Jones 1909). See also Paul Timmons, "Peace Officers."

2. Eugene Hall was named a U.S. deputy marshal in February 1896. See Shirley, *West of Hell's Fringe*, 339, 343.

3. Ben Wolforth was a Woodward deputy sheriff.

4. J. D. F. Jennings (1831-1903) was born in Virginia. A college-educated, Methodist Episcopal circuit rider, Jennings studied medicine and served as a Confederate surgeon during the Civil War. After the war he practiced law in Illinois, Ohio, Missouri, Kansas, and Colorado before making the land run into Oklahoma in 1889. Active in Democratic Party politics, Jennings was appointed the first probate judge in Woodward County with the opening of the Cherokee Outlet. His sons Al and Frank Jennings became notorious outlaws. Jennings eventually moved to Shawnee, Oklahoma, and finally to Missouri, where he died. See Shirley, *West of Hell's Fringe,* 384-85.

5. Former Canadian County, Oklahoma, prosecutor Alphonso J. Jennings abandoned a promising career as a lawyer at age thirty-two to join with his brother Frank, a former court clerk, brothers Morris and Pat O'Malley, Little Dick West, and Dynamite Dick Clifton in an outlaw gang. In 1897 the Jennings gang began to rob stores, post offices, trains, and banks. U.S. marshals soon pursued the thieves, killed Dynamite Dick, and captured the O'Malleys and the Jenningses before the end of the year. Officers killed Little Dick West in 1898.

Frank Jennings and the O'Malley brothers were sentenced to five years each in the federal penitentiary at Fort Leavenworth. President William McKinley commuted Al Jennings's life sentence to five years, and Theodore Roosevelt granted him a full pardon. Jennings later ran for governor of Oklahoma and was the subject of a popular motion picture biography. See ibid., 385, 390-99, 408-11, 422-25.

6. Temple Houston shot farmer J. B. Jenkins on Main Street in Woodward on October 8, 1896, exactly one year after he had killed Ed Jennings. Jenkins had abused Houston's second son, Sam, over the boarding of a horse. A lenient court assessed the irate attorney only a three-hundred-dollar fine in the case. See James, *Below Devil's Gap,* 119.

7. The tiny town of Kenton briefly served as the seat of Cimmaron County. See Fugate and Fugate, *Roadside Oklahoma,* 257-58.

8. Gober refers here to a small creek taking the Spanish name for the reed grass growing along its banks. See Shirk, *Oklahoma Place Names,* 39.

9. The *Woodward News* of January 31, 1896, reported that Jim Gober had recently established the Equity Saloon, probably named for a famous

Tascosa drinking hall. Gober soon opened a restaurant, and on February 28, 1896, the newspaper noted that the "Palace Equity Restaurant and Saloon" was enjoying liberal patronage.

10. Taloga was surveyed and designated as the county seat of "D" County, present-day Dewey County, before the opening of the Cheyenne-Arapaho reservation to settlement. A post office was established there in 1892. See Fugate and Fugate, *Roadside Oklahoma,* 305-6.

11. Economic stress and social dislocation during the early 1890s gave rise to a phenomenon known as Populism, particularly in the South and West. Populists in the West advocated the free and unlimited coinage of silver, free homesteads, protection of school land leases, and a graduated service pension. Represented by the People's Party, Populists won seats in Congress and control of several state legislatures, including that of Kansas, in the 1892 election. Many Populists settled in western Oklahoma during the runs of 1892-93, and by 1894 Populist candidates controlled some county governments and claimed key seats in the territorial legislature. In 1896 the Populists forged a political alliance with elements of the Democratic Party and nominated William Jennings Bryan for president, on a "free silver" platform. With Bryan's defeat the Populist movement declined. See Shirley, *West of Hell's Fringe,* 375-76.

12. Jim Gober was appointed under sheriff to Sheriff Robert "Big Bob" Benn in January 1897, not 1898. See *Woodward News,* January 8, 1897.

13. Jeff Mynatt had served as a deputy sheriff of Woodward County under Bob Benn. When Benn did not run for reelection, Mynatt defeated C. E. Hall (the Populist candidate) and James R. Gober (running as an independent). Mynatt served from January 1899 to January 1901. See ibid., November 4, 1898.

14. Cattle baron Granville Stuart led a war against rustlers in Montana in 1884. Stuart's vigilante movement took the lives of thirty-five cattle and horse thieves. See Granville Stuart, *Forty Years on the Frontier,* 2 vols. (Cleveland: Arthur H. Clark, 1925); Howard R. Lamar, *The Reader's Encyclopedia of the West* (New York: Thomas Y. Crowell, 1977), 1148.

15. Reference here is to a Woodward, Oklahoma, financial institution owned and operated by the Gerlach family.

16. According to the *Woodward Dispatch,* April 26, 1901, J. R. Gober was a deputy to Albert S. Woods.

A Return to the Cowboy Life

1. Antelope Creek rises in northwestern Carson County northwest of the Panhandle, flowing north twenty-two miles into the Canadian River in southwestern Hutchinson County. See *Handbook of Texas,* 1:52.

2. Located in northwestern Oklahoma Territory, Woods County was named for Kansas political leader Sam Woods. The territorial county was

divided at statehood, with one part retaining the Woods County designation. See Shirk, *Oklahoma Place Names,* 225.

3. Between 1888 and 1892, the notorious Dalton gang terrorized the West from Kansas to California. Grat, Bob, and Emmett Dalton began their criminal careers while serving with the Osage Indian Police in Indian Territory. The gang engaged in horse theft in Oklahoma and robbed a gambling house in New Mexico and trains in California. On October 5, 1892, Bob, Grat, and Emmett and several associates attempted to rob two Coffeyville, Kansas, banks at once. Irate citizens killed all but Emmett, who was seriously wounded. He was paroled after fourteen years in prison and lived until 1937. Bill Dalton, who did not accompany his brothers to Coffeyville, briefly joined Bill Doolin's gang, then formed his own. He was killed by law officers at Ardmore, Oklahoma, on June 8, 1894, after a botched bank robbery in Longview, Texas. Robert B. Smith chronicles the Daltons' jaded careers in *Daltons! The Raid on Coffeyville Kansas* (Norman: University of Oklahoma Press, 1996). The Daltons also figure prominently in Shirley, *West of Hell's Fringe.*

4. George Waightman, a horse thief and murderer better known as Red Buck because of the reddish tint of his hair and mustache, hailed from Texas. Arrested by Marshal Heck Thomas in 1890 and sentenced to nine years in federal prison, Waightman escaped incarceration. He joined Bill Doolin's Wild Bunch and survived the famous 1893 gun battle with law officers at Ingalls, Oklahoma. Two years later Waightman organized a new gang that stole cattle, robbed stores, and murdered citizens in the sparsely populated western reaches of the Oklahoma Territory. A posse killed Red Buck in a shootout at a dugout near Arapaho in February 1896. See Shirley, West of Hell's Fringe, 139, 158-59, 341-51.

5. An associate of George "Red Buck" Waightman, George Miller was wounded in the same 1898 fight with lawmen that claimed Waightman's life. Miller served about twenty years in the penitentiary for his crimes but later became deputy sheriff for the town of Three Sands. He was killed while attempting to arrest a drunk. See ibid., 348-50; Thrapp, *Frontier Biography,* 2:987.

6. Cattle commission merchants, such as the Drumm-Flato Commission Company, provided credit to the cattle industry, secured with mortgages on herds. Established in 1893, Drumm-Flato was one of the largest cattle commission firms in the nation, maintaining offices in Kansas City, St. Louis, and Chicago. See *Financing the Western Cattleman* (Fort Collins: Colorado Experimental Station, 1928), bulletin no. 338, 18-20; Eva L. Atkinson, "Kansas City's Livestock Trade and Packing Industry, 1870-1914: A Study in Regional Growth" (Ph.D. dissertation, University of Kansas, 1971), 336-37; David Murrah, *Oil, Taxes and Cats: A History of the Devitt Family and the Mallet Ranch* (Lubbock: Texas Tech University Press, 1994), 18, 38-39.

7. This Dewey County agricultural community was founded in 1894 and named for the owner of the town site, Louis A. Seiling. During early 1900s it

was home to Carrie Nation. See Fugate and Fugate, *Roadside Oklahoma,* 257-58.

8. Kaffir corn is a grain sorghum cultivated in dry regions and used as animal fodder.

9. Griener Canyon and the ghost town of Griener are located in Major County, west of Orienta. See Shirk, *Oklahoma Place Names,* 93.

10. Alva, the seat of Woods County, acquired a post office in August 25, 1893. The town took the name of railroad attorney and Colorado Governor Alva Adams. See ibid., 8.

11. Ohioan Andrew Drumm (1829-1919) joined the California gold rush but soon found hog raising and meat packing more profitable than mining. By the 1870s Drumm was driving Texas cattle to Kansas railheads. During the early 1880s he established the U Ranch on more than one hundred thousand acres in the Cherokee Strip. Drumm moved to Kansas City in 1881, where he oversaw various business interests, including banking. In 1893 he joined commission merchant F. W. Flato, Jr. and veteran cattleman R. G. Head to form the Drumm-Flato Commission Company. See Meade L. McClure, *Major Andrew Drumm,* 1829-1919 (n.p., 1919), 5-10; "Monument Erected to Major Drumm," *The Cattleman* (Aug. 1932): 7; Skaggs, *Cattle Trailing Industry,* 33; Dykstra, *Cattle Towns,* 210-11.

12. In 1877, F. W. Flato, Jr. of Fayette County, Texas, opened the Fort Worth branch of Hunter, Evans & Company, a cattle commission house. He became manager of the firm's St. Louis office before joining several other investors in buying out Hunter in 1888 and forming the Evans, Snider & Buel Commission Company, Inc. Organization of the Drumm-Flato Commission Company followed, in 1893. Flato sold his share of this company in 1902. See Skaggs, *Cattle Trailing Industry,* 82-83; Cuthbert Powell, *Twenty Years of Kansas City's Livestock Trade and Traders* (Kansas City, MO: Pearl, 1893), pp. 304-5; "Obituary," *The Cattleman* (Dec. 1941): 52; Murrah, *Mallet Ranch,* 18, 38-39.

Becoming A Cattle Sleuth

1. Born in Gonzales, Texas, in 1857, Joseph Henry Nations began ranching at an early age, purchasing yearlings with his earnings as a cowboy and borrowing money from friends to add to his herd. In 1882 Nations and his father removed their stock from the Gulf Coast to Presidio County. Fifteen years later he became partners with E. S. Newman in the Clabber Hill Ranch, near Midland. He eventually acquired a second ranch in Texas and another in New Mexico, where he ran large numbers of sheep. Nations eventually became a resident of El Paso, where he owned meat and transfer companies and became director of the First National Bank. In 1898, Nations left El Paso for a brief residency in Kansas City, where he lost heavily in livestock. After settling his debts he returned to El Paso. See *History of the Cattlemen of Texas* (Austin: Texas State Historical Association), 153-55.

2. Named by Albert Pike in 1832, the Salt Fork of the Brazos River rises in the breaks of the Llano Estacado in Crosby County and flows southeast across Garza, Kent, and Stonewall Counties, uniting with the Double Mountain Fork to form the main Brazos in Stonewall County. See *Handbook of Texas,* 2:535.

3. The son of a Methodist circuit rider, John Wesley Hardin (1853-1895) killed his first man at age fifteen. He added nearly twenty more during the lawless turbulence of Reconstruction Texas. In 1874 he murdered deputy sheriff Charles Webb and fled Texas for Alabama and Florida, where he added a half dozen or more homicides to his bloody roster. Texas Rangers captured him in Pensacola, Florida, in 1877, and returned him to Texas, where he was sentenced to twenty-five years in prison for Webb's murder. In Huntsville Penitentiary, Hardin attempted escape, headed the Sunday School program, and read law. He was pardoned in 1894 and admitted to the bar. Hardin went to El Paso in 1895, where he was murdered by Constable John Selman. Hardin wrote his own autobiography, *The Life of John Wesley Hardin as Written by Himself,* in 1896. Briefer accounts of his life include Webb, *Texas Rangers,* 297-304; and J. Evetts Haley, *Jeff Milton: A Good Man with a Gun* (Norman: University of Oklahoma Press, 1948), 226-48.

4. Colorado City, the seat of Mitchell County, owed its birth to the Texas & Pacific Railroad in 1880. The arrival of the first train the following year inaugurated an economic boom that brought five thousand residents to the town in a matter of months. See *Handbook of Texas,* 1:378.

5. Tom Powers later moved from Colorado City to El Paso, where he operated a saloon. Powers became a close friend of Pat Garrett and helped bury the old lawman after his murder in 1908. See Metz, *Pat Garrett,* 252-254, 306.

The Major Turning Point

1. The town of Gage, Oklahoma, named for President William McKinley's secretary of the treasury, Lyman J. Gage, lies seven miles northeast of Shattuck in Ellis County. A post office was established there on February 5, 1895. See Shirk, *Oklahoma Place Names,* 85.

2. Oil cake is a form of cattle feed made from cottonseed or linseed pressed free of its oil.

3. In 1902 Drumm bought out his partner and renamed the business the Drumm Commission Company. See Murrah, *Mallet Ranch,* 38.

4. On Wednesday afternoon, June 15, 1904, Wade Bowie, employed in Jim Gober's saloon for several years and a boarder in Gober's home, shot Belle Gober while she slept, then killed himself. The murder shocked Amarillo citizens, and the atrocity was widely covered in the press. One report noted that Bowie, normally quiet and reserved, had been drinking heavily prior to the incident and that Belle Gober had warned him to stay away from the Gober home while her husband was absent. Belle Gober, age thirty-one,

was found by her children, who were playing outside when the shots rang out. See Key, *Cattle Country,* 281; "Terrible Tragedy," and "A Sad Tragedy," undated newspaper clippings, Gober Family Collection.

A Racing Attempt at Escape

1. Indiana-born Sam Bass (1851-1878) came to Texas in 1870. He worked as a cowboy and a teamster before launching a career as a horse thief and a stage and train robber in Wyoming, Nebraska, and Texas. Bass was mortally wounded by Texas Rangers during a thwarted bank holdup at Round Rock, Texas. See Thrapp, *Frontier Biography,* 1: 70-71.

Gober may have seen Sam Bass race a swift quarter horse, known as the Denton mare, at an improvised track in Dave Fry's pasture north of the Denton town square. See Clarence Allen Bridges, *History of Denton, Texas: From Its Beginning to 1960* (Waco: Texian Press, 1978), 144-45; *Handbook of Texas,* 1: 119.

The Quest for Peace and a Meaning to Life

1. Near Union Station was a district of gambling dens, saloons, and prostitution known as the Bowery. Home to transients and thugs of every description, it was the scene of recurrent crime and violence. See Price and Rathjen, *Golden Spread,* 75.

2. Barney Plemons was the son of Judge W. B. Plemons and Gober's brother-in-law.

3. Gober was probably among a group of Woodward homesteaders, including Temple Houston, who immigrated to present-day Cimmaron County, Oklahoma, during the summer of 1901. At least some of the new arrivals also planned to prospect for copper deposits in nearby Colorado. See "Woodward Colony Stakes Claims," *The Boise City News,* Summer, 1968, F:4.

4. Jim Gober's 125-acre homestead was located on North Carrizo Creek about five miles north of a seven-hundred-foot-high lava plateau known as Black Mesa. See Louis Maynard, *Oklahoma Panhandle: A History and Stories of No Man's Land* (Boise City, OK: Louis Maynard, 1956), 38-39.

5. Garnett Lee, who ranched and homesteaded on the Canadian River in Potter County, often assisted travelers in fording. See Key, *Cattle Country,* 76, 127, 291.

6. Located in Dallam County, in the northwest corner of the Panhandle, Buffalo Springs became headquarters for one of the divisions of the XIT Ranch. See Haley, *XIT Ranch,* 44, 19, 147.

7. The town of Texline was established in 1888 on the Fort Worth and Denver Railroad in western Dallam County, on the Texas-New Mexico border. Between 1891 and 1893 it was the county seat. See *Handbook of Texas,* 2:768.

8. Named for Boise, Idaho (although pronounced differently), Boise City, Oklahoma, was named county seat of Cimarron County in 1908. See Shirk, *Oklahoma Place Names*, 26.

9. The town of Texhoma straddles the Texas-Oklahoma border in Sherman County, Texas, and Texas County, Oklahoma. See *Handbook of Texas*, 2:768; Shirk, *Oklahoma Place Names*, 204.

10. Animal-powered scrapers and slips were employed to build dams, reservoirs, and roads before the advent of motor-powered machinery.

11. Gober may have been experiencing the effects of marijuana.

12. Indian corn is distinguished from maize by the color and character of its kernels.

13. The organic act that established Oklahoma Territory reserved two sections in each township that would be opened to settlement for the benefit of public education. The same practice was followed with the opening of the Cherokee Strip. School lands were leased at first and later sold, the revenues disbursed to finance normal schools, agricultural colleges, and universities. See Grant Foreman, *A History of Oklahoma* (Norman: University of Oklahoma Press, 1942), 341-42.

14. On February 3, 1913, Gober mortgaged his Cimmaron County land to Kenton merchant D. K. Lord for $250, giving a promissory note at ten percent interest for a year. Having completed the government homestead requirements, Gober received a certificate of title from the General Land Office on June 5, 1913. The following month he reduced and renewed his note with Lord for another year, this time for $150. Gober satisfied this obligation on May 27, 1914, and the mortgage on his homestead was released. See deed and mortgage records, county clerk's office, Cimmaron County Courthouse, Boise City, Oklahoma.

Laverne Hanners, *The Lords of the Valley* (Norman: University of Oklahoma Press, 1996), which includes the complete text of Ed Lord's previously unpublished memoir "Our Unsheltered Lives," provides a social history of Kenton, Oklahoma, and the Black Mesa region during Gober's time.

15. Located between the Cimarron and Beaver Rivers in Beaver County, Oklahoma, Forgan was promoted as a town site in 1912 by J. N. Cook, who hoped to capitalize on the arrival of the Wichita Falls and Northwestern Railway. The community was named for Chicago banker and railroad financier James B. Forgan. See Fugate and Fugate, *Roadside Oklahoma*, 284.

16. The settlement known as Norice took the name Shattuck in 1893, in honor of George O. Shattuck, a Santa Fe Railroad official. After statehood a county reorganization made Shattuck the seat of Ellis County and produced an influx of population. See ibid., 252; Shirk, *Oklahoma Place Names*, 190.

17. James D. Horan adequately surveys the organization and operation of Pinkerton's National Detective Agency in *The Pinkertons* (New York: Crown, 1967).

Grasping the Vision of a Detective Agency

1. Lee Bivins (1862-1929) was a native of Grayson County. A merchant in Sherman and Farmington before coming to the Panhandle, Bivins established a flour mill in Claude, Texas, near Amarillo, in 1890, and began to speculate in land and cattle. In 1906, he bought the LX brand and one hundred thousand acres of range south of the Canadian River. In time he acquired several other Panhandle ranches; another near Midland, Texas; and two more in New Mexico. By the time of his death he was one of the largest individual livestock operators in the country, owning as many as sixty thousand head of cattle. His ranch lands also yielded significant reserves of oil and gas.

Bivins moved to Amarillo in 1895 and eventually developed a housing addition that bore his name. In the 1920s, he became president of an aerial charter service and helped develop the city's first airport. Bivins served as an Amarillo alderman (1910-13) and city commissioner (1913-17). He was elected mayor of Amarillo in 1925 but died during his second term in office. See Key, Cattle Country, 312-13; Robertson and Robertson, *Cowman's Country,* 117; Hamlin, *Flamboyant Judge,* 29, 80-81.

2. Gober probably met John Snider when he worked for the LS Ranch and at Tobe Robinson's Tascosa livery stable in the 1880s. Snider served as city marshal (and unofficial chief of police) of Amarillo from 1910 to 1914. The Amarillo Police Department was not officially created until 1914. See Hammond, *Amarillo,* 35; Sullivan, *LS Ranch,* 152; Millie Jones Porter, *Memory Cups of Panhandle Pioneers* (Clarendon, TX: Clarendon Press, 1945), 528.

3. The ten-story Oliver-Eakle Building, Amarillo's first office skyscraper, was built in 1927 by prominent businesswoman Melissa Dora Oliver-Eakle. See B. Byron Price, "Melissa Dora Oliver-Eakle: Community Financier," *Amarillo Daily News,* December 18, 1982.

4. Located at Third and Pierce Streets in Amarillo, the fourteen-story, six-hundred-room Herring Hotel was begun in 1926 by pioneer west Texas rancher, oilman, and banker C. T. Herring and leased by Colonel Earnest O. Thompson before its completion and opening on January 1, 1928. See Hamlin, *Flamboyant Judge,* 116-17; Cox, *Historical and Biographical Record,* 533.

5. A Georgian by birth, B. T. Ware (1853-1937) settled in Amarillo in 1889. He worked briefly as a mercantile clerk before becoming Potter County's third treasurer in 1890. After his first term, he left politics to represent Kansas City and Chicago cattle commission firms. In 1900 he became president of the Amarillo National Bank. Between 1903 and 1906 Ware also operated the Channing Bank & Mercantile Company. In 1906 he organized the Western Bank & Trust Company, which merged with Amarillo National in 1908, with Ware as the principal stockholder. Ware's banking empire later passed into the hands of his sons and flourishes today. B. T. Ware's career is amply surveyed in Thomas Thompson, *The Ware Boys: The*

Story of A Texas Family Bank (Canyon, TX: Staked Plains Press, 1978). See also Hamlin, *Flamboyant Judge,* 21; Hammond, *Amarillo,* 211-12.

6. W. H. Fuqua attended colleges in Tyler and Waco before entering the cattle and livery stable business. Fuqua arrived in the Panhandle from Ellis County, Texas, in 1890. Two years later he became a vice-president of the First National Bank of Amarillo, and by 1895 he was president of the institution and a financial and community leader until his death. Hamlin, *Flamboyant Judge,* 6, 10-11; Cox, *Historical and Biographical Record,* 504-5; Hammond, *Amarillo,* 218.

7. Ray Wheatley was a nephew of Amarillo sheriff Jerome Wheatley, and at age eighteen he briefly served as his uncle's deputy in the mid-1890s. Wheatley later became a clerk for the Amarillo National Bank and eventually became president of the Amarillo Bank and Trust Company. He died of a heart attack in 1943. See Paul Timmons, "Peace Officers," 4; Hamlin, *Flamboyant Judge,* 10-11.

8. The Gober family possesses a badge bearing the name "Gober Detective Agency."

The Final Roundup

1. W. M. D. Lee's later life was not the failure Gober thought. After leaving the cattle business in the Panhandle, Lee succeeded in developing of Texas's first deepwater harbor at Velasco. He also prospered as an oil prospector, developing fields in Brazoria County and at Spindletop. Lee died of kidney failure in Houston in 1925 at the age of eighty-three. See Schofield, *W. M. D. Lee,* 92-139.

2. W. C. Isaacs arrived in the Panhandle in 1883 from Taylor County, his brothers John and Sam a year later. The younger Isaacs brothers worked for ranches with leases in the Indian Territory until 1885, when they relocated the Mallalay and Forbes herds to near Endee, New Mexico. William Isaacs became a cattleman on the Tierra Blanca, south of Tascosa, in 1887. Two years later Sam moved his employers' cattle to Red Deer Creek, near the town of Canadian, Texas. In 1893 Sam and Will Isaacs bought out Mallalay and Forbes at Canadian and formed a ranching partnership on thirty thousand acres that lasted until 1912, when the brothers divided up the assets. See L. F. Sheffy, "Sam Isaacs," *Panhandle-Plains Historical Review* 19 (1946): 40-44; *Tascosa Pioneer,* August 27, 1887.

3. The historian of Tascosa claims that Harris committed suicide. See McCarty, *Maverick Town,* 124.

4. The robbery of the Union Pacific at Big Springs, Nebraska, by Sam Bass and several associates is recounted in detail in Larry D. Ball, "The United States Army and the Big Springs, Nebraska, Train Robbery of 1877," *Journal of the West* 34 (Jan. 1995): 34-45. Tom Spotwood is not listed as among the robbers.

Appendix

"A Philosophy of Morals and Ethics"

by Jim Gober

It's the degree of confidence and trust one places in me that measures my interest in them. If anyone comes to me in trouble and confides their grievances to my keeping, I immediately reciprocate with sympathy to the value of their spirit of confidence. As time goes on, that spirit of sympathy grows in my heart until I am ready to go to battle for the ones that trust and respect me and confide in me, whether they be right or wrong. I have been placed on the side of injustice in some few instances on account of this irresistible spirit that nature planted in my heart.

I defend my conscience by reflecting on the mighty words, "lend your aid to the weak, pass not your neighbor in the mire, at any cost." My sympathy had always been, and always will be, for the underdog. I love and demand equity and justice and a square deal. There is no room, in my system, for the smallest degree of hypocrisy or policy of selfishness. The older I get, the more lonesome I get for friends of my own nature and disposition, and I really pass many lonely hours because it is not convenient to be with company of my choice.

Of all the things of God's or of man's making, the human mind is no exception in importance. A continually disturbed mind will slowly, but surely break the heart and destroy the courage and turn the spirit of pride and moral character to despotism and recklessness. These facts I know from personal experience. I have been at the breaking point, many times, and can only thank God for reinforcing the strained cords of my brain by His providential spirit.

I can look back into past events of my life and recall, many times, that the least inducement or slightest provocation would have led me to despotism, and most likely, destroyed any chance of my being a civilized peaceable man. For that reason, I have long since decided that circumstances and general surroundings are largely, if not wholly responsible for our nature, disposition and general spirit of life. Therefore, I must admit that there is some degree of sympathy, in my heart, for all humanity no matter what their downfall might be, for I always reflect my mind back to the things I might have done in these periods of life that were so trying on my mind and heart, and realize the superior strength I was created with over the average man.

Then I console myself that my Creator intended for me to be a faithful servant of weaker men and I have always been faithful to that cause and will be until I am retired form this earth.

Index

Note: Page numbers given in italics refer to illustrations.

D

E

M

McCarty, John, 5

McDonald, Tom, 22, 26

McDonald, W. J. (Bill), 148, 301 nn6,9

McDowell, Tip, 90-96, 99

McGee, Thomas F., 151, 301 n12

McGuire, Dutch, 93-97

McIntyre, Jim, 131-32

McKinney, Al, 163

McMurray, Sam, 137-38, 149, 299 n3, 301 n6

McNeal, Cleve, 115-20, 237

McPherson, Mr. (deputy sheriff), 234-35

Main Creek, 194

Major County, Oklahoma, 308 n9

Manskers, Ike, 226-27

Martin, Burns, and Johnson, 112

Martin & Russell law firm (Amarillo), 154

Mason, Joe, 166

Matagorda County, Texas, 290 n1

Mathis, Gus, 240, 242

Maverick brands. *See* Cattle rustling

Maxwell, Will, 193-94, 196

Merchant, Claiborne (Clabe), 101, 104, 109, 111, 121-23, 149, 294 n2

Merchant, John, 149

Mexican Plaza, 103, 295 nn9-10

Mexico, 109

Miama, Texas, 245

Middleton (bookmaker), 236

Miller, "Deacon" Jim, 4

Miller, Dr., 164

Miller, George, 193, 307 n5

Miller ranch (Clayton), 224-25

Missouri Pacific Railroad, 120

Mitchell County, Texas, 309 n4

Mobeetie, Texas, 38-39, 45, 161, 166, 283 n11, 284 n13

Montague County, Texas, 12, 30

Montana, 51, 112, 189

Moore County, Texas, 114, 289 n20, 297 n2

Moore, R. M. (Mack), 102, 109, 111, 130-32, 136-38, 140, 143, 295 n6, 297 n23, 299 n10

Morris, Cap Ed, 193-94, 196, 199-200

Mosely, John, 196

Motley County, Texas, 282 n1

Mulberry Basin, 71, 292 n16

Munson, W. B., 285 n18

Murphy, Jesse, 18, 20

Murphy, Jim, 278-29

Murphy, Pat, 174-76

Murry, Jim, 88-89, 97, 105

Mynatt, Jeff, 189-91, 306 n13

N

Nations, Joseph H., 203-6, 223, 308 n1

ND Ranch, 288 n11

Nebraska, 278

Negro Sam, 201, 224

Neutral Strip, 181

New Boston, Colorado, 187

Newman, Jim, 67, 291 n6

New Mexico, 49, 50, 109, 155, 158, 172, 225, 242, 270, 284 nn14-15, 286 n5, 287 n7, 290 n2. *See also* individual locations

No Man's Land, xiii, 119, 170, 181, 253, 297 n3, 302 n8

Norwell, Bob, 180, 182

O

Odem, Tobe, 172, 179-82, 189-90, 304 n12

Oklahoma City, 207, 258

Oklahoma Territory, xiii-xv, xxi, 1, 160, 164, 168, 179, 189, 207, 215, 225, 242, 250, 256, 258, 281, 289 n20, 297 n3, 304 n10, 311 n13. *See also* individual locations

Oldham County, Texas, xxii, 2, 30, 52, 84, 86, 284 nn13,15, 285 n3, 288 n17, 289 nn20,23

Oliver, Bally, 211, 212

Oliver-Eakle Building (Amarillo), 265-266, 312 n3

Omaha, 225

O'Malley, Morris, 186, 305 n5

Ouray, Colorado, 279

Overland Park racetrack, 235, 238

Owens, R. A., 258

T

U

V

W

photo by Jack Newsom

As a child, James R. Gober was fascinated by tales of his grandfather, a story-book sheriff of the Old West. But it wasn't until he inherited a disheveled bundle of age-discolored and faded papers that he realized Sheriff Jim Gober had composed his memoirs.

An Annapolis graduate, James R. Gober enjoyed careers in the U.S. Army and in engineering management for the electronics industry before he began editing *Cowboy Justice*. As an author, he draws upon a rich pioneer heritage and military background.

B. Byron Price is executive director of the Buffalo Bill Historical Center in Cody, Wyoming. A native Texan, Price is a graduate of West Point and Texas Tech University. Formerly executive director of the National Cowboy Hall of Fame and Western Heritage Center in Oklahoma City, and director of the Panhandle-Plains Historical Museum in Canyon, Texas, he has written several books and numerous articles on western subjects.

File name: author page.eps; Page no. 1 of 1